THE THREE KHANS

THE THREE KHANS

AND THE EMERGENCE OF NEW INDIA

KAVEREE BAMZAI

WESTLAND
NON·FICTION

First published by Westland Publications Private Limited in 2021

1st Floor, A Block, East Wing, Plot No. 40, SP Infocity, Dr MGR Salai, Perungudi, Kandanchavadi, Chennai 600096

Westland and the Westland logo are the trademarks of Westland Publications Private Limited, or its affiliates.

ISBN: 9789390679959

10 9 8 7 6 5 4 3 2 1

Typeset in Dante MT Std by SÜRYA, New Delhi
Printed at Manipal Technologies Limited, Manipal

*This is for my two boys, Samvit and Kartikeya,
my constant companions during countless hours of
movie-watching, and for my husband, Sourish,
who used that free time to come up with
the idea for this book.*

Contents

Preface

There are two primary reasons why I am writing this book. One is that I have, like the three Khans, been fortunate to live through this period, often volatile, usually turbulent, but never boring. Two, not only have I had the privilege of watching most of their movies, but I have also had the pleasure of meeting them in the course of the last twenty years. My meetings with them have usually taken place on the sets of movies they were shooting, or in their homes, or sometimes at special screenings. Most of what you will read in the book is a mix of my own observations, that of their friends and co-workers, and their own words chronicled over the years in reams of magazine pages.

I remember meeting Shah Rukh for the first time on the sets of *Chalte Chalte* in 2003. He was shooting with Rani Mukerji at the international airport in Mumbai and the man in the director's seat was his mentor, Aziz Mirza, a large bear of a man, at whose office Shah Rukh would often crash when he was new in Mumbai and whose generous wife, Nirmala, would often make him dinner. Aziz's son, Haroon, was there too, helping his father on set as Shah Rukh switched between crying on cue in an intense scene (Mukerji, his wife in the movie, has decided to leave him) and bantering behind the monitor. Between advising Mukerji to tell her mother to lose weight and discussing the scene with Haroon, Shah Rukh was energetic and excitable. Haroon was an old friend, with whom Shah Rukh had spent many days and nights while shooting for three serials produced by Iskra, a production company set up by Mirza, his elder brother Saeed, and Kundan Shah. Saeed channelled urban angst in movies such as *Albert Pinto ko Gussa Kyon Aata Hai* (1980) and *Salim Langde Par Mat Ro* (1989), and Shah was the iconic director of *Jaane Bhi Do Yaaron* (1983). The serials were *Umeed, Wagle ki Duniya*, and Shah Rukh's last work on the small screen as an actor, the twenty-episode *Circus*.

Over the next eighteen years, I would meet him often. Sometimes the relationship was adversarial, like the time after I did a cover story for *India Today* in 2007 on his feud with Amitabh Bachchan. One of the many things at stake was the hosting of *Kaun Banega Crorepati* (KBC), the show that had reinvented Bachchan's image and career in 2000. In a bid to renegotiate his ₹40-lakh-per-episode fee, Bachchan had written to Star Plus that he would not be able to honour his commitment to *KBC*. This prompted Shah Rukh to step in to save the day for the channel, then under siege from a resurgent Zee TV, with a heftier pay cheque—₹70 lakh per episode. Shah Rukh had infamously, without mentioning my name, said he would slap me after he saw the *India Today* story. That was my first and last brush with fame.

In my experience, Shah Rukh is as generous as he is temperamental. Recently, when my husband took ill in Dubai, he offered to help with the hospital, remarking with his trademark humour that he had more clout there than he had in Mumbai.

As a conversationalist, he is fascinating, quick to share his latest look from whatever film he is working on, and even quicker to offer advice—I remember once on the sets of *Paheli* (2005) in Film City, when Lara Dutta dropped in to say hello, he asked her why she was working so much. To which she cited advice from her co-star Akshay Kumar, whose philosophy is to take on at least four films a year.

Shah Rukh is perhaps one of the smartest men I have met. He is equally at ease talking cricket with Lalit Modi at 3 a.m. in his Kolkata hotel room after a match involving his team Kolkata Knight Riders (KKR, which he co-owns with former co-star Juhi Chawla and her businessman husband Jai Mehta) in the Indian Premier League (IPL), as he is playing FIFA on his brand new Playstation 4 with Boman Irani after pack-up on the sets of *Happy New Year* (2014) in Karjat outside Mumbai.

Aamir Khan is less exuberant and more thoughtful than Shah Rukh. I remember meeting him in a busy coffee shop in Delhi while he was in the city. It was 2007. He was accompanied by his new publicist. Over the years, I have spent a lot of time with him, and his lovely wife, Kiran Rao, whom I knew as a young girl of eight practising the scales on her piano at home. She is the younger sister of Suman Rao, now Suman Bhat, who was my best friend when we were both in Loreto House, Kolkata. I remember bumping into Kiran again in a queue outside the Siri Fort auditorium in the days when it still hosted the International Film Festival of India. She was then a post-graduate student of filmmaking at Jamia Millia Islamia. She remains exactly as she was, bubbly, full of ideas, and passionate about cinema.

I have seen a great deal of Aamir, sometimes as the exacting director agonising over a particular scene in his debut as filmmaker, *Taare Zameen Par* (2007). Another time, he was the patient subject of an interview at 2 a.m. at his Pali Hill apartment. And yet again, he was a concerned voice at the other end of the line when he found out I had fallen ill in Berlin after the Berlinale, in 2010—yes, I know, hospitals feature in a major way in my relationship with the Khans. Unlike Shah Rukh, whose silences can sometimes stretch for a year or more, Aamir is always unfailingly polite and responsive when asked about something—until recently, when he decided to give up his phone to stop wasting time.

Salman Khan is someone I met more recently, in 2010, when he had just re-established himself after the success of *Dabangg*. Compared to many of my contemporaries, who have been greeted with quirky sights such as the actor performing a self-manicure with a knife, I have had better luck. Salman has been in a mood to answer questions and often even candidly, talking about his childhood and his complicated relationship with his father. He has an innate intelligence and a twisted sense of humour. Political correctness is not his strongest suit. I remember his idea of a joke was to narrate an incident featuring Katrina Kaif, his then girlfriend. She was watching TV in their bedroom when she called out to him to come and see something. It was someone who looked just like Salman in an old movie, she said. It turned out to be Salman himself. Another time, he said, there was a young man who came and stayed with him for a year, telling him he was his brother Sohail's friend. It turned out that Sohail thought he was Salman's friend. By the time the truth was out, the stranger had indeed become a friend.

Salman is given to doling out advice, much like Shah Rukh, especially if he likes you. The advice can range from what fitness regime to follow to the telephone number of a hair transplant surgeon in Dubai who worked on him because, as he once told me, 'You seem to have a personal interest in the subject. Is someone close to you balding?' Of the three Khans, Salman is the least rehearsed and also the least likely to engage in long conversations. Once he feels comfortable, though, he can be quite voluble, more so as the mugs of coffee give way to shots of Bacardi. He is not the most comfortable in public, and I remember him looking particularly miserable before going on stage and being interviewed before a 1,000-strong crowd at the India Today Conclave in Delhi in 2014.

This book is more than a composite of my memories. It is an account of the irrepressible rise of three talented young men who found fame in a changing and challenging time for the film industry, for the country and for themselves. They have negotiated failures and tasted heady success, been friends and rivals, lost and found love, and made an indelible impact on India's imagination through their movies and the memorable characters they played.

I feel honoured to have been a witness to it.

Introduction

'I am young,' Rajiv Gandhi told the US Congress in Washington DC, in 1985, to thunderous applause. 'I too have a dream.'

The mid-Eighties were the era of Rajiv Gandhi, of India's consumer boom, the computer culture, the relaxation of economic restrictions and a new political language that called out power brokers who had transformed the Congress from a mass movement into a feudal oligarchy.[1] It was the era of the Anti-Defection Act aimed at ending arbitrary party hopping by legislators, a new economic policy that encouraged capital-goods imports, relaxed industrial regulations and rationalised the tax system, as well as political reform that encompassed the spectrum, from lowering the voting age to legislating panchayati raj.

Forty years old when he took over as prime minister in November 1984, Rajiv Gandhi truly symbolised a new India. A professional pilot, he had taken to politics after the traumatic death of his brother, Sanjay, in 1980, but once in politics, he showed flashes of the old upwardly mobile lifestyle he had enjoyed as a pilot—family holidays in wildlife sanctuaries and on sunlit beaches; patriotic 'Run For My Country' jogs down Janpath; a love of adventure, whether para-jumping or driving at breakneck speed; and a passionate relationship with a wife he would often hold hands with, even at public events.

It was the year 1988. A senior civil servant in Punjab, Rupan Deol Bajaj, had just accused 'super cop' K.P.S. Gill of sexual harassment, one of the first such allegations against a public figure. B.R. Chopra's *Mahabharata* was making waves every Sunday morning on State-run Doordarshan, the only television channel available then, while two strong-willed women (J. Jayalalithaa and the now-forgotten Janaki Ramachandran) fought over the political legacy of the legendary Tamil Nadu leader, M.G. Ramachandran (MGR).

Indian society was changing, this change reflecting in the kind of stories that *India Today* magazine, then a fortnightly, was doing—on such varied trends as the fitness craze, the rise of women entrepreneurs, urban decay, and the entry of foreign brand names.

On the economic front, controls over electronic and computer imports were relaxed. A new education policy was drafted. Festivals of India were held in many foreign countries with much panache, and secret approval for nuclear weaponisation was given.

On the political front, by 1988, the Teflon had worn thin and the promise of the initial Rajiv Gandhi years had gone down the tubes with the Shah Bano case, the bungling over the Punjab Accord, the aborted Defamation Act (that made an attempt to muzzle the press) and worse, the allegations of kickbacks for recommending the Bofors gun to the Indian Army.

What was happening at the movies that year? It was a vast wasteland, in which two violent movies stood out. One was N. Chandra's *Tezaab*, which created a blockbuster song in *Ek*

Do Teen ..., picturised on Madhuri Dixit, who played Mohini, a dancer and the daughter of an alcoholic gambler. The movie reinforced, as Ashish Rajadhyaksha and Paul Willemen observed in the *Encyclopaedia of Indian Cinema*, the fanatic communalism evident in the director's earlier film, *Ankush*. 'The hero, identified as a Maharashtrian, disposes of several outsider thugs suggesting that "local" Maharashtrian criminals are revered by the people who dislike outsiders interfering with their home grown racketeers.'[2] The other movie was *Khoon Bari Maang*, directed by Rakesh Roshan, a revenge saga in which a woman, played by Rekha, returns with a new face, courtesy plastic surgery, to wreak vengeance on her murderous husband. It sparked a series of similar women-oriented movies and unveiled a chic new avatar of Rekha, with big lips, bigger hair, padded shoulders and leather jackets.

And then there was the biggest box office hit of 1988: *Qayamat Se Qayamat Tak (QSQT)*. It heralded the arrival of twenty-three-year-old Aamir Khan in a teen romance directed by Mansoor Khan, who had managed to drop out of IIT, Cornell University ... and MIT! Son of the famous producer/director Nasir Husain (whom Aamir had assisted in previous years, and in whose movie *Yadadon ki Baraat* he had appeared as a child actor), Mansoor Khan kept it all in the family when he cast cousin Aamir. Mansoor may have opened the doors to Aamir's career but Aamir stood apart in his own right as an actor and was soon a teenage heart-throb. His performance in the film won him an army of fans and led *India Today* to declare that he was 'the kind of guy who you'd like to take home to your mother'. The said object of attention could only respond by fretting over no longer being able to 'take my wife for a walk on the beach'—Reena, who worked in a travel agency, continued to take a bus to work every day.

Meanwhile, in Delhi, another twenty-three-year-old, Shah Rukh Khan, with unruly hair and deep dimples, was playing

Captain Abhimanyu Rai in a thirteen-episode serial for Doordarshan called *Fauji*.

In Mumbai, yet another twenty-three-year-old, Salman Khan, clad in an undershirt and jeans, was dancing to music in a room filled with posters of Michael Jackson and Madonna as Vicky, in a film called *Biwi Ho To Aisi*, starring Rekha and Farooque Shaikh.

All three young men, now in the thirty-fourth year of their careers, embodied India as it was then.

Coming at the tail end of India's fascination with Amitabh Bachchan (*Shahenshah* and *Ganga Jamuna Saraswati*, released in 1988, had announced his sell-by date) and the last years of pre-liberalisation innocence, the rise of the Khans coincided with the opening up of the Indian economy, the emergence of religious fundamentalism and the return of caste politics.

In 1989, as the world was redrawing its map, celebrating the fall of the twenty-eight-year-old Berlin Wall and the rise of Perestroika in the former Soviet Union, India was hurtling towards the Dark Ages. A desperate V.P. Singh, having come to power in December 1989 on the back of a campaign against Rajiv Gandhi's alleged corruption, took a long-festering report out of cold storage to keep his coalition government in power. The Mandal Commission report allowed the mobilisation of Other Backward Classes (OBC) but agitated upper castes to such an extent that it sparked protests in the streets, one of these ending in a Delhi student named Rajeev Goswami setting himself on fire in full public view. Goswami, a commerce student of Deshbandhu College, became a symbol of upper-caste rage against the new quotas. He died in 2004 because of severe health complications as a result of his self-immolation bid, but the image of his body on fire remains one of the most powerful portraits of protest against the government decision to activate 27 per cent quota for OBCs.

The BJP, a party which had had little success till then, ever since its inception in 1980, was fashioning its own answer to caste politics—its plan to unite Hindus across caste lines got a big fillip when L.K. Advani took off on a Rath Yatra to mobilise the masses to build a temple in Ram's Janmabhoomi, Ayodhya. It would culminate in the demolition of the Babri Masjid in 1992 and spark violent riots in Mumbai.

But the three Khans, Aamir, Shah Rukh and Salman, products of Nehruvian socialism and its deep-rooted secularism, were unaffected by the poison that was slowly finding its way into society.

Aamir Khan's father, Tahir Husain, was the less successful of two film producer/director brothers (Nasir Husain, who created the swinging, singing playboy template for Shammi Kapoor in *Tumsa Nahi Dekha* released in 1957, being the other). A film of Tahir's which stalled for eight years, *Locket,* would impoverish the Husain family, and inculcate in young Aamir a value for money that ensured he continued to believe in living a fairly middle-class life. He has on occasion recalled how he and his three siblings would regularly be late in paying their school fees, and, humiliatingly, have their names called out in school.

Aamir recalls being present at countless story and music sessions with both his father and uncle. He remembers his father listening to writers narrating movie plots and asking them: 'If I were to ask you for the gist in one line, what would would it be?' He started working young, having decided to embrace cinema. A role in Ketan Mehta's *Holi* and another in *Raakh,* for his friend Aditya Bhattacharya (director Basu Bhattacharya's son), saw him land a role as Raj. *QSQT*, with its lilting music, great locales and a fresh young heroine conspiring to make the film into a huge hit, appealed to a new demographic that wanted to see itself on-screen and share the hero's ambition of making it big as articulated in the song, 'Papa kehte hain bada naam karega'. Aamir Khan's Raj, well-spoken, funny, capable of looking good while lip syncing to hummable songs, afraid of his father yet made brave by love, seemed to be just what India needed. As Gautam Chintamani notes in his book, *The Film That Revived Hindi Cinema: Qayamat Se Qayamat Tak*, Aamir's ascent was possible because in a country devoid of any young icons, he quickly became the poster boy.[3] Sachin Tendulkar, the cricketing wunderkind, would not appear on the national scene until the end of 1989 when he made his international test debut for India against Pakistan at the age of 16. Once he appeared on the cricket pitch, he won hearts and minds with his youthful maturity and incredible batting skills. His playing career lasted till 2013 but he endures as an icon.

Salman Khan, meanwhile, was getting ready to reprise *Biwi Ho To Aisi*'s Vicky with a lot more charm and a better physique in 1989's iconic *Maine Pyar Kiya*. The film was directed by Sooraj Barjatya, whose father, coincidentally, had given a break to a young Salim Khan, Salman's famous writer father, when he had come to Bombay fresh out of Indore. Salim's family—he had five children—kept an open house even though money was tight. Salim Khan remembers that for ten years he was a struggling actor and even when he started earning as a scriptwriter, the money was not excessive. 'I got all of ₹10,000 for our script for *Haathi Mere Saathi*,' he told me once.

Mahesh Bhatt, the director, collaborated with Salim Khan on *Naam* (1986) and would often spend time with him at his home. 'I used to drink heavily those days and young Salman was often deputed to drop me home,' Bhatt said to me with his characteristic candour.

Salman started working as a model when he was fourteen, after dropping out of a series of schools. Even now, he says, he sometimes dreams about Scindia School (a well-known boarding school in Gwalior) and when he wakes up, his pillow is wet with tears. He had a taste for the good things of life and he once told me how he treasured a pair of Wrangler jeans an uncle had brought from abroad, wearing it until it tore.

If Aamir Khan was the middle-class boy next door, Salman Khan was the quintessential rebel, the entitled insider who was rude to his on-screen sister-in-law, Rekha—who, if the *Stardust* gossip columns of October 1991 are to be believed, had a crush on the young actor and even ensured that he was part of a Morani Brothers' stage show that she was headlining in London.

The third arm of the troika was Shah Rukh Khan, an outsider to Mumbai but not an outsider to the profession of acting. Trained under the UK-born Indian theatre director and actor, Barry John, he had worked in theatre in Delhi for a long time along with friends such as Sanjoy Roy, Rituraj and Divya Seth Shah. Shah Rukh came from a middle-class background. His father, he has often emphasised, was a freedom fighter who was not very successful in business, including one that involved catering at the National School of Drama canteen. His mother was a go-getter, employed as a special magistrate in the Juvenile Court. After her husband's death in 1981, she ran a small restaurant called Khatir near Jor Bagh in Delhi, as well as an agency for oil. They moved from a rented apartment in Rajendra Nagar to another in Gautam Nagar. They didn't always have enough money but his parents never let him feel that absence, and at St Columba's where he studied, though he was part of the cool C-Gang, money was never discussed among friends. But once, in 1990, when he came to Bombay with two friends and ₹10,000 in his pocket to look for then girlfriend (and later wife) Gauri Chhiba, he apparently promised himself, standing on Marine Drive, that he would one day become the king of Bollywood.

By popular reckoning, he did.

The Delhi boy was willing to experiment, and so hungry for success that he would accept anti-hero roles that fellow actors steered clear of, whether it was playing the killer in *Baazigar* or the stalker in *Darr*. He would eventually go on to fulfil the ultimate yuppie dream, becoming everyone's favourite NRI with his role as Raj, the beer-drinking but eventually tradition-observing London-bred boy in *Dilwale Dulhaniya Le Jayenge*. Raj may have been brought up in the West but he would draw the line at taking advantage of the tipsy heroine, inscribing what sociologist Patricia Uberoi has called the 'tyranny of tradition' because *'Main ek Hindustani hoon, aur main jaanta hoon ki ek Hindustani ladki ki izzat kya hoti hai!'* (I am an Indian and I know what honour means to an Indian girl.) The construction of Indianness, so imperative for the diaspora and Indian audiences in India was carefully done—however much the NRI heroes enjoyed their lavish consumerist lifestyle, their hearts beat for India.

MYTHS, MANUFACTURED AND CAREFULLY MAINTAINED

What has made the three Khans such enduring stars, so adaptable to the changed India, and so relevant even thirty years on? It is because they have, along with their audiences, constructed myths about who they might be and, in particular, who their audiences would like them to be. These myths were by-products of their movies.

This book will examine the persona of the three Khans—the myths and the realities, how these leading stars have influenced the Indian male's idea of masculinity, and in doing so, influenced the idea of romantic love and family life; how they have negotiated their Muslim identities, especially in an increasingly anti-Muslim and toxic environment; and how they have redefined our ideas of India, in a post-Rajiv Gandhi era where social divisions are more deep-rooted, where communities are more clearly defined by markers of caste, religion, language or geography. As Ramachandra Guha remarks in *India After Gandhi: The History of the World's Largest Democracy*, 'Even by the standards of Indian history, the 1980s were an especially turbulent decade. The republic had always been faced with dissenting movements but never so many, at the same time, in so many parts of India and expressed with so much intensity.'[4]

There is no doubt that movies influence life and these three movie stars are as much a product of their times as they are an influence on many millions of people. Their following is almost immeasurable.

Even today, there are at least fifty young men outside Salman Khan's Galaxy Apartments in Bandra, waiting to catch a glimpse of 'bhai', or brother, and is a title given to him by his adoring fans. Some want to talk to him about their grievances, some ask him for help, while others want money; yet others just want his presence to be that moment of magic in their lives. Shah Rukh Khan's home, down the road on Bandstand from Salman Khan's, has a bus stop named after it, and at any time of the day, there are small groups of people taking pictures standing next to the high, well-guarded door of his dream house called 'Mannat' (Boon). Shah Rukh, with typical self-aware hyperbole, calls it the second most famous address in India, after Rashtrapati Bhavan. On Pali Hill, not very far away, Aamir Khan lives two floors down from the flat in which he grew up. There are no crowds or fans waiting on the street for him, but to gauge his popularity, all one needs to do is to ask a taxi or auto driver to take you to Aamir Khan's home. They all know it.

As the Indian viewer changes the way he/she consumes entertainment, no longer waiting only for tent-pole movies on much-awaited Fridays or weekly soaps by appointment, the era of the star with universal appeal is ending. The industry is at an inflexion point, as it was in the Eighties when Amitabh Bachchan's era, which began with his breakout role as the brooding, revenge-driven police officer in *Zanjeer* (1973), was ending. His *Ram Balram, Naseeb, Namak Halal, Lawaaris, Yarana, Mard* and *Coolie* had done well. But then, wannabe blockbusters like Ramesh Sippy's *Shaan*, B.R. Chopra's *Burning Train* and Yash Chopra's *Silsila* tanked. As Bachchan's charisma faded, dance choreographers and fight directors gained popularity with movie-makers in Mumbai copying regional or foreign films. Two star sons were launched in 1981 with *Rocky* and *Love Story*: Sanjay Dutt (son of yesteryear stars Nargis and Sunil Dutt) and Kumar Gaurav (son of the man known as 'Jubilee King' for the number of weeks his films ran in the theatres, Rajendra Kumar). They would eventually become brothers-in-law.[5]

Two years later, another trio was launched in leading roles. Anil Kapoor was cast in the lead in his father Surinder Kapoor's production *Woh Saat Din* after doing a few bit parts. Producer-director Subhash Ghai selected a model with Gujarati and Kazakh blood, dropped his first name, Jaikishan, and used his pet name to launch him in *Hero* as Jackie Shroff. And Rahul Rawail cast Dharmendra's elder son Sunny in *Betaab*. None of them filled Bachchan's shoes, though forty years on, Kapoor has built a remarkable career encompassing dramatic roles, comedic turns and significant Hollywood appearances, including the role of game show host Prem Kumar in 2009's multiple Oscar winner *Slumdog Millionaire.* But back then, the hero was shrinking in size and importance, embodied best by Kapoor's character in *Parinda* (1989), who is not afraid of tears, is reluctant to take to the gun, and is killed in his marital bed with his new bride. The villain was thriving, whether it was Mogambo in *Mr India* (1985) or Dr Dang in *Karma* (1986). Meanwhile, colour TV had come to India in 1982 and the threat of the video cassette recorder (VCR) loomed large. Star director Manmohan Desai famously called it the AIDS of the movie industry.

Technology continues to play a part in keeping audiences at home. The rise of streaming services such as Disney+Hotstar, Netflix and Amazon, various thieves of time like social media networks, and social distancing norms and closed cinemas enforced by COVID-19 lockdowns across the world have meant that there are far fewer theatre-goers. It has also accelerated the changes in our idea of the screen hero by allowing us access to greater diversity in storytelling at home, both from India and elsewhere. With big movies now rubbing shoulders with smaller, independent fare, the playing field has become much more democratic. The cost of watching a big budget movie, a longform series, and more experimental fare is the same on streaming services. The hero can now encompass the spectrum from Akshay Kumar to Nawazuddin Siddiqui to Ayushmann Khurrana. The growth of multiplexes—2019 data points to 6,300 single screens and 3,200 multiplex screens—as well as the ticket price differential has also enabled different kinds of cinema creating more than one kind of hero. But just as Bachchan was the gold standard of stardom for the three Khans, the troika has become the touchstone for all newcomers to aspire to.

AAMIR KHAN: THE MIDDLE-CLASS ICON

Aamir Khan, the boy next door from *QSQT*, later emerged as a middle-class hero, reinventing himself virtually every year in a different kind of role. It began in 2001 with the irreverent and youthful *Dil Chahta Hai* and the epic *Lagaan*. As Akash in *Dil Chahta Hai,* he was the archetypal young man sleepwalking through his father's money until he's woken up by love, signifying the 'friends as family' dynamic for the youthful audiences who were increasingly studying and working in places far from their homes and reminding them of their 'chamkile din' (salad days). With *Lagaan*, set in 1893, he told the story of a group of diverse villagers (including the Muslim Ismail and the 'untouchable' Kachra) taking on the might of their colonial masters by playing better cricket. *Lagaan* tried to reinvent patriotism for the Noughties, consciously assembling a team that cut across all social divides and celebrated a newfound confidence in India's soft power.

With these two very different films, Aamir Khan re-established his credentials as the thinking man's superstar, making films that invariably carried a message, whether it was *Taare Zameen Par* (2007) about a dyslexic child, *3 Idiots* (2009) about the futility of the straitjacket educational system, or women's empowerment in *Dangal* (2016). *Satyameva Jayate* (2012), his provocative TV show about real-life issues ranging from domestic violence to toxic food, only burnished his reputation as a thoughtful man interested in making a difference to society.

SHAH RUKH KHAN: THE NRI HERO

Shah Rukh Khan's emergence as the NRI hero dates back to the iconic *Dilwale Dulhaniya Le Jayenge* (1995) and the less-celebrated *Pardes* (1997) with its 'I Love My India' ethos. Both films marked a distinct change for the actor's persona, created by *Baazigar* (1993) and *Darr* (1993), which broke through the clutter of the early Nineties with the emergence of the 'psychotic as protagonist' ('From Subjectification to Schizophrenia', Ranjani Mazumdar, in *Making Meaning in Indian Cinema*). As Mazumdar writes, the psychotic hero of contemporary cinema no longer speaks the broad social language of the earlier 'angry man' but remains within a world of seemingly unrelated individual obsessions.[6]

From there to the individualism of the overseas Indian was a swift leap, and the theatre-trained Delhi boy who came to Mumbai with ₹10,000 in his pocket and a shovel-full of dreams, was the perfect vehicle for this transition. As Ashish Rajadhyaksha writes in the *Encyclopaedia of Indian Cinema*, a remarkable feature of *Dilwale Dulhaniya Le Jayenge* is the elimination of the staple Bachchan formula of the State as a contested site, being replaced here by an unproblematic subsumption of feudal patriarchy into 'postmodern' globalisation and the selling of 'authentic' identity as something that can only be achieved via consumerism.[7]

In many ways, Shah Rukh Khan made the passage to the West, with its attendant traumas of racial adjustment, worth the pain. His subsequent roles have been varied but they always underline his level of comfort with Western ways even while retaining his innate Indianness, most clearly seen in *Swades* (2004), where he plays a NASA scientist driven by the ambition of improving conditions at home. In his travels between India and America, between building a hydroelectric power generation unit for his ayah Kaveri Amma's village and completing his project in NASA, Shah Rukh Khan's Mohan Bhargava embodies the NRI's increasing ease with living in the West while being happy to embrace his roots.

This new take is a far cry from Manoj 'Bharat' Kumar's *Purab Aur Paschim* (1970), where the West is shown as a deeply corrupt place that turns good Indians like Preeti, played by Saira Banu, into smoking, drinking, immoral creatures with dyed blonde hair. Preeti soon sees the errors of her 'immoral ways' but not before we are made to acknowledge India's intellectual superiority as the land which pioneered everything from the zero to the decimal system and where every man is Ram and every woman is Sita.

There was no such conflict, however, in the development of the NRI hero. What we are fed is a celebration of his success. In his off-screen life too, Shah Rukh Khan has reiterated this, saying, 'I am just an employee of the Shah Rukh Khan myth.'

He has revelled in the material wealth he has acquired, often saying, 'Don't philosophise until you're rich first. I used to be poor, and I can tell you there's nothing romantic about it.'

SALMAN KHAN: WORKING-CLASS CHAMPION

In the third Khan, Salman, one finds the working-class hero, a reinvention that happened with *Tere Naam* (2003). In this remake of the Tamil film *Sethu* (1999), he plays Radhe, a college rowdy who becomes obsessed with the local priest's daughter to the point where he abducts her and loses his mind over her. In the 2009 film, *Wanted,* he played another Radhe, this time a mysterious killer-for-hire, who stalks the woman of his dreams while terrifying the local police inspector and generally hanging about the city. This set the template for a series of Salman Khan movies, from *Dabanng* (2010) to *Bajrangi Bhaijaan* (2015), where he is the simple, good-hearted man who would do anything for a friend.

This late career remaking followed Salman's iconic portrayal of the naughty but nice Prem in *Maine Pyaar Kiya* (1989) and *Hum Aapke Hain Koun* (1994). The latter established Salman Khan as part of the story of the Indian family as a 'form of imagined community' as well as an 'icon of national society'.[8] But with *Tere Naam* and *Wanted*, he acquired a new audience, the ordinary working-class Indian who wanted to watch a stylised version of his own self on-screen. Salman Khan was able to connect with the anxieties of the working-class male, about work, love and life, which explains the popularity of the crooked but loveable police officer Chulbul (Robin Hood) Pandey of *Dabangg* (2010).

It is interesting to examine how the Hindi film hero has changed, from the Five Year Plan (FYP) hero, a term suggested by Sanjay Srivastava[9] and exemplified by the Nehruvian heroism of Dilip Kumar to the Modernists (typified by the Nasir Husain hero) to the Angry Young Man brought to life by Bachchan, to the emergence of the three Khans, representing the middle-class hero, the NRI icon and the working-class champion. The FYP hero represented, in a broad sense, a particular formulation of Indian masculinity where manliness comes to attach not to bodily representations or aggressive behaviour but rather to being scientific and rational.

As Akshay Manwani writes in his book, *Music, Masti and Modernity: The Cinema of Nasir Husain*, there was a magic in-between period post-Partition and before the rise of the Angry Young Man.[10] This gave birth to a kind of hero whom he describes as the Modernist. The disillusionment following Independence and what was promised for a young India had yet to solidify into youthful angst, says Manwani, quoting Anuradha Warrier, who runs the popular blog, 'Conversations Over Chai'.[11] The Modernist (epitomised by Shammi Kapoor in *Dil Deke Dekho*, 1959, and Shashi Kapoor in *Pyar Ka Mausam*, 1969) appealed to a younger generation of the 1960s who wanted, even needed, optimistic and aspirational stories. They wanted music, they wanted romance, they wanted colour, the promise that a Nasir Husain hero held out. They didn't want their lives to be lived in stark black and white. They were middle class, they were educated, they wanted to hear that they could get a job, get a lover, have the romance of their lives, and a life filled with music. They didn't want major conflict: they didn't mind the tiny hurdles that the Nasir Husain hero faced, for they knew things would be all right in the end.

This was followed by the Angry Young Man, or what Kishore Valicha calls the 'industrial hero', a reflection of the political violence in India at the time.[12] Of his anger, Javed Akhtar says to Rachel Dwyer in *Yash Chopra: Fifty Years in Indian Cinema*: 'As an actor, Amitabh's anger was never ugly. Other actors mix anger with arrogance. But Amitabh's anger was mixed with hurt and tears. So you accept it, you get fascinated by it, and you find justification for it.'[13] The mix of emotions is best exemplified in a scene that Javed Akhtar scripted with Salim Khan for Yash Chopra's *Kaala Patthar* (1979), when he says to Raakhee, the doctor treating him: 'Pain is my destiny and I just can't avoid it.'

THE IDEA OF MUSLIMNESS

From its personnel, to film titles, to the language of the screenplays and lyrics, Hindi cinema has been deeply shaped by Muslim influences, according to Mukul Kesavan.[14] However, over the years, as Srivastava points out, one can identify the emerging discourse of middle-class Hindu respectability where the 'Muslimness' and 'debauchery' became conjoined. Kalyani Chadha and Anandam P. Kavoori talk of the cinematic 'othering' of Muslims that has occurred through a variety of representations ranging from exoticisation and marginalisation to demonisation, which are widely recognised by anthropologists as critical to the production and maintenance of social and cultural difference. In *Global Bollywood*, its editors Kavoori and Aswin Punathambekar argue that this othering has been a long-term trend within the discourse of popular Hindi cinema and is not a recent result of a movement away from traditional secular moorings.[15] They point to the time when Dilip Kumar and Madhubala had to change their names to appear Hindu and note that Hindi cinema's purported secularism has always had significant limits. In recent years, it has even become comfortable in the shadow of saffron, with anti-Khan and anti-Muslim trolling acquiring virulent proportions.

The three Khans themselves are at pains to show they are more a product of their class than their religion. It helps, as Javed Akhtar says in *Talking Films and Songs* by Nasreen Munni Kabir, that the Hindi film hero is a kind of composite character:

'He is from everywhere and from nowhere.'[16] Both Aamir Khan and Shah Rukh Khan married Hindu women (in Aamir Khan's case, his second wife, Kiran Rao, is also a Hindu), while Salman Khan's mother was a Hindu (Sushila, who took the name Salma). All three stars have frequently chosen to champion their Indianness over their faith. In reply to a question from a court in connection with the blackbuck poaching case in 2017, Salman Khan said, 'I'm Hindu and Muslim both. I'm Bharatiya.' In a 2003 interview quoted by Chadha and Kavoori, Shah Rukh Khan says that while he is a Muslim, he is also a 'true blue Indian' and that 'no one can take this right away from me'.

In an even older interview, published in *Communalism Combat* in 1998, Aamir Khan says about his then wife Reena, 'We both come from very cosmopolitan backgrounds—neither Reena nor I hail from "Hindu" or "Muslim" ghettos respectively. We both hail from very similar cosmopolitan backgrounds within Bombay. Reena, until we got married (she was nineteen at the time) had spent half her life abroad and the rest in Bombay.'

The three actors have only rarely played Muslim characters on-screen, nor have they spoken about their faith. It is only of late, with the atmosphere in the country having become vitiated, that they have spoken up in response to questions, whether on rising intolerance (in the case of Aamir Khan), on Pakistani cricketers playing in the IPL (in the case of Shah Rukh Khan) or on the war between India and Pakistan (in the case of Salman Khan). On such occasions, the Shiv Sena, which is a powerful regional party with a strong presence in Mumbai, where all the three Khans live and work, invariably organises a protest, unleashes goons, and ensures enough controversy to fuel several hours of television airtime and online trolling. In 2018, when news of Aamir Khan playing the role of Krishna in an ambitious remake of *Mahabharata* broke, a war of words was sparked off on Twitter between right-wing writer Francois Gautier and poet and lyricist Javed Akhtar.[17]

All this has made the Khans circumspect about airing their political opinions in public, belonging as they do to an industry that is increasingly seeing itself divided on pro- and anti-government lines. The battle-lines have not manifested on-screen yet, though it is undeniable that post the destruction of the Babri Masjid and post 9/11, terrorists have almost always been portrayed as Muslims in Hindi cinema, whether from within India or outside.

An analysis of the Khans' on-screen Muslim characters reveals a rather mixed bag. Shah Rukh Khan's Muslim personas are closest to real life, whether it is the nationalist archaeologist Amjad Ali Khan in *Hey Ram* (2000), hockey coach Kabir Khan in *Chak De! India* (2007), who is pilloried for losing a game to Pakistan or as a man petitioning the US President in *My Name is Khan* (2010) to explain why his religion or his name does not make him a terrorist—a comment on post 9/11 America which acquired even greater significance when news emerged that Shah Rukh Khan was strip searched twice by authorities upon landing in that country. In private, Shah Rukh Khan has often joked about his being a 'good' role model for Muslims globally, as opposed to alternative icons like Osama bin Laden. And though he continues to find humour in the attacks—he once told me that if the Hindu right wing wants him to be exiled to another nation, why couldn't they at least pick a First World country instead of Pakistan? But it is clear that he has become far more cautious and therefore less vocal. Perhaps he is letting his work speak for him, as he plays a proud Pathan (his father's heritage) in a forthcoming spy drama produced by Yash Raj Films.

Salman Khan's later movies, *Bajrangi Bhaijaan*, where he returns a Pakistani girl to her nation, and the two Tiger movies (*Ek Tha Tiger* and *Tiger Zinda Hai*) where he falls in love with a Pakistani spy and lives happily ever after with her, clearly point to a larger goal of peace between communities and nations. The only time he played a Muslim on-screen, in the eponymous *Sultan,* he is shown proudly waving a green flag and, in one scene, wrestling against an opponent bearing a saffron flag.

Aamir Khan has played Muslim characters thrice, all three less than savoury. In Deepa Mehta's *Earth* (1998), he is the ice-candy man, Dilnavaz, who betrays the Hindu ayah hiding in the Parsi family's midst out of pique, while in *Fanaa* (2006) he plays a brain-washed terrorist. In *Dhoom 3* (2013) he played the villainous twins, Sahir and Samar Khan.

As Dilnavaz, in an interview to *rediff.com*, Aamir Khan makes it a point to draw a distinction between the character's faith and his action. In response to a question, he says: 'The role has an amazing graph, that of the transformation of an innocent, lowly but charming rogue faced with the atrocities of Partition. Being an average human being, he is shaken to his roots and loses all control over his actions. I have a dialogue that gives you an insight into his behaviour and which goes something like this, "It's not a question of Hindu, Muslim or Sikh. All of us are like caged beasts waiting for the cage to open. And when that happens only God is the maalik!" It's not a role you interpret in absolute black and white terms.'[18]

The Khans have had contemporaries whose careers have lasted as long as theirs. Ajay Devgan, son of fight director Veeru Devgan, began his career as an action star in *Phool Aur Kaante* (1991) performing a split as he balanced on two motorcycles. He went on to do serious roles in a series of acclaimed films by directors such as Mahesh Bhatt (*Zakhm*, 1998, for which he won his first National Award for Best Actor), Rajkumar Santoshi (*The Legend of Bhagat Singh*, 2002, for which he got his second National Award), Prakash Jha (*Gangaajal*, 2003) and Vishal Bhardwaj (*Omkara*, 2006). He continues to make movies that are commercial and critical successes, the most recent being the historical *Tanhaji: The Unsung Warrior* (2020).

Another action star made his debut in 1991, a martial arts expert who had worked in Bangkok as a cook. Akshay Kumar had auditioned for the part that eventually went to Deepak Tijori in the Aamir Khan starrer *Jo Jeeta Wohi Sikander* (1992). Tijori played Aamir's antagonist in it, the spoilt rich brat named Shekhar Malhotra. Akshay eventually made his debut in *Saugandh* (1991), directed by Raj Sippy, but found popular success in *Khiladi* (1992). He remained trapped in the action star image for long until he was rescued, after three years of flops, by Tanuja Chandra with *Sangharsh* and Suneel Darshan through *Jaanwar*, both in 1999. Later comedic roles sparked by the success of Priyadarshan's *Hera Pheri* in 2000, as well as exercises to deepen his voice, have ensured a long career. In his fifties, Akshay Kumar has evolved into a dramatic actor, winning a National Award, albeit controversially, for playing Rustom in the eponymous film loosely based on the well-known Commander Kawas Manekshaw Nanavati trial in Mumbai in 1959. Much like Devgan, he has chosen to stay on the right side of the establishment, even snagging a much-watched interview with Prime Minister Narendra Modi on the eve of the 2019 general elections. While not as popular as the Khans, Ajay Devgan and Akshay Kumar have also shown remarkable agility in remaining relevant to the times.

In the midst of so much change, the ability of the three Khans to negotiate their way through the world is a fascinating study in reinvention, reinterpretation and rebirth.

Let's see how.

1

1988–1993

Then There Were Three

'Every ten years, the audience says, "Hey, I've changed." Aamir has swept a whole new generation, just the way Zeenat Aman once did.' That was Shekhar Kapur on *QSQT* in a 1988 *India Today* story.[1] Director of *Masoom* (1983) and *Mr India* (1987), Kapur was a filmmaker in demand back then, even if he was later labelled as someone who had a penchant for abandoning films midway. *Time Machine*, started in 1992, starring Aamir, Naseeruddin Shah and Rekha was one such movie that he did not complete. *Barsaat*, the 1992 debut of Bobby Deol, and *Dushmani* in 1995, starring Sunny Deol and Jackie Shroff, are other examples. Most notorious amongst his half-finished or never-started films is *Paani*, which he was to make for Yash Raj

Films and in which the late actor Sushant Singh Rajput was to star.

Acknowledging Aamir Khan's impact on audiences, the *India Today* article written by Simran Bhargava described QSQT's cult status, saying youngsters were re-watching certain scenes over a hundred times. 'Like the cutely passionate one in the woods where Aamir is alone with Juhi Chawla: he is desperately attracted to her and yet has to keep away. By the end, he says, "to hell with it" and kisses her.' The article called QSQT a 'real' film, noting that the hero fights with six guys and gets beaten up and that he is dead scared of his father and lies to him. 'Aamir is awkward,' says Bhargava, 'but it is an awkwardness that works.'[2]

A state-level tennis player, Aamir Khan chose not to continue his studies after Class XII at Narsee Monjee College. Adamant that he wanted to work in films, he decided to assist his uncle Nasir Husain on *Manzil* (1984) and *Zabardast* (1985). *Manzil* featured Sunny Deol and Dimple—she was returning to films after separating from Rajesh Khanna—while *Zabardast* starred Sanjeev Kumar, Sunny Deol and Rajeev Kapoor. It was during these years that Aamir also acted in Ketan Mehta's *Holi* in 1984, based on Mahesh Eklunchwar's play. Mehta's film, shot mostly on the campus of the Film and Television Institute of India (FTII) in Pune, co-starred Naseeruddin Shah and Ashutosh Gowariker. It was during the making of *Holi* that the seeds of a close friendship with Gowariker were sown. A moustache and short cropped hair made Aamir (credited as Aamir Hussain) barely recognisable as Madan Sharma, one of the college students in *Holi* who goes on a strike after an altercation between the principal's nephew and another student.

But it was QSQT that made him a real star. The movie came in the middle of a tumultuous year in which Rajiv Gandhi pushed through a Constitutional amendment that would lower the voting age from twenty-one to eighteen. This extended voting rights to fifty million more people and acknowledged the country's youth power. In 1991, when Census figures were released, the proportion of fifteen to thirty-four-year-olds in the population was estimated at 33.5 per cent of 846 million, or 283 million, compared to 168 million in 1971. In 2011, this rose to 422 million. This rising number of young people would subsequently be described as the 'demographic dividend'.

In 1988 though, India and the film industry were in the throes of middle age. Having won independence in 1947, India was still grappling with the promise of a sovereign, socialist, democratic republic. The early promise of 'Mr Clean' Rajiv Gandhi's tenure at the top had disintegrated with the taint of the Bofors arms scandal, and his former finance minister V.P. Singh had raised the banner of revolt against him with full force. In 1988, the young, progressive prime minister was obliged to fall back on conventional Congress politics, which included overturning a Supreme Court judgment that had previously ruled that the Muslim divorcee Shah Bano was entitled to maintenance like any other Indian woman. To invalidate the judgment, he cited Muslim personal laws which did not call for maintenance beyond the three-month post-divorce iddat period.

This capitulation by the government appeased Muslim fundamentalists but it also gave a fillip to the Vishwa Hindu Parishad's campaign of '*Garv se kaho hum Hindu hain*' (Say it with pride, we are Hindu). In trying to win over the Hindus, Rajiv Gandhi had earlier, in 1986, given orders to open the locks of the Ram Janmabhoomi–Babri Masjid structure, allowing religious rites to take place in the disputed complex. Three years later, the foundation stone ('shilanyas') of a future Ram temple was laid—an act that continues to bedevil Indian politics even today. It was an act that continues to bedevil Indian politics till today.

In Hindi cinema, the old order was looking, well, distinctly old. Amitabh Bachchan had top billing in *Shahenshah* and *Ganga Jamuna Saraswati* but at forty-six, he was no longer the force he used to be. In *Shahenshah*, Bachchan played a bumbling and comically corrupt Mumbai police inspector by day and an imposing figure of dread for the city's criminals by night. In *Ganga Jamuna Saraswati*, he was cast as a truck driver who has been wrongfully imprisoned for two years and who goes looking for his estranged wife once he is a free man again. This was the last film to be directed by Manmohan Desai. *Ganga Jamuna Saraswati* was a dismal failure and *India Today* promptly declared that Bachchan's 'future looks uncertain'. The other movies of the year were symptomatic of late '80s Bollywood. Among them were masala entertainers such as *Tezaab* and *Dayavan* (a remake of Mani Ratnam's *Nayakan*), loud revenge dramas like *Khoon Bhari Maang* and *Zakhmi Aurat*; and multi-starrers including *Vijay* and *Khatron Ke Khiladi*.

When Mansoor Khan's *Qayamat Se Qayamat Tak* hit the screens on 1 March 1988, it offered audiences fresh energy and a sense of novelty with its cast of newcomers. Writer Aysha Iqbal Viswamohan observes that Aamir Khan was not cast in the mould of the big heroes of the time—the tough and macho Sunny Deol, Jackie Shroff and Sanjay Dutt. Instead, he was softer, closer to the Rishi Kapoor and Kumar Gaurav mould.[3] Director Mansoor Khan introduced several new ideas in the narrative; one such example is a reversal of gender dynamics: Aamir is first seen in the story strumming a guitar while Juhi Chawla, the heroine, is riding a horse.

Again, setting a trend that was to be followed by Sooraj Barjatya in *Maine Pyaar Kiya* with Salman Khan, the hero, and not the heroine, was presented as an object of desire. Scholar Jyotika Virdi notes that in their first encounter in QSQT, Rashmi (Juhi Chawla) gazes voyeuristically at Raj's (Aamir Khan) athletic body as he stands against the setting sun.[4] Here again, the hunter becomes the hunted, with the girl making the first move, saying *'Hum par aapka bada achcha* impression *pada hai'* (I have a really good impression of you) and then, in a later scene, asking to sleep next to him when they spend the night in the jungle. She says: *'Aa jaayen aapke paas?'* (Can I come closer to you?) This was refreshing, notes Virdi, because it brought in a new kind of heroine, sweet, innocent and yet determined, unlike the more overtly sexualised heroines of the '70s and '80s.

The Romeo and Juliet theme was something even the youngsters associated with the film could identify with. Gautam Chintamani describes the film's crew as being in much the situation and experiencing the same realities as the film's characters.[5] Cinematographer Kiran Deohans, Mansoor Khan and Aamir were either dating their future wives or were newly married. Chintamani quotes Deohans as saying: 'It wasn't tough to fall in love with the way the story was written,' adding that he could sympathise with Aamir's character. Deohans was a Hindu dating a Parsi, Mansoor was dating Tina, who was Christian, and Aamir was with Reena, a Hindu. All three of them could understand the dilemma of Aamir's character.

Aamir's life changed after QSQT. The *India Today* story of 1988 noted, 'His servants have become star servants in his neighbourhood and keep bringing autograph books for "Aamir baba" to sign. Aamir lives in a simple, non-filmi house where little girls keep peeping in through the windows. "They don't know what to say to me, they're embarrassed," he says. "And I don't know what to do with them, I'm embarrassed."'

Of the three Khans, Aamir was the first to acquire fame. He had heard of the other two, with whom his name would come to be permanently hyphenated. In an *Al Jazeera* interview in 2017, he recalled that the first time he met Salman was in Class II, at St Anne's, at Pali Hill, Mumbai. Though they were in the same class, they didn't know each other then. The second time was at the home of Aamir's friend, director Aditya Bhattacharya, who is called Babla by his family and friends. Aditya is the son of filmmaker Basu Bhattacharya. They were all fifteen then. Aamir was at Babla's house to discuss a short film called *Paranoia*, in which he was the actor, spot-boy, production head and first assistant director, all rolled into one. They shot the film over the course of a month, and it was the first time Aamir had ever acted as a young man, though he had appeared in uncle Nasir Husain's *Yaadon Ki Baaraat* as a child in 1973. That film, written by Salim-Javed, is considered by many scholars to be Indian cinema's first masala film, with its template of lost-and-found brothers, a self-sacrificing mother, and a fortuitous reunion just before the climax.

One day, Salman Khan, who lived close by, was cycling on Carter Road and rode past Babla's house. He knew Babla too. Aamir recalls: 'We stood on the balcony and talked. He told me about how he also wanted to become an actor. I thought of him as a sweet chap.' By 1988, the sweet chap was getting restless. In April that year, he was signed on to play the lead in Sooraj Barjatya's *Maine Pyaar Kiya*, but the movie that first made it to the theatres was J.K. Bihari's *Biwi Ho To Aisi*, in which he played Vicky, the younger brother of Farooque Sheikh. In the film, we see him dancing to Western music, clad in singlet and jeans, the walls of his room adorned with posters of Madonna, Rod Stewart, and Michael Jackson.

It so happened that J.K. Bihari had approached many actors, but they had all refused the role of the hero's young brother. In a *rediff.com* interview, Salman recounted how he came to be cast: 'I remember he had his office in a garage. A couple of actors had met him but things couldn't be finalised. Out of frustration, he said, "*Ab koi bhi* next idiot *aayega, main usko sign kar dunga.* (I will sign up the next idiot who comes). After some time, I walked in. I was the lucky idiot (laughs)."'[6]

At twenty-three, Salman was a veteran of the glamour world, having modelled for Campa Cola with Arti Singh, who later married a leading director of ad films, Kailash Surendranath. He had also appeared in a commercial for Lakhani shoes with Sangeeta Bijlani, his girlfriend at the time. His portfolio had been shot by Gautam Rajadhyaksha, who was working with Lintas and was soon to become the most celebrated photographer in Bollywood. He had also assisted Shashilal Nair on his film *Falak*, taking a bus to work every day.

It was around the same time, in the late '80s, that Sooraj Barjatya of Rajshri Productions was looking for a new face for his first film—*Maine Pyaar Kiya*. The film was supposed to revive the family banner and the 1965-born Sooraj, who was the same age as the Khans, knew he needed a newcomer—teenage romance films had traditionally done well as vehicles to launch the careers of young actors. The oft quoted example was Raj Kapoor's *Bobby* (1973) that made stars of Rishi Kapoor and Dimple. Someone suggested Salman Khan to the Barjatyas—at that point, Salman was known only as scriptwriter Salim Khan's son.

Sooraj Barjatya recalls: 'Heroes looked big and burly but Salman looked so small! But when I saw his photographs they were a world apart, so we decided to do a screen test one week before his birthday. The screen tests were rejected because no one liked the way he said "Kyon?". There was this girl, Shabana Dutt, who also suggested Salman's name to us. After four months, I started meeting people and *Biwi Ho To Aisi*, as it was produced by Suresh Bhagat, had an impressive cast. Salman was playing a side role. Suresh Bhagat also suggested Salman's name to us. We finally decided to cast him as the hero.'

Salman remembered being nervous about *Biwi Ho To Aisi*, which saw the light of day on 22 August 1988. 'The moment me and my brother Arbaaz saw the film, we cringed. I called Sooraj and told him that I am horrible in the movie. Then came the casting for the heroine for *Maine Pyaar Kiya*. We liked a girl who was the niece of a big star and her name was Shaheen Jaffrey [actor Saaed Jaffrey's niece, who was also Salman's girlfriend at the time]. Later Sooraj showed me pictures of Bhagyashree who was chosen by Raj Babu (Sooraj's father). I asked him, "Are you going to cast her as a sister in the film?"'

Barjatya says the sound mixing technician saw the rushes and said they would have to dub Salman's voice or else the film would not do well. But eventually they decided against dubbing. The actor remains grateful: 'A twenty-three-year-old boy had the courage to cast me. The film went on to become a hit. It was an expensive film, with a budget of ₹1 crore 11 lakh. Raw stock was expensive too. [This was the era before digital cameras were in common usage in India.] *Tabhi life ka* ambition *tha* ₹10 lakh *kamana*, which I made in my two films. I thought I'll put the money in the bank and get back to writing and modelling,' Salman recalled in an interview.[7] He was aware there was another Bandra boy, Aamir Khan, who had become a star. 'It was a big *bojh* on my *chaati* [burden on my chest]. I felt if I didn't do well, I would be screwed. I was like Bandra *mein toh koi nahin puchega toh Bhayandar main jaake rehna padega* [no one will ask for me in Bandra; so I'll have to live in Bhayandar.].' Luckily, *Maine Pyaar Kiya* (December 1989) was a huge hit.[8]

Back in 1988, another Khan was making waves in a medium that Aamir and Salman would embrace much later. Producer Lekh Tandon had been casting for the Doordarshan serial, *Dil Dariya*. State-run Doordarshan was then the only channel providing both news and entertainment. Tandon had left a message at veteran actor Sushma Seth's home, saying he would like to work with her daughter, Divya, who by then had become quite a star thanks to her role as the wannabe actress Majhli in *Hum Log*, a soap based on a quintessential middle-class family's trials and tribulations, which was also telecast on Doordarshan.

A few days later, Sushma, who played the grandmother in *Hum Log*, sent her daughter to the producer's house. Tandon recalled in an interview with *rediff.com* that he was sitting on the veranda when Divya Seth got out of her car, which was being driven by Shah Rukh Khan. Shah Rukh, who lived in Gautam Nagar, a middle-class neighbourhood, with his mother Lateef Fatima and sister Shehnaz Lalarukh, was mates with Divya. They were both part of the Theatre Action Group, led by Barry John and would act together in a now-forgotten film, *In Which Annie Gives it Those Ones*, directed by Pradeep Krishen and written by and starring Arundhati Roy. Recalls Tandon: 'He (Shah Rukh) dropped her off and was leaving when I asked her to call him back. I told him that if he cut his hair, I would give him work in my serial. He asked, "What if I cut my hair and you don't give me the job?" I told him to cut his hair and come and we would see. He cut his hair and I gave him a role in *Dil Dariya*.'

Tandon's friend, Colonel Raj Kapoor, saw Shah Rukh in *Dil Dariya* and subsequently cast him in *Fauji*, which aired from 18 January 1989. *Dil Dariya* was telecast after *Fauji* due to a delay in production. *Fauji* propelled Shah Rukh into the spotlight, even though he was cast by default. His character, Abhimanyu Rai, loosely based on Lieutenant Colonel Sanjoy Bannerji of the Bombay Sappers, was supposed to have been the second lead. However, Col. Kapoor, TV's endearing 'ketchup' uncle (those of a certain age might remember the immortal lines 'Ketchup *hota kaddu bhara*' [this ketchup is full of pumpkin] in the 1985 Volfarm commercial), said in an interview that the camera 'loved him so much' that they had to change the script to make him the lead. As journalist Chandrima Pal writes, 'At a time when the most popular television serials were about bows, arrows, clubs and crowns (*Ramayana* and *Mahabharata*), *Fauji* gave Doordarshan's younger demographic an insider's view into army life. Hand-to-hand combat, parachutes, machine guns with almost-real ammunition, bombs and a band of boys who nursed their cigarettes and their crushes were a hit, as were the lanky commandos in tiny boxers and their romantic interludes featuring women in puff-sleeved dresses (this was the '80s, after all).'[9]

Fauji brought Shah Rukh to the attention of producers in Mumbai. And at least one of his famous contemporaries, Aamir, remembers meeting him briefly when he was shooting with Juhi (Chawla) somewhere on the road in Mumbai. The film was Aziz Mirza's *Raju Ban Gaya Gentleman*. 'He was sweet, and it was a warm meeting,' said Aamir.

Shah Rukh was also cast in the TV series *Circus* and *Wagle Ki Duniya*, for which he flew in and out of Mumbai, but it was not until 1992 that he was seen on the big screen in his debut film, *Deewana*. Yet, in a 1991 interview with Nishi Prem, editor of *Stardust*, an influential film magazine of the time, he was already sounding like a star. Titled 'Rebel With a Cause', the story included a photograph of him sitting in the middle of a street, with a cigarette between his lips, saying outrageous things—soon to become his trademark: 'I don't understand why you want to interview me? Why are you writing about me? Yours is not a TV magazine to write about television stars. I have performed only on the small screen (so far).' He had been signed on, though, by Hema Malini for *Dil Aashna Hai*, Rakesh Roshan for *King Uncle*, G.P. Sippy for *Raju Ban Gaya Gentleman*, and Lalit Kapoor for *Deewana*, which ultimately released first. Shah Rukh already had the star system in his firing line. In the same interview, he spoke of how he perceived the early days of stardom: 'I find the entire set-up quite funny, you know, I've been shooting in Bombay for the past one month, and suddenly there are guys waiting to hold my cup of tea, tie my shoelaces, hold an umbrella over my head. Why? I am not a fucking retard.'

He was also already thinking about the end of stardom. 'Six years from now when people stop thinking about you, you're a fuck-up. And you'll realise it yourself, but by then you've lost yourself. You are only a fabrication, an image conjured up in the minds of other people. You don't even know what to think about yourself because it's been so long since you gave yourself a thought. You were leading a superficial life.'

Even Salman, in his less articulate way, spoke of his insecurities in a May 1990 interview.[10] In the interview, the journalist asks why he has not signed many films after *Maine Pyar Kiya*'s huge success. 'What's the hurry anyway? I am not without a roof over my head. I can take a chance and relax. Besides, signing twenty films isn't going to get you security. I'd call it risky. The next release flops and the others could soon be on the shelves. I know I can't cope with too many films. I can't go to the set, ask for my lines, say them and rush off. I need time to work things out. I improve only with practice.' He is asked the popular question often asked of celebrity children: Do they have it easy because they have something to fall back on? He answers with characteristic humour. 'Forget a room. I don't even have a pillow to fall back on. It all belongs to Dad. And that's why I want to make it big. I want to make lots of money.'

So bad was the work situation that Salim Khan had to call up his old friend, producer G.P. Sippy, and ask him to announce in trade magazines that he had signed on Salman. Sippy, in typically grand style, said he would not merely announce a film but make it as well. And that is how the 1991 film *Patthar ke Phool* happened. It was written by Salim Khan and starred debutante Raveena Tandon. The film was a hit and Salman's career was on track again.

It's important to remember that, like the other two Khans, Salman too is a product of pre-liberalisation India. When the

Filmfare journalist asked him about the Kumar Gaurav jinx—Gaurav had stormed the film scene with *Love Story* but lost the hearts of audiences soon after, to remain a classic one-film wonder. Surprisingly, Salman turned the whole thing on its head and answered with matter-of-fact sincerity: 'Wow! Who wouldn't want to be in Kumar Gaurav's shoes? He's got a beautiful home, is happily married, has a BMW, a Mercedes, he's happily settled and has got work. Besides, he's a nice guy. If I'm compared to him, I take it as a compliment.'

Around this time, Aamir Khan was involved in a flurry of activity. He had signed six films immediately after QSQT. There was one film that he had signed even earlier and it was *Raakh*, for his old friend Aditya Bhattacharya. The film cast Aamir as Aamir Hussain, who seeks vengeance for the rape of the woman he loves, played by Supriya Pathak, daughter of Bollywood's iconic 'mother', Dina Pathak. The film also starred Supriya's future husband, Pankaj Kapur. It had a young Santosh Sivan as cinematographer and Sreekar Prasad as editor, ensuring that even though it took a year-and-a-half to shoot, working on *Raakh*, as Aditya described it in a 2012 book on Aamir, was 'a joy and somehow untouched by the day-to-day cynicism that marks our trade'.[11] The film featured in the official selection at various film festivals, including Mannheim, Montreal, Moscow and Cairo, establishing Aamir as not just the star/boy next door but also as an actor who could play a complex role.

High praise was followed by the bruising the next six releases would inflict—they most definitely dented Aamir's confidence and were nothing short of mediocre and entirely forgettable fare. He played a star-crossed lover in *Love, Love, Love*; a promising cricketer in *Awwal Number*; a devoted hero in *Deewana Mujh Sa Nahin*; an anti-dowry activist in *Jawani Zindabad*; a playboy in *Afsana Pyar Ka* and Juhi Chawla's boyfriend, yet again, in the treasure-hunt-cum-romance, *Daulat Ki Jang*. All six movies failed dismally to appeal to the audience. Quite aware of the films' shortcomings, in a May 1990 interview, Aamir reflected: 'Sometimes the compromises you make for your career boomerang. I've learnt the intense fan following for QSQT was for something new rather than for something good.'[12]

The competition among the newbies in the film industry was becoming intense. Salman Khan's star had risen, even Rahul Roy was being feted for his role in Mahesh Bhatt's *Aashiqui*—whose music, best described as 'ghazal lite'—was the prototype for later movies such as *Saajan, Phool aur Kante, Dil* and *Deewana*. Released in June 1990, *Dil* managed to salvage Aamir's career, and he admitted as much: 'Suddenly it gave me a new lease of life. It gave me the power to begin again.'[13] Though the film had a youthful spirit and also starred the gorgeous Madhuri Dixit, it had a vastly different flavour from QSQT and lacked its polish. Aamir's Raja (in *Dil*) was not a nice boy to know, and in his own words, Raj was a brash brat who was rude to his father and rough with the girl.[14] He considered the role a departure from his performances so far, and perhaps embarrassed by the brazenness of the character, he said he was convincingly 'bad' simply by imitating Indu (director Indra Kumar) and his mannerisms.

On the political front, from even before the time QSQT had caught the nation's imagination, things had been going downhill for Rajiv Gandhi. The hope and hype around him had been extinguished by severe setbacks such as the AB Bofors arms scandal that broke in April 1987 when Swedish Radio claimed that the company had paid massive bribes to top Indian politicians and defence personnel in the ₹1,437 crore deal between India and the Swedish arms manufacturer, for the supply of 400 155mm Howitzer guns to the Indian Army. In the same month, Rajiv Gandhi famously told the Lok Sabha that no kickbacks were paid and no middlemen were involved.

In August 1987, a Joint Parliamentary Committee (JPC) was set up under former Union minister B. Shankaranand to investigate the allegations. A few months later, Indian investigators visited Sweden to probe the issue.

In a widely read cover story in 1988, *India Today* detailed Rajiv's decline, calling it 'The Changing Face of Rajiv Gandhi'. When he took office, he was not only 'Mr Clean' but also 'Mr Kool'. The man had a certain panache about him then. Steady under pressure, enjoying to the hilt his new workaday existence, goofing off once in a while with old buddies. Even holidays with the Bachchans didn't make the public mad at him. After all, every prime minister needs a break. In his public speeches, Rajiv Gandhi positively exuded verve. At a Congress Centenary speech in Bombay, he vowed to reform the party and kick out all power brokers. Those were the days when the '21st century' didn't sound like a cliche. When Rajiv could attack party chieftains like Pranab Mukherjee and Kamalapati Tripathi with nary a peep from the party. He talked good, he sounded good, he looked good. Khushwant Singh called him the 'handsomest prime minister in the world'.

But then, things began to change. The magazine reported, in the same cover story, that 'in the process of surmounting his crises, Rajiv now appeared to be sluggishly mired down in the status quo. He had "sort of ducked" away from crisis to crisis. No longer did he hold out the promise of magical change, dazzle and excitement—the pizzazz that had so electrified the middle class. South Block had snuffed out Camelot. The 'handsomest prime minister in the world' was now taking on a faint and jowly resemblance to his cousin Arun Nehru. Those who knew Rajiv agreed that he had become frustrated and disappointed because he could not bring about the changes he wanted to, in the time he promised. He realised that all the advertising ideas worked out by his personal media advisers did nothing, either to change his image or to establish a climate for speedy change.'

Yet, there were many positive changes that he brought about, which created an atmosphere where young people and youthful ideas could flourish. He deepened and widened India's democracy by not only ensuring that the voting age was brought down to eighteen, but also creating a new generation of women leaders through the 73rd Constitutional amendment, which reserved one-third of all panchayat seats for women.

It was a tremendous shift, recalls Mani Shankar Aiyar, Joint Secretary in the prime minister's office between 1985 and 1989. 'The world's largest democracy was also the least representative,' he told me. 'Rajiv Gandhi grasped the idea that India cannot have a responsive administration unless it is a responsible administration. And it cannot be responsible to the people being administered unless it is representative of those being administered. Democracy, where it mattered, was either non-existent or was in transient existence. In its failure to devolve powers formally, panchayats had become vehicles of mobilisation as vote banks. And so it was in 1988 that the focus shifted from Centre-State relations to the relationship between the State and the people of India. It was a revolutionary new idea, turning on its head the one that the Indian elite has inherited from the British that they knew better than the people of India.'

Those were also the years of two great foreign triumphs for Rajiv Gandhi. The first was a visit to China and an eight-and-a-half minute handshake in Beijing's Great Hall of the People with the country's Grand Old Man, Deng Xiaoping. It was a demonstration that India was no longer the militarily weak nation that had lost the 1962 war against China, as well as proof that whatever their differences, the two countries would work towards eventual reconciliation. There was also a trip to Pakistan at the end of 1988 for the fourth SAARC summit, which became the first bilateral visit by an Indian prime minister to Pakistan since 1960. In 1989, Rajiv would make a formal bilateral visit. The sight of two prime ministers who came of age after 1947—Benazir Bhutto was the first democratically elected leader of her country since 1977—was enough to make even hardened foreign reporters somewhat giddy with excitement.

As Steve Coll, reporting for *The Washington Post* wrote in 1989: 'Under a blistering sun on the airport tarmac this afternoon, Gandhi and Bhutto walked side by side to inspect a Pakistani military honour guard. Later, after being whisked through the city, guarded by federal security police stationed along Islamabad's main streets, Gandhi was feted at a state dinner. The two also were scheduled for private talks in advance of a joint press conference Monday. Gandhi and Bhutto have developed an apparently comfortable personal relationship based on shared generational and political experiences.'[15]

1989 was also the beginning of the software revolution in India, with a breakfast meeting between Jack Welch and Sam Pitroda in the Chambers of the Taj Mansingh Hotel in Delhi. Welch, CEO of General Electric, wanted to sell aircraft engines and turbines to India. Pitroda was a man of many titles: Adviser to C-DOT (Centre for the Development of Telematics). Adviser to the Prime Minister on Technology Missions. Chairman of the Telecom Commission. Secretary to the Department of Telecom. Pitroda wanted to sell GE Indian software.

In my conversation with Pitroda, he told me: 'Thirty days after the Welch meeting, eleven GE executives appeared in Delhi from their plastics, consumer goods, appliances and other divisions. Our job now was to show them around and give them a sense of our software capability. We had several government-sponsored organisations with software people, including C-DOT, the Centre for the Development of Advanced Computing (C-DAC), the country's supercomputer operation, and a national informatics centre. But in the private sector there wasn't much, and the GE executives would want to assess our consulting potential. The truth was that the Indian software-consulting industry was just being born. Tata Consulting had a few people, Infosys had five, Wipro eight or ten. When I called to set up meetings, Infosys called back to say, "Sam, you've set up this meeting with GE, but we don't even have an office." I told them, "Don't mention that. Arrange the meeting at one of the five-star hotels. Say that you will be there anyway for some other meetings. You might as well meet them there."'

While India didn't have the proper organisational infrastructure back then, it definitely had software engineering talent. What Pitroda wanted to do was show GE the quality of India's software engineers. It turned out that the GE executives were very pleased with the visit. At its conclusion, they announced that they would be giving India a 10-million-dollar order. Today, these software companies have gone global. Together, they have over half-a-million employees and a market cap in the area of hundreds of billions of dollars.

Yet, by November 1989, it was all over for the Congress. It was defeated in the general elections. Rajiv Gandhi was followed by V.P. Singh as prime minister and then, in late 1990, for six months by Chandra Shekhar, with outside support from the Congress.

On 21 May 1991, Rajiv Gandhi was brutally assassinated in Sriperumbudur, Tamil Nadu, while campaigning for his party before a crucial election that may well have seen him return to power. It was a suicide bombing carried out by Thenmozhi Rajaratnam (also known as Kalaivani Rajaratnam or Dhanu), a member of the Sri Lankan Liberation Tigers of Tamil Eelam (LTTE) which was fighting for a separate Tamil nation. India had ended its involvement in the Sri Lankan civil war by withdrawing the Indian Peace Keeping Force (IPKF). The Supreme Court held that the decision to eliminate Rajiv was perhaps triggered by the former prime minister's interview to *Sunday* magazine in August 1990 where he said that if he returned to power, he would send the IPKF to disarm the LTTE.

When the new government came to power—a Congress-led coalition with P.V. Narasimha Rao as prime minister—its first priority was economic reforms following the financial downturn during the Chandra Shekhar interregnum which saw India pledging her gold reserves. Added to that was the first Gulf War (January–February 1991), which was possibly the first globally televised war in history. It opened up India as a potential market for satellite broadcasters from all around the world, as a collective of strong, albeit unregulated cable television networks came up. This gave Indians access to foreign news channels such as CNN and BBC, as well as American soaps such as The *Bold and the Beautiful* and *Santa Barbara*. Economic liberalisation and social transformation were happening simultaneously. This was the backdrop against which three young Muslim men rose to prominence as icons for India's youth, echoing the 1950s when three Muslim women—Nargis, Madhubala and Waheeda Rahman—embodied beauty, intelligence and passion for India's moviegoers.

Aamir Khan's next release, in 1992, was his cousin Mansoor Khan's *Jo Jeeta Woh Sikander.* The film was plagued by casting problems and took two years to make. Milind Soman shot for the role eventually played by Deepak Tijori, but he didn't get along with the director—30 per cent of the film, shot with Soman, had to be scrapped. Girija Shettar, whom Mansoor Khan had seen in Mani Ratnam's *Geetanjali* (1989), shot for Ayesha Jhulka's role but left the film because it was way behind schedule. Akshay Kumar was also screen-tested but lost out, according to choreographer-turned-director Farah Khan, because he was 'doing strange things with the ball instead of playing volleyball as the scene required'. Pooja Bedi's role was initially offered to Nagma, whose mother felt the 'gold digger' character would not go down well with her image.

Farah Khan had recently returned from Bangalore, where she was assistant director on the post-production of *Malgudi Days*, and Mansoor Khan hired her as fourth assistant director. Her primary task was to find extras who had to look like they were middle-class college students. But when choreographer Saroj Khan didn't turn up one day, Farah was given charge of the songs. The first song she choreographed, with Aamir performing, was *Pehla Nasha*, which became a super hit. She still remembers Aamir giving her a lesson on perspective by drawing on the ground with a stick—two screens which showed the left and right perspective. Farah can reproduce these diagrams on paper to this day. She also remembers Aamir's relentless quest for perfection, repeating a long uphill cycle run several times because he wasn't satisfied with the expression on his face.

Meanwhile, after *Maine Pyaar Kiya*, Salman's superstardom seemed a foregone conclusion, with the media coining the term 'Salmania' because he had become an object of love and fantasy for his fans. In May 1990, Mumbai's most prestigious film magazine, *Filmfare*, put him on the cover with the story headlined 'Salman Khan: The New Craze'. In November 1991, he was once again *Filmfare*'s solo cover boy. A photograph of Salman was also the dominant one on a 1991 cover about the year's achievers.[16] But, despite this coverage, there were already signs that Salman would never be the critics' favourite. At the Filmfare Awards (1989), while his *Maine Pyaar Kiya* co-star, Bhagyashree, was awarded 'Most Outstanding New Face' and Barjatya the 'Most Sensational Debut of the Year', Salman's arrival went unrecognised in award terms. It marked the start of Salman's apparent prosecution at the hands of the media. Social media chatter by the star's fans even today testifies to the fact that they have still not forgiven the magazine for not giving their hero an acting debut trophy that year.

Rauf Ahmed, who was then the magazine's editor, clarified that *Filmfare*, in fact, had no such acting debut trophy at the time. 'The "Most Sensational Debut of the Year" was not meant to be only for acting,' he said. The winner of that particular award was chosen after deliberations between the editor and his team. 'We gave it to Aamir Khan for 1988's *Qayamat Se Qayamat Tak* because we thought his was a good performance ... For 1989, we gave it to Sooraj Barjatya for directing *Maine Pyar Kiya* because he had made a sensational beginning with that film. We didn't think Salman's was a great performance, but everyone had assumed it would go to Salman because I had earlier given it to Aamir.' According to Rauf Ahmed, it was only from the following year that awards were given specifically to male and female newcomers. And so Shah Rukh bagged the prize for 1992.

Salman appeared deeply affected by the snub. 'He stopped talking to me, there was a cooling off with his family and he did not turn up for the awards the next year,' Ahmed said. He heard that 'they were upset because they felt I had deliberately avoided giving the award to Salman. So I said, it is not charity that I would give it to him. The performance did not merit the award.' The rift with the press would deepen further in years to come.

In Deepak Shivdasani's *Baaghi: A Rebel for Love* (1990), in which Salman was credited for the story idea, he played a college student braving murderous pimps to save the woman he loves (Nagma) from a life of prostitution. After that, he did a series of films in 1991 and 1992, the most successful being *Saajan* (1991). Salman plays Sanjay Dutt's younger brother in the movie. Dutt is lame, a poet who writes under the pen name Sagar, and is in love with Madhuri Dixit, as is Salman, a playboy. Dutt's role was first offered to Aamir Khan, who declined it, in a casting pattern repeated in later movies.

1991 was the year Shah Rukh's mother passed away. The young actor, who was twenty-six, finally took a chance and came to Mumbai at the invitation of his friend Viveck Vaswani. Journalist Bharati Pradhan describes meeting him in her editor's cabin at *Showtime*: 'I was excited to meet him because I found him charismatic and impressive in *Fauji* and *Circus*, and wanted my staffers to interview him. Simi Chandoke, Zoom TV's glamour anchor today, still remembers wondering why I was asking her to interview this unknown boy from Delhi. She also recalls that I spoke highly of his screen charm, and had pushed her to do his first interview for our magazine.'

Shah Rukh couldn't keep away from his cigarettes even then. Publisher Nari Hira, who had turned health-conscious, had declared the entire building a 'No Smoking' zone (long before it became fashionable to do so) and there were no ashtrays anywhere in the office. So Shah Rukh helped himself to the dustbin and dropped ash into it. But smoke he did.

Since he was never the sort of eager wannabe who carried his portfolio around, they shot Shah Rukh's pictures in publisher Nari Hira's cabin. And even the publisher wondered who this boy was.

Shah Rukh returned to Delhi soon after his first interview and quietly married his girlfriend, Gauri Chhiba, on 25 October 1991, the anniversary of their first interaction at a Delhi party seven years earlier. They married at a registrar's office in Delhi, and a traditional Hindu wedding followed—Shah Rukh rode to the venue on an elephant, wearing a suit borrowed from the costume department of *Raju Ban Gaya Gentleman*, which he was then shooting for in Mumbai. Though he had managed to convince Gauri's family that he would be a worthy husband, there was still tension because it was an inter-faith union.[17]

Walking down the nostalgic lane, actor-producer Viveck Vaswani, who had appointed himself Shah Rukh's mentor in Mumbai, helping him meet directors and producers, told IndianExpress.com: 'He didn't want to act in movies initially. He stayed with me because he didn't have a house then. When I asked him if you would like to act, SRK said, "No, I can't think of anything worse." It's only after his mother passed away that he decided to act in films. That's when we decided to make *Raju Ban Gaya Gentleman* so that he would have a platform. I took him to meet a whole bunch of other producers who were able to sort of give him work. I was playing a very safe game because I didn't want *Raju* to be his first film. You become a celebrity when your film is sold. *King Uncle* and *Dil Aashna Hai* may not have been very big, important roles but these are roles that got sold as opposed to all the other rival competitors like Rahul Roy and Armaan Kohli who were doing solo hero films but not getting their movies sold or released. SRK slowly understood the business of films and the result is there for all to see.' That was also when Shah Rukh became friends with Arbaaz, and he would often hang out at Galaxy, playing chess and generally being part of Salim Khan's extended family.

The movie Shah Rukh was cast in first was Hema Malini's *Dil Aashna Hai*, co-starring Divya Bharti. *Chamatkar* with Urmila Matondkar and *Raju Ban Gaya Gentleman* with Juhi Chawla also released in 1992. In an interview to *Filmfare* after *Deewana,* Shah Rukh said, 'I'm glad the film has done so well. I feel happy for the producer, the director. A hit is good for the industry as well. But I don't think I've contributed in any way to its success. My performance was awful—loud, vulgar and uncontrolled. I overacted terribly and I take full responsibility for it. But that's what happens when you work without a graph. I didn't even have the script with me. I was to start shooting for the film much later but then some of my other schedules got cancelled and I allotted my dates to this film. I am my worst critic and when I saw myself on the screen, I was appalled. Isn't it amazing that people have liked me in the film? Perhaps that's because I am a fresh face. It's not a performance I'd care to repeat or remember.'

Shah Rukh was also aware of the Khan competition. To the question on who he thought was his closest rival, he said: 'Well, there's Aamir Khan, I can't call him competition, he is a far better actor. If there's a superb actor in a country today it's Aamir. I've heard that he wants to retire after thirty and turn director. I plan to quit at thirty too.' Clearly, that didn't happen.

India was also changing, perhaps forever. On 6 December 1992, the Babri Masjid was demolished by kar sewaks. It was, as *India Today* said then, 'the death of secularism, the ideal India had long cherished'. The seeds of hate were germinating with alarming rapidity.

Shah Rukh's life was also about to change forever. The mahurat of Abbas and Mustan Burmawala's *Baazigar* was filmed in December 1992 and the main shoot was scheduled to start soon, with a view to wrapping up work by January or February. The movie chronicled the story of a young man with a vendetta against a business tycoon and his plot to destroy the rest of the tycoon's family. The film hit a roadblock after communal riots broke out in different parts of the country post the Babri Masjid demolition. It was only after things settled that shooting could resume.

Shah Rukh played the anti-hero effortlessly, but he had not been the first choice for the role. The producers, Venus Worldwide, had approached Salman, who at that point was doing Sooraj Barjatya's film, *Maine Pyaar Kiya*, and felt the negative role might not work for his good-boy image. Anil Kapoor, according to Mustan, felt he would not be able to carry off the negative role. Shah Rukh had come to meet producers at

Venus for the narration of a film which he did not like, but that led to a chance encounter with the director duo which landed him *Baazigar*.

Bombay was on fire during the 1992–1993 riots, in which 900 people were killed. Everyone in the city lived in fear. Businesses were shut for days and no one could leave their homes. The city saw two rounds of horrific communal violence, according to Justice B.N. Srikrishna, who led the Srikrishna Commission of Inquiry into the riots and blasts. The first bout of rioting in December was 'spontaneous' (a word used in the Srikrishna report), the result of angry Muslims hitting the streets to protest against the demolition of the mosque in Ayodhya. The Shiv Sena did get involved after the first forty-eight hours, but the initial flare-up pitted local Muslims against a worryingly partisan Mumbai police.

The second round of violence was far more complex. The immediate trigger was the burning of a Maharashtrian Hindu family in a Jogeshwari slum in January 1993, but there were a series of minor incidents and the inexplicable killings of mathadi (labour) workers in central Mumbai that suggested a deliberate attempt to instigate communal trouble. The Shiv Sena's cadres too had armed themselves with knives and kerosene bombs, and its sustained campaign of maha-aartis and Bal Thackeray's vitriolic speeches added a communal edge to the city's charged atmosphere. A toxic mix of crime and communalism was responsible for the 'second burning of Mumbai'. In an interview in February 1993 to journalist Rajdeep Sardesai, then Maharashtra chief minister Sudhakar Naik would dramatically claim that a land-mafia-underworld-neta nexus had orchestrated the January riots to oust Naik from office because he was trying to rein them in.[18] Just days after the interview, the chief minister was removed and replaced by Sharad Pawar.

Just before that, actor Sunil Dutt had requested his colleagues to unite and do their bit to end the riots. They formed a delegation of forty industry members who met Naik and told him to do whatever it took to put an end to the violence. Their job didn't end there—the delegation held a silent protest close to Mahatma Gandhi's statue near Mantralaya. Sadly, there were no cameras to capture and highlight the unity of the industry. As Aamir recounts, they stood and protested without the presence of any security or media. Sunil Dutt decided to protest around the clock till the riots stopped. So they would take turns and spend the night below the statue. On the first night, Sunil Dutt, Yash Chopra, Aamir Khan and Johnny Walker decided to stay back. Some others joined them in the morning and got them tea and breakfast. Aamir told NDTV, 'It was a wonderful time. It was a memorable night for me because I was sitting with stalwarts like Dutt Saab, Yashji and Johnnyji.'[19] The protest was called off and the actors and filmmakers went back home only when the chief minister took some action and the city returned to normal. Imagine this happening now in the age of establishment cheerleaders and hyper-nationalistic movies.

On 12 March 1993, there were twelve coordinated terror attacks on the city's iconic buildings, from the Bombay Stock Exchange to Zaveri Bazaar. Over 250 people were killed. The attacks were planned by Mumbai's underworld, which had undergone a fundamental metamorphosis. Till December 1992, the underworld was mostly 'secular': Dawood's gang, for example, included the likes of Sharad Shetty, Chhota Rajan, among others, all of whom had split the city's growing real estate riches amongst themselves, and were, in fact, perceived to be attached to local politicians. By January 1993, the same Dawood gang was sharply divided between Hindus and Muslims. In the second phase of rioting in that month, and even more specifically, by the time the blasts of 1993 took place, Dawood's prime gang-leaders were all Muslims: Tiger Memon, Chhota Shakeel and Abu Salem were key accomplices in the blast conspiracy. The

1992–93 riots communalised the underworld, perhaps forever. It certainly ended the age of Mumbai's wide-eyed innocence that had never heard of RDX; the underworld 'don' was no longer the local neighbourhood toughie aka Arun Gawli or even a 'supari' assassin, but a frightening enemy waging war against the state and citizenry.

Pre-December 1992, Dawood was a much-feared gangster and gold smuggler, but there is little evidence to show that he was a terrorist or, indeed, an ISI agent. The 1992–93 riots changed all that: from being a flag-waving 'patriot', Dawood was now an RDX-wielding Pakistan-sponsored terrorist targeting the city of his childhood; Tiger Memon was his chief henchman (Tiger's travel agency office, a cover for his criminal activities, was attacked in the January riots) while Tiger's brother Yakub, who was hanged in 2015, ran a successful chartered accountancy firm in Mumbai's Mahim area with a Hindu partner, Chetan Mehta.

It wasn't just Indian cricketers, but also much of the film industry that would happily attend Dawood's parties in Dubai and even agree to dance at them in the '80s. The industry was being increasingly financed by the underworld: producers would even be called to Dubai to finalise which actors would star in their films. Among these producers were Samir Hingora and Hanif Kadawala of Magnum Video. They were not small-time film-makers. Samir was the treasurer of the Indian Motion Pictures Association (IMPA), an influential industry body. Samir and Hanif had signed Sanjay Dutt for their film *Sanam*, which was to be shot during the period when the riots erupted. A year earlier, Sanjay had been introduced to Dawood for the first time, in Dubai, by filmmaker Feroz Khan during the making of *Yalgaar* and had attended a private dinner. Sanjay was gradually drawn into Dawood's film circle like many other stars, for whom a relationship with the don was both a financial necessity and a social obligation.

The venom was spreading. Sunil Dutt was threatened for his relief work during the riots by those who had split Mumbai into Hindu versus Muslim. He was targeted as a '*Musalmano ka tarafdar*' because he had tried to help families in Behrampada, a Muslim-dominated slum in his constituency that the Shiv Sena had labelled as a 'den of illegal Bangladeshis'. Significantly, Sunil Dutt had little support within the Congress then: he was never in any political camp and the Narasimha Rao government was already being seen as 'soft Hindu' for allowing the Babri Masjid to be demolished. Maharashtra's strongman Sharad Pawar was being attacked for failing to call in the army swiftly enough as Union defence minister, while the chief minister, Sudhakarrao Naik, was considered politically weak and mostly somnolent. Sunil Dutt was a bit of a solitary figure during the riots and it left him vulnerable. Whether there was any realistic threat to his life is uncertain but this was, one must remember, a city that was badly scarred and fearful, sharply divided by escalating communal violence.

While the Congress in Mumbai was on the retreat in 1992–93, the Shiv Sena and Bal Thackeray were on the ascendant. Thackeray had been in Maharashtra politics since the 1960s but it was only during the riots and its aftermath that he acquired a political saliency that went beyond his original 'Marathi manoos' constituency. This is the period when he was transformed into a 'Hindu Hriday Samrat', a saviour of the Hindus, in the polarised narrative of communal riots, a larger-than-life image that would win him the 1995 Maharashtra elections. (In a twist of fate, it was Thackeray who later pushed for Sanjay Dutt's charges to be watered down after Sunil Dutt paid him umpteen visits seeking help for his son).

The Shiv Sainiks were on a high during this period as the Srikrishna Commission of Inquiry (which was abandoned the moment the Sena-BJP government came to power in 1995) has graphically documented. The Sena 'controlled' Mumbai's graph of riots as the state government receded to the margins. Not only was Thackeray 'proud of his boys' for the Babri demolition, local Shiv Sena leader Pramod Navalkar admitted to Sardesai in an interview that, 'Yes, our Sainiks were involved in the Mumbai violence to protect Hindus'.[20] As it turned out, only one Shiv Sena leader, Madhukar Sarpotdar, was later convicted (in 2008) for his role in instigating the riots. He too was granted bail soon afterwards. More than a thousand people died in the Mumbai riots of December and January, a majority killed by sword-wielding thugs owing allegiance to political parties, but there were less than a dozen major convictions. In effect, the riots were treated like most riots in post-independence India, with the ringleaders getting away scot-free (just like the 1984 anti-Sikh pogrom and the 2002 Gujarat riots). Over 100 accused were convicted under the Terrorist and Disruptive Activities Act (TADA), the exceptions remain the chief conspirators, Dawood and Tiger who still reside in Pakistan. As filmmaker Mahesh Bhatt says, for a generation that hadn't seen Partition, the 'other' was created in 1992. And the other was invariably 'the Muslim'.

In the UK newspaper, *The Independent*, Tim McGirk reported that until then, religious discrimination was alien to the Mumbai film world. There were as many Muslim stars as Hindus, and movie plots never had a communal twist, as confirmed by Subhash Ghai: 'The heroes of our movies are always secular. If anyone tries to divide by religion or caste, they're the villains.'[21] But the Shiv Sena gained strength after the riots, which Thackeray described as a victory of the city's Hindus against Muslims. 'The powerful third eye of Hinduism is opening,' he proclaimed.

Soon, the industry that had once paid homage to Dawood started celebrating Thackeray, who often became their first port of call when in trouble, whether it was Amitabh Bachchan[22] or

Sunil Dutt.[23] *The Independent* reported that a 'famous actress once appealed to Mr Thackeray for protection after thugs hired by a rival kept heckling her during her stage performances. He sent over twenty boys with knives. They were ready to stab to death anyone in the audience who booed or walked out during the middle of the show, said the actress, who preferred not to be identified. Luckily, everyone stayed in their seats that night.'[24]

Luck may have favoured her, but it was slowly deserting the city of Mumbai.

2

1993–1999

A Split Nation, Divided Stars

The huge impact that Shah Rukh Khan made on Hindi cinema and its audience was running parallel to profound changes in Indian society and politics. The city he had made his home—Mumbai—was also the heartland of Hindi film production. This great metropolis had changed and, by the end of 1993, fear and suspicion ruled, following the bomb blasts that had shaken the core of a seemingly all-inclusive space where people of all states and religions slid into the fabric of the city.

The deep emancipatory potential of the urban modern, which spoke to new visions of community, independence and freedom, was shattered. The city of many citizens was transformed into a city of strangers marked by the ubiquity of 'evil', wrote scholar Radhika Subramaniam in her analysis of the culture of suspicion engendered by the Mumbai riots.[1]

It was also during this time that the underworld's role in film financing came to the fore. In April 1993, actor Sanjay Dutt, who was tipped to become the industry's number one star, was arrested under the Terrorist and Disruptive Activities Act (TADA) and the Arms Act for having accepted an AK-56 assault rifle from the underworld-linked producer duo, Hanif-Samir, of Magnum Video. TADA, an anti-terrorism law, had come into being during the height of the Punjab insurgency, in 1985, and remained in force across India till 1995.

Released on bail in May 1993, Dutt was able to witness the success of *Khalnayak*, where, in one of life's many ironies, he played a terrorist. Directed by Subhash Ghai, the movie sparked controversy for the suggestive lyrics of its chartbusting song, '*Choli ke peeche kya hai?*', picturised on the heroine, Madhuri Dixit. Dutt was re-arrested in July 1994 and finally released in October 1995, after being granted bail by the Supreme Court. Over the next two decades or so, he would be arrested and released several times. His roles in *Munnabhai* M.B.B.S. (2003) and *Lage Raho Munnabhai* (2006), the beloved franchise, did much to improve his image. He was finally released in February 2016 after completing his forty-two-month sentence.

The arrest of Sanjay Dutt in 1993 uncovered what by then had become a five-year-old relationship between the Hindi film world and the notorious Dawood Ibrahim. High on Mumbai police's wanted list for the murder of Samad Khan, a rival gangster, Dawood had fled to Dubai, from where he organised the lucrative export of gold to India and also acquired an iron grip over other underworld operations in the nation's financial capital.

Around the time when Shah Rukh Khan was making his presence felt through *Fauji,* a new breed of producers and financiers was producing films in Mumbai, and some of them allegedly had a Dubai link. Some named producer Sudhakar Bokade as one such producer who benefitted from dubious help. A former cargo-handler with Air India, Bokade produced his first film, *Izzatdar*, in 1988, with Dilip Kumar, Govinda and Madhuri Dixit. The film flopped, yet he went on to make *Nyay Anyay* for ₹1 crore and then *Saajan* for ₹1.5 crore, starring Sanjay Dutt, Madhuri Dixit and Salman Khan. Then there were Mukesh Duggal (who made *Fateh*, starring Sanjay Dutt, in 1990) and Dinesh Patel (who produced *Phool Aur Kaante*, starring Ajay Devgan, in 1991). Both owned nondescript garment shops before turning producers.

Before Shah Rukh made inroads into Mumbai films, the industry was loosely divided into three categories. There were the big banners with producer/directors at the helm, such as Yash Chopra and Subhash Ghai; independent directors who owned their own production companies, including Mahesh Bhatt and Vidhu Vinod Chopra; and purely commercial filmmakers who catered to the 'the front-benchers' (the audiences seated in lower priced seats, closer to the screens in theatres). According to the 15 May 1993 issue of *India Today*, it was the third category of filmmakers whose films were regarded as entertainment for the masses and were said to be backed by underworld money.

Dawood wasn't the first mobster to invest in film production. The most famous before him was Haji Mastan Mirza, a gold-smuggler-turned-politician and businessman. But Dawood was the first non-resident don to invest in Bollywood, flying top stars to Dubai for private parties or cricket matches and lavishing expensive gifts on them. India, during this period, appeared to be in the grip of what *India Today* called a 'graftocracy'. The heroes of liberalisation were quickly becoming villains—the most infamous of them being Harshad Mehta, the star stockbroker who had proudly showed off his expensive imported cars and had photographers take countless photos of his 15,000 sq. ft. home on Bombay's Worli Seaface. His house, with its billiards room, mini-theatre and a nine-hole putting green was exposed as little more than the reward for fraud and the illegal raising of money from banks to bump up share prices.

In June 1993, Harshad Mehta had, with typical braggadocio, staged a press conference to claim that he had given a one crore rupee bribe to prime minister P.V. Narasimha Rao. (His story was most recently retold on SonyLIV in a streaming series called *Scam 1992*. The series won much praise for its deft portrayal of the politics and financial markets of the time. It was quickly followed by a movie on the same subject, *The Big Bull*, starring Abhishek Bachchan.)

Narasimha Rao, who came to power in mid-1991 and ran a minority government, was bedevilled by several other problems. There were challenges to his authority from his own party members, most notably from senior Madhya Pradesh Congressman Arjun Singh, who made an unsuccessful bid to lead the Congress (I). Narasimha Rao's relationship with Sonia Gandhi, the widow of former prime minister Rajiv Gandhi, was also not particularly easy. There were a series of scandals, old and new. In July 1993, Rao's government faced a no-confidence motion. It was alleged that he had, through a representative, offered bribes to members of the Jharkhand Mukti Morcha (JMM), and possibly a breakaway faction of the Janata Dal, to vote for him during the no-confidence motion. Shailendra Mahato, one of those who had accepted the bribe, turned approver.

Two more cases haunted him. One was the Lakhubhai Pathak cheating case dating back to 1983. Pathak, an Indian businessman living in England, alleged that Narasimha Rao, along with two shadowy aides, Chandraswami and K.N. Aggarwal alias Mamaji, had cheated him of $100,000. The amount was given in return for the promise of allowing supplies of paper pulp to be imported into India, and Pathak alleged that he spent an additional $30,000 entertaining Chandraswami and his secretary. The second case dated back to 1989 when Narasimha Rao, former minister K.K. Tewary, Chandraswami and K.N. Aggarwal were accused of forging documents showing that Ajeya Singh had opened a bank account in the First Trust Corporation Bank in St. Kitts and deposited $21 million in it, making his father, former prime minister V.P. Singh, its beneficiary. The alleged intent was to tarnish V.P. Singh's image.

By mid-1996, after demitting office, the man who had wisely steered India away from the troubled waters of virtual bankruptcy towards liberalisation, was named in the JMM bribery case; a month later, he was summoned in the Pathak cheating case, and by September, he was an accused in the St Kitts forgery case. However, by the time he died in 2004, Rao had cleared himself of all accusations.

The 1990s was a decade of contradictions, and as much about the eroding of faith in state institutions as the growth of the private sector; economic liberalisation and religious revivalism; mounting consumerism and rising social anomie. In 1991, the Indian skies had re-opened to private airlines, with Jagson Airlines becoming the first to commence operations in 1992. In October 1993, Coca-Cola returned to India after sixteen years of exile. In 1995, Mobilink began pager services in Delhi. By September of the same year, cellular services began through private operators, and a month later, the cabinet cleared tie-ups worth ₹3,100 crore with foreign car makers. In 1998, it allowed 26 per cent foreign equity in the insurance sector, and a year later, the Insurance Deregulation Bill was passed. Internet services were rolled out in 1995 by Videsh Sanchar Nigam Limited and in November 1998, the government opened them up to the private sector. By 1999, there was a new telecom policy which drastically reduced the cost of calls. FM radio was also opened to private players although news broadcasts were, and still are, restricted to the terrestrial state radio.

It was a time of angst and aspiration. There were great global conquests from victories in beauty pageants, with Delhi girl Sushmita Sen becoming Miss Universe and Mumbai model Aishwarya Rai becoming Miss World (both in 1994), and the Booker Prize in 1997 being won by Arundhati Roy for *The God of Small Things*. There were some terrible tragedies too, from the 1994 pneumonic plague outbreak in Surat to the 1999 killing of Australian missionary Graham Staines by the extremist Hindu group, Bajrang Dal, in Odisha.

Shah Rukh Khan had captured the anxiety of a nation at war with itself in 1993 with his psychotic anti-hero roles in Abbas-Mustan's *Baazigar* and Yash Chopra's *Darr*. In her iconic book *Bombay Cinema: An Archive of the City*, Ranjani Mazumdar wrote of how these films with their unhinged heroes reinvented the withdrawn anti-hero as a self-destructive force. The changed circumstances required a different kind of narrative, she stated. The desire here was to move away from the social context into a world where despair had turned into a personal nightmare. Javed Siddiqui, who wrote *Baazigar,* saw the psychotic as an extension of Salim-Javed's 'angry man', the only difference being in motivation and impact. The angry man's compulsion contains a dialogue with society on issues of justice. The psychotic fights only for himself. This drive toward death, imbued with a radical evil, was surely Bombay cinema's Nietzschean moment.

Mazumdar quotes scriptwriter Javed Akhtar's explanation for this fascination with Shah Rukh's anti-heroes: 'I suppose we respect perfection. We respect freedom. There is evil in all of us, there is a sadist hidden in each one of us, but our morality has imprisoned it and when we see somebody whose evil has broken all the moral norms and now he's a complete person in himself, even in his ill-doing, we admire that person because he is a law unto himself, he's a morality in himself. We respect that power. We don't want to imitate him, but that power fascinates us.'

The rise of the deranged man was explained by the culture of materialism, money and success in a jungle-like society where only the fittest survived. So the anti-hero who would tolerate no obstacle on the path to his self-declared true love (*Baazigar*, *Darr* and *Anjaam*) could also morph into Rahul, the almost-pimp who works for Aditya Pancholi's boss character, Siddharth, in *Yes Boss* (1997). He will do anything to become rich, including sexually entrapping women. As Rahul puts it: *'Zindagi ki har baat sirf sach ya jhoot nahin hoti. Hum sab mein kuchh na kuchh kamiyan hain jo kabhi kabhi humein aisi cheezen karne par majboor karti hain jisse kisi na kisi ko thes pahunchahti hain. Hum sab adhure hain.'* (Everything in life is not about truth or lies. We all have some flaws which force us to do things that hurt others. We are all incomplete human beings.)

In all these roles, Shah Rukh, though fairly new to the industry, showed a rare dynamism, perhaps drawing on his own experience of life in Delhi, moving seamlessly from a middle-class Muslim household to a school run by Christian missionaries, to a cosmopolitan theatrical group where he did a variety of jobs—from lighting to set coordination—to marrying an upper-class Hindu young woman from a conservative army background. In *Baazigar*, his character, Ajay moves between different social classes—he is educated, and though we do not see him holding down a job, he leads the life of an urban, upper-class man. The shifting between genres is an established form in Hindi films, and so Ajay is many things at once. Perhaps for visual effect and to emphasise his access to many worlds, the murders he is guilty of take place in a college hostel room, in a five-star hotel room, and on the top floor of a skyscraper.

In real life, Shah Rukh possesses a similar measure of obsessiveness, amply demonstrated in his relationship with his wife Gauri. In the first season of *Koffee with Karan* in 2004, Gauri says as much, when speaking about the early years of them knowing each other: 'He was too possessive of me and I just couldn't handle it. I wanted to be by myself, meet people, go out, hang out, he couldn't handle it. I wanted my own space. I did it for a while and then I went back to him.' The host and director of some of Shah Rukh's best-loved movies, Karan Johar, intervenes saying how Shah Rukh came running after her to Mumbai and looked for her everywhere, heading to every beach in town because he knew that she loved swimming, and that he finally found her on Gorai beach. To which Gauri replies: 'Wherever I would go, he would be there and I couldn't bear it.' 'So he was very well cast in *Darr*,' says Karan, to which Gauri replies: 'Totally.'

The bipolarity afflicting society was also something Shah Rukh Khan was said to be suffering from. As Anupama Chopra writes: 'Gauri called him Shah Rukh One and Shah Rukh Two, which she explained as "two sides: one is saying one thing, the other is saying the complete opposite, and both in the space of a minute".'[2] This prompted writer Javed Akhtar to jokingly ask Gauri once, 'How are they?'

As the nation was being divided along religious, social and economic lines, Shah Rukh's cinematic transformation was also underway, often effectively capturing the zeitgeist. In 1995, he played Raj in *Dilwale Dulhaniya Le Jayenge* (DDLJ), and suddenly there was a new way of negotiating the liberalisation and globalisation unleashed in India—the opening up of the country as a marketplace for the world could still co-exist with its deep rootedness in tradition and culture.

This also meant the image of the second-generation NRIs as wasted hippies or drunk tarts, permanently etched in the Indian psyche by the hugely successful *Purab aur Paschim* in 1970, was altered forever. Now Indians could be as comfortable in London as they were in Punjab, whether they were from a rich NRI family like that of DDLJ's Raj or a working-class NRI family like that of the heroine, Simran.

In Raj, Aditya Chopra gave the NRI and new India what it was desperately seeking: every girl's fantasy lover who would keep her chaste till marriage, every mother's virtuous son who would promise to fulfill her daughter's dreams, and every father's ideal son-in-law who would show that he respects age-old conventions. DDLJ offered us a new template for a hero. Raj replaced Vijay, the prototype of Amitabh Bachchan's Angry Young Man. That image was soon buried and gone. No longer did the hero rage at the establishment or an unfair world, nor did he have to make it from rags to riches the hard way, and no longer did he have to avenge someone (in particular, his wronged mother). Raj was a yuppie who worked the system to get the desired results, he was not any kind of anti-establishment rebel. An articulate global Indian, he was equally comfortable in a nightclub in Paris or a village in Punjab. Depending on the situation, he could be progressive or conservative. He played by the rules but also tweaked them when necessary. Unlike Vijay, Raj was not larger than life. He was scripted, as Aditya Chopra put it, as life. 'The herogiri was gone. It was the age to be chilled out.'[3] He was the new Indian man, comfortable when peeling vegetables with the women of the house, fasting along with the love of his life on Karva Chauth, but also able to win over the more blatantly chauvinistic men in the film, Simran's father and her fiancé. More than playing the prototype, Shah Rukh played himself. He was the best of the East and the West, a fusion star for a confused country torn between economic liberalisation and social conservatism.

The media loved Shah Rukh, and he loved it right back, giving them quotable quotes in countless interviews. In January

1994, fresh off the success of *Baazigar* and *Darr* and dressed in a tuxedo, he got his first *Filmfare* cover shot by the ace stills photographer, Rakesh Shreshtha. In an interview to *Filmfare* in June 1994, he holds forth on the new computer he has bought, which the magazine calls his 'new playmate': a computer with a fax and a colour printer, as well as a laser disc player. Asked a question about his superstardom, he says that it is heady and scary, but 'interesting roles, top banners, big bucks, rave reviews, much-coveted awards, super hits, a happy family life—I've had it all in the last six months.' He talks about complacency, putting on weight, and his wife telling him off, asking him to focus on a goal. Because 'when you're supremely content, you die'.

In the same interview, when asked about doing three similar movies, *Darr, Baazigar* and *Anjaam*, he says that perhaps Aamir should have accepted *Darr* and Salman should have done *Baazigar*. He also speaks of how his face is not as clean-cut as Salman's or as cute as Aamir's. 'I'm just an okay-looking, ordinary guy, which makes it easy for me to slip into any role. I can never be slotted.'

His relationship with Salman Khan, it appears, was already coming under strain. In a November 1993 *Filmfare* interview, he alluded to this when he said that a joke he had made earlier about 'the body building role' while doing a shoot for Rakesh Roshan's *Karan Arjun* misfired, with Salman getting very angry. In the same breath, he added: 'I told Salman if I wanted to be nasty, I'd tell him so on his face. C'mon, I wouldn't hurt a guy like him. His family and Chunky's [actor Chunky Pandey] have really looked after me during my early days in Bombay. My wife's always at Salman's place. Gauri and his sister Alvira are close friends. And if I had any objections to working with body builders, I'd only be surrounded by girls. Most of the guys are all brawn and muscles—Salman, Sunny, Jackie and Sanjay Dutt. I think Rishi Bhai [the late Rishi Kapoor], Anil Kapoor and I are the only weaklings.'

In 1995, he won the Filmfare Best Actor award for DDLJ, over Aamir Khan's endearing performance in Ram Gopal Varma's *Rangeela*. Shah Rukh, unintentionally or intentionally, rubbed it in when it came to his acceptance speech at the award ceremony. 'How I wish,' he said, 'I could dance like Govinda, I could act like Aamir, look like Salman, fight like Ajay. But you don't just get everything. You have to work hard.'

Indeed, Munna, Aamir's tapori character in *Rangeela*, was hard work. He's a carefully crafted little guy who is unable to confess his love to Mili (Urmila Matondkar), his neighbour in the chawl, who breaks into Bollywood's big league. Munna embodies the lower middle class, dazzled by the gifts of liberalisation—from five-star hotels to foreign cars—but not swept away by them. There is a certain integrity in the life that he leads, albeit on the margins of society. Catering to cine-goers in a movie-mad nation, Munna is a ticket tout, selling movie tickets in the black market at higher prices, a phenomenon that has disappeared from most big Indian cities owing to the multiplex boom. He is unashamed of his profession, and at one point taunts a policeman by saying: '*Bombay mein danga fasad karnewale ko chhod dete hain; share bazaar mein hazaaron karodon ka gapla hua, kisi ko pakda kya? Nahin pakda. Apun seedha saadha aadmi, picture dekhne ko aaya, apun ko pakadta hai. Pakdo bhai pakdo, aapka raj hai.*'(They didn't arrest the trouble-makers in the Bombay riots and in the stock market, thousands of crores went missing—was anyone caught? No, no one was. And a straight-forward guy like me who's just come to the movies—you wanna catch me? Go ahead, brother! You're the boss.)

An interview by *Rangeela* director Ram Gopal Varma given to then *Filmfare* editor Khalid Mohamed added to Aamir's already frigid relationship with the movie magazine and the movie media in general. Years later, Varma recalled: 'The famous controversy between me and Aamir happened six to seven months after

Rangeela released. Khalid Mohamed was doing an interview with me in which I was giving an explanation that the audience can rarely understand the difference between a character and an actor. I cited the scene in *Rangeela* when Aamir takes Urmila to a restaurant. Now the waiter of a five-star hotel steward is higher in social status than Munna, but being a waiter he has no choice but to serve him. But on a human being level he can barely hide his disgust hearing Munna's lines. So I told Khalid that the lines are being delivered by Aamir but the look on the waiter's face is what is making the audience laugh. So in that particular scene it calls for more complex acting on the waiter's part compared to Aamir's. Khalid who apparently had a personal axe to grind with Aamir went ahead and printed this article which read as though I said, "The waiter was better than Aamir."'

Varma continued: 'By the time the article came out I was off on a Telugu film shoot in interior Andhra Pradesh. Aamir tried to contact me and in those days there were no cell phones. The fact that I was not getting in touch with him and him not knowing where I was, he thought I was avoiding him as the media was hounding him to react. He went ahead and reacted and the media blew the thing up into a full-scale war. The moment I realised what had happened, I met Aamir and explained it to him. He wanted me to give a statement in print against Khalid that I was misquoted to which I said I can't, because I did say all those things, it's just that it's too technical for a layman at that time to understand and I should not have spoken to a man like Khalid about that and that was a mistake. Some cold vibes still remained with good reason till years later we met at a party and had a long chat and since then we are cordial with one another.'[4]

In 1994, Aamir was still speaking to sections of the movie media. Reporting from the sets of two films, *Baazi* and *Akele Hum Akele Tum*, *Movie* magazine stated that the actor had started three new films that year, the third being *Raja Hindustani*. It also spoke of his 'sullen silence' towards the majority of the English language press. The author of the article found in Aamir a prim, polite and principled actor who thrived on the attention of his fans, which he considered a 'belated ovation'; a man who read Dostoevsky, Somerset Maugham, Daphne du Maurier and P.G. Wodehouse; and was very clear that there should be no vulgarity or obscenity in his films. 'If you want pelvic thrusts and dialogues brimming with double meaning, don't even bother leaving your visiting card,' wrote journalist Sonali Kotnis.

In Aamir Khan's early decision to make movies that matter, you see the birth of the actor as character. 1994 was also the year the Khans acted together in pairs, for the first time. Aamir Khan and Salman Khan starred in Rajkumar Santoshi's *Andaz Apna Apna*, a comedy where the two male leads did not talk to each other for much of the duration of the shoot, nor did the two female leads, Karisma Kapoor and Raveena Tandon. (Karisma who was then dating fellow actor Ajay Devgan had forbidden him from associating with Raveena, with whom he had been friends for a long time.) Though the two Khans strenuously denied rumours of dissension, Aamir Khan did acknowledge later how difficult it was to work with Salman, who was 'moody' and 'mercurial'.

Salman Khan started the year as a has-been. In October 1993, *Dil Tera Aashiq* with Madhuri Dixit had flopped, and so did *Chandra Mukhi* with Sridevi. *Andaz Apna Apna* was yet to be released, and though it would not be a commercial success. It gathered critical appreciation and became a cult film with a loyal fan club that swells annually. Salman was then shooting for old friend Sooraj Barjatya's *Hum Aapke Hain Koun*, and that is where Rakesh Roshan met him on the sets in Filmistan, 'looking fresh' in jeans and a T-shirt. Roshan offered him *Karan*

Arjun, to replace Ajay Devgan, who had walked out. Salman didn't hesitate, even leaving the choice of role to the director. This was to become the first time that Salman Khan acted with Shah Rukh Khan.

Devgan, by all accounts, was not amused. He had been ready to do the film but Shah Rukh had talked him out of it, only to return to it. Shah Rukh explained it in an interview to *Stardust* in 1993: 'I wasn't too happy with the film to begin with. In fact, Ajay and I wanted to switch roles, When Rakeshji wouldn't agree, we both decided to drop out. Salman was taken on for Ajay's role, I went off to Delhi. I'd planned to return a couple of days before the mahurat to tell Rakeshji I wasn't doing the film. Before that could happen, I learnt that my remark about not working with body builders had been misinterpreted.' Shah Rukh went on to reiterate: 'Salman thought I wasn't doing the film because of him which just wasn't true. His family was very kind to me when I had first come to Bombay. How could I hurt Salman? I drove straight from the airport to the Holiday Inn gym where Rakeshji was working out. I told him I was doing the film. By then, they had already started negotiating with Govinda for my role but Rakeshji was good enough to take me back. So there are no regrets.'

A *Filmfare* piece on Salman Khan from June 1994 reads almost like an obituary: 'While hysterical girls want to know whether he will marry Sangeeta Bijlani or keep her dangling, industry-wallahs are wondering whether he will ever swerve into the spotlight again—with the much-awaited *Hum Aapke Hain Koun* ...! Once Salman craved for glory and adulation, now he curls a lip at the world at large. He has paid heavily for the mistakes in the tradition of Rajesh Khanna. He could not handle overnight fame.' It quotes Rakesh Roshan as saying: 'When a film is a hit, the actor tries to hog the credit. He begins working with new producers, directors, writers—people he can dictate terms to.

He wouldn't be able to do this with established directors. This is where he goes wrong.'

The article, written by Nilufer Qureshi, who went on to become a film publicist, has Rajkumar Santoshi saying that Salman has 'an excellent script sense'. 'Very often he would come up with very good lines of dialogue. Most of the time I would give the lines he suggested to Aamir because they were more suitable to Aamir's character. Salman did not mind that.' There were also rumours of affairs with women other than his long-time girlfriend, Sangeeta Bijlani. Pakistani actress Somy Ali was specifically named. Another Pakistani actress, Zeba Bakhtiar, said he had propositioned her in Kulu Manali, as did starlets Neela and Anita Ayub. Santoshi predicted that his *Andaz Apna Apna* and Barjatya's *Hum Aapke Hain Koun ...!* would bring him back. He said: 'He is one of the few actors who can be both vulnerable and macho at the same time. He has a long innings ahead.'

Barjatya echoed Santoshi's words when he said Salman could not be written off, but added he had two weak points: a perpetual cold that affected his dubbing and an urbane sophistication which didn't allow him to play rural characters. 'But we are working on these shortcomings,' Barjatya commented. He believed that 'with time, everything should be fine with him'. An accompanying interview quoted Salman Khan as saying he would like to be a director one day. Asked about acting, he said: 'I just do it. If I have to have to cry for a scene, I break into tears. If I have to laugh, I break into laughter.'

Hum Aapke Hain Koun ...! was released in August 1994. With two weddings and a funeral, over three hours of celebrations of Indian rituals, nuptials, and an honouring of the united Hindu joint family, critics rubbished it as an extended wedding video. But viewers loved it so much that it became the highest grosser in recent Bollywood history and got many VCR-addicted audiences back into theatres after a long time. The credit went largely to the music of the film.

As an *India Today* cover story, 'Music Mania' (November 1994), put it: 'The movie, which prompted sniggers in the trade pre-release, is the biggest hit in the eighty-one-year history of Indian cinema.' So what's the magic, the article asked. Songs, songs and more songs—amongst them the enormous hit, '*Didi tera devar deewana*', it answered. The article went on to argue that the 'white collar bhais' of the music industry had replaced underworld money.

In the mid-'80s, the Hindi music market was valued at a little less than ₹100 crore, monopolised by HMV and, to a lesser extent, by Music India. Tapes (or cassettes) priced at ₹35 or more were bought only by the well-heeled few. Film producers, concentrating on Amitabh Bachchan-inspired action, tended to sideline music altogether. A royalty payment of ₹1 lakh from a music company was an occasion for a producer to throw a party. And then, fruit-juiceman-turned-music-mogul Gulshan Kumar lowered the price of tapes to less than ₹25 and hiked audio payments to several lakhs. In 1990, he released his breakthrough album, *Aashiqui,* the soundtrack of a Mahesh Bhatt-directed film starring Rahul Roy and Anu Agarwal. An estimated two crore tapes were sold, and at one point, T-Series was producing 80,000 to 90,000 units in a day.

The article went on to argue that the post-Bachchan era belonged to the audio-cassette star. One hit song could lay the foundation of a career. Madhuri Dixit came into the limelight with '*Ek do teen*' in *Tezaab* (1988), following it up with '*Dhak dhak*' in *Beta* (1992) and '*Choli ke peeche kya hai*' in *Khalnayak* (1993). Saif Ali Khan, said the article, was being taken seriously after swivelling to '*Ole ole*' in *Yeh Dillagi* (1994). Raveena Tandon, earlier considered jinxed, was now the '*Mast mast*' girl from *Mohra* (1994). Just the sexy walk in '*Chura ke dil mera*' from *Main*

Khiladi Tu Anari (1994) took Shilpa Shetty's career five steps ahead. Even Shah Rukh, who insisted that an actor needed more than songs to become a star, said that with ten hit songs behind him, he was an 'audio-cassette hero'. For too long, the industry had been hunting for another Bachchan, said the article. It hadn't found a reliable name on which to hang its ventures. Until the emergence of new stars with the charisma to floor millions, music may well be considered the new hero.

Even though music was deciding box-office success, Shah Rukh Khan, with a growing number of blockbusters under his belt, was only too willing to proclaim himself the next Bachchan, perhaps a subtle way of shaking off any competition and placing himself firmly in the same league as the Angry Young Man. In December 1994, in a *Filmfare* interview, he stated: 'Whenever I'm asked to do a drunken scene I think of Amitabh Bachchan.' A few months later, in a July 1995 interview, he elaborated: 'I'm waiting for the day they say "do it the Shah Rukh Khan way". Right now they're doing it the Amitabh Bachchan way.' The December 1994 edition of *Movie* magazine had Shah Rukh and Amitabh Bachchan on the cover, with the headline 'Heir Apparent?'.

It was a theme that Shah Rukh and his work would return to again. The next decade would begin with the face-off between Bachchan and Shah Rukh Khan in Aditya Chopra's *Mohabbatein* (2000). The competition was on many levels—screen performance, tradition versus modernity, and conflict between the past and the future. Bachchan played the strict principal of a school called Gurukul who believed in honour, tradition and discipline, while Shah Rukh was a progressive music teacher who believed in love. The film's dialogue articulated the music teacher's world view: '*Duniya mein kitni hain nafratein ... phir bhi dilon mein hai chaahatein ... jao kehdo is jahaan se, is zameen se, aasman se ... rok na sakenge ab yeh mohabbatein.*' (There is so much hatred in the world, yet so much love in the heart. Tell the world, the earth, the sky, love cannot be stopped.)

On- and off-screen, the clash was squarely between the Angry Young Man of the 1970s and the New Age Man of the 1990s. The Angry Young Man had not aged well, it seemed, with his ambitious plans to corporatise film production under the banner of ABCL having come a cropper. It left Amitabh Bachchan so broke that, by his own admission, he had to go to see Yash Chopra for work. In contrast, the New Age Man had just taken a chance on the idea of corporatisation, setting up a studio called Dreamz Unlimited with his friends, director Aziz Mirza and actress Juhi Chawla. *Phir Bhi Dil Hai Hindustani*, their first film, would be released in the first month of the new millennium.

There were other neat parallels. Salim-Javed and Yash Chopra were the men who did the most to craft the Angry Young Man image with *Deewar* (1975), *Trishul* (1978) and *Kaala Patthar* (1979). Chopra took a chance on the young Shah Rukh to give him the part in *Darr* that consolidated his stardom. His son Aditya Chopra added to Shah Rukh's aura by casting him in what became the iconic role of Raj in DDLJ. In a memorable scene from the movie, Raj and Simran spend the night together when they find themselves stranded on a Eurorail trip. Simran is in a drunken stupor and when she wakes up the next morning, Raj convinces her that they have had sex. When she breaks down, he tells her the truth, that he is an 'adarsh Hindustani aadmi' (the ideal Indian man), as much as she is the 'perfect Hindustani aurat' (the ideal Indian woman): '*Main itna bhi gira hua nahin hoon. Main ek Hindustani hoon, aur main jaanta hoon ki ek Hindustani ladki ki izzat kya hoti hai. Main sapne main bhi tumhaare saath aisi harkat nahin kar sakta hoon.*' (I cannot stoop so low. Simran, I am an Indian and I know what honour means to an Indian girl. Not even in my wildest dreams can I imagine behaving inappropriately with you).

Never mind all the red flags that it raises on what it means to be a Hindustani woman: chaste, virginal, pure.

In yet another iconic scene in the movie, when Simran wants them to elope and escape her domineering father, Raj stops her, saying he is a Hindustani and will marry her only when her father gives him her hand in marriage. A love marriage must also be arranged. Tradition plus modernity. Swoon.

This transformation as the poster boy of the 90s was further solidified by Yash Chopra's *Dil To Pagal Hai* (1997) whose tagline was 'someone ... somewhere ... is made for you'. He was Rahul, Raj's hipper avatar, a role he was to play again, in an even trendier version, a year later, in Karan Johar's *Kuch Kuch Hota Hai* (1998). As the overseas market for Bollywood films became bigger, the financing also changed, and the gore and violence favoured by the shadowy underworld of the previous decades was replaced by a return to family values and a conservative sense of morality. Even as Hindi films started looking at worldwide distribution as a separate box office territory, 1997 saw the attempted assassination of high-profile producer-director Rajiv Rai and the brutal killing of T-Series founder Gulshan Kumar.

Following the informal blacklisting of Dawood Ibrahim by the film industry in 1993, the dons—including Dawood's main hitman Abu Salem and former associate Chhota Rajan—began extortion operations. In its 25 August 1997 issue, *India Today* reported on the murder of Gulshan Kumar, saying the attacks were a comeback by the dons. With the real estate industry in the dumps, the smuggling of white goods and gold on the wane and narcotics a risky proposition, the underworld found soft targets in Bollywood.

Gulshan Kumar was reportedly asked to part with ₹10 crore. Producer-director Rajiv Rai was assaulted in his Mumbai office on 29 July, not long after he turned down the demand of extortionists. Director Subhash Ghai reportedly received two calls demanding ₹5 crore. Crime branch officials said that Mukesh Duggal, a small-time garments-trader-turned-producer was assassinated in March after he ran into trouble with his financiers, among them, Anees Ibrahim, Dawood's younger brother. Industry veteran Yash Chopra said: 'We are living in perpetual fear. How can we create?' Director Mahesh Bhatt called it 'urban terrorism'. Unlike Duggal, Rajiv Rai had not been linked to Dawood's organisation, the D-Company, as it was known in common parlance. Yet, Abu Salem, Dawood's man of the moment, owned up to the attack on him. And within twenty-four hours of the Gulshan Kumar murder, the police confirmed that it had indeed been an Abu Salem hit.

At least fifteen more people, even 'clean' ones with independent sources of finance, were apparently on D-Company's list. Dawood's challenger Chhota Rajan told *India Today* that he was aware of Salem's plan to eliminate Ghai. 'I sent him (Ghai) a message through a friendly police officer … told him to be careful,' he said. He further disclosed, 'I spoke to three boys hired by Salem to attack Ghai. They had been given revolvers and ₹1.5 lakh.'

Gulshan Kumar's murder was typical of the way D-Company dispensed its brand of justice. Although he had paid a few lakh rupees as the first instalment of protection money, he had reneged on the second instalment, police sources said. Such examples of bullying and extortion were aplenty and Kumar's death was a message. The story went on to say that the phones at TOPS, the security company that took care of bigwigs like the Bachchans, Shah Rukh Khan, Dharmendra and Jackie Shroff, hadn't stopped ringing since the murder. 'They have to take the threat perception seriously. It costs a few lakhs but a lot less than one's life,' said TOPS managing director Diwan Rahul Nanda. 'Gulshan Kumar took a bad risk.'

The industry tried to offset this terror and inevitable tightening of free flowing but dubious financing by catering to the twenty-million strong Indian diaspora. Yash Chopra opened a distribution office in the UK and their first theatrical release *Dil To Pagal Hai* made a million pounds. A year later, Yash Raj Films opened an office in the US, and *Kuch Kuch Hota* Hai grossed $7 million worldwide. In the UK, *Dil Se* became the first Indian film to break into the box office top ten. Clearly, there was a demand from the diaspora for their stories, old and new, to be told.

That didn't stop the continuing reign of terror and extortion by the mafia in the Mumbai film industry, now divided on religious lines. Abu Salem's threatening calls to Shah Rukh, who then required protection from Mumbai police, as well as Chhota Rajan and Chhota Shakeel's attempts at dabbling in funding and profiting from movies, were open secrets in the industry. In 2000, there was an assassination attempt on Rakesh Roshan, after the stupendous success of his son Hrithik Roshan's debut film, *Kaho Na ... Pyaar Hai*.

In 2001, well-known producer Bharat Shah, with a track record of having bankrolled movies from *Darr* to *Devdas*, was arrested following an investigation into the possible involvement of the mafia in a film he financed, *Chori Chori Chupke Chupke*. In 2003, he was convicted for not disclosing fellow producer Nazim Rizvi's links to Chhota Shakeel.

Abu Salem, who began his criminal life as a driver for Dawood, transporting arms and contraband, was arrested in 2002 in Portugal and extradited to India. He was arrested on the charge of carrying a fake passport, and tried as well as convicted in some cases. He was sentenced to life imprisonment in 2015. Chhota Rajan was extradited from Bali to India in November 2015 after twenty-seven years on the run, and is currently in Tihar Jail in Delhi after being sentenced to life imprisonment in 2018 for the murder of a journalist, J. Dey, in 2011. Chhota Shakeel had become one of the most-wanted men in India after his alleged participation in the 1993 Mumbai blasts. He was considered to be responsible for the day-to-day functioning of Dawood's gang and was also wanted by the US government for international drug trafficking. He is reported to have died in 2017. Dawood survives though, and is supposedly living in Karachi, Pakistan. Designated as a 'global terrorist' in 2003 by India and the United States, he carries a reward of $25 million on his head for his alleged role in the 1993 Mumbai blasts.

But all of this would come later.

By 1995, Salman, Aamir and Shah Rukh were acquiring well-defined personas. Salman was the troubled star, the boy who had burnt up his father's salary of ₹750 and got beaten up for it. According to *Khantastic: The Untold Story of Bollywood's Trio* by Sanjukta Nandy, Salman had run out of paper to burn while celebrating Diwali and had gone to find some more in his father's study. He burnt what he found.

In 1995, the twenty-nine-year-old still lived in a matchbox-sized room in his father's house and still hoped to please his father by completing his college degree through correspondence. *Karan Arjun* had just come out and Khalid Mohamed did an interview with Salman for *Filmfare* in March 1995. He wrote: 'In recent weeks, he's being gabbed about ... with a smidgen of respect once more ... thanks primarily to his impressively underplayed act in *Karan Arjun* ... Shah Rukh Khan was the boisterous one, he the subdued one. Nine times out of ten, it is the lively, bright-eyed one who steals the show. This time though, Salman's studied approach—as if he was controlling himself with Herculean effort—hit home. The actor who had nearly become a pariah, following a spate of flops, is no doubt having the last laugh at his detractors today.'

Khalid Mohamed went on to say that at twenty-nine, Salman was going on twenty-four. He'd had his share of controversies. He'd been branded a brat. He'd split with Sangeeta Bijlani, his long-time girlfriend. It's his life, let him be, Mohamed wrote, adding that Salman was entering an interesting phase as an actor. He's still a natural, he said. He doesn't overdo things. He may not ever become a Bachchan or a Dilip Kumar. Why should he be? Mohamed continued: 'Why must his story be a story of arrested development? His peers, Shah Rukh Khan and Aamir Khan, to name two, are inward looking actors. They're extending their artistry and their craft. Salman Khan can too. The camera likes him, which is half the battle won. If only he'd look deeper within, he could be an actor and not only a charismatic star. Success breeds confidence and memorable performances. *Karan Arjun* is the beginning. If only this Khan would take himself more seriously, then there would be no stopping him. Seriously, did you say? Yes, it isn't a dirty word.'

Yet, in February 1997, when *Filmfare* wrote about the Khans, Salman didn't even feature in the piece. The focus was on Aamir and Shah Rukh. Both were young and too innately confident to be burdened by Amitabh Bachchan's long shadow. Their innovativeness and assurance had helped jumpstart Indian cinema from its doldrums in the late 1980s. Now, said *Filmfare,* they were well on their way to reshaping the film industry on their terms. Both of them, at the age of thirty-one, had dilemmas of their own. Just how bold and inventive do they want to be, now that they have made their mark, now that they have arrived, asked the article.

The *Filmfare* story did a good SWOT analysis of the two. It praised Aamir Khan for his diligent attention to detail and his predilection for the low key. It said Shah Rukh had a restless energy, furious emotion, and innate complexity and curiosity. Each had been a risk-taker with his own strengths, but neither was an 'all-rounder' yet. Aamir, it added, had a temperament and talent akin to a cerebral, workmanlike, doggedly determined athlete. His mental preparation and dedication ensured few mistakes, but also limited the real chances he took. Shah Rukh was closer to being 'a natural', but with the wildness, the inherent drama, and mastery of skills that are neither fully measured nor fully controlled. Shah Rukh was capable of stunning audiences and surprising even himself, but equally capable of deeply disappointing all concerned. Aamir was steady, it said; Shah Rukh was volatile.

Aamir was so steady that by 1998, when *India Today* profiled him on the sets of *Mela*, it was calling him Mr Perfectionist. The relentless pursuit of perfection had become the hallmark of Aamir's career; in an industry marked by chronic unprofessionalism, a committed actor was a rarity. And Aamir's dedication was well-known. For *Ghulam*, he'd been dubbing at 5 a.m. because he felt his voice was better in the mornings. For the film's climax, he didn't wash his face for eight days so that he looked appropriately 'battered'. He also infamously did his own stunts for *Ghulam*, missing an oncoming train by a mere 1.3 seconds. On a bitterly cold night in Jaisalmer, he was up at 2.30 a.m. giving cues to co-star Naseeruddin Shah for director John Matthew Matthan's *Sarfarosh*.

The directorial endorsements in the article were glowing. '"Aamir is one with the project," says *Ghulam* director Vikram Bhatt. "He's always part of the solution, not the problem." For *Earth* director Deepa Mehta, Aamir was "a director's dream". "He's a world-class actor and the first one on the set every day." *Mela*'s Dharmesh Darshan is equally effusive: "Aamir is an actor willing to grow. Twenty years hence when you look back, he will be a legend."'

The Aamir myth was not just about being a well-behaved star. It was about an actor assiduously honing his craft to perfection. Shah Rukh may be the flashier actor and Salman the pretty boy, but Aamir's performances had rare depth. Shah Rukh, no matter what the role, was always Shah Rukh, but Aamir became

Raghu in *Dil Hai Ki Manta Nahin* and Munna in *Rangeela*. The transformation was difficult. And Stanislavsky didn't work in Mumbai. Aamir, an untrained actor, had concocted his own method: 'First, I understand what the director has in mind for the film. Then what he wants out of me. I understand the character's mind. I come on the set prepared with the lines. How many rehearsals I need depends on how cooked I am. I try to achieve a state of semi-consciousness where I am that character but I can also take instructions. I try to give an honest shot. Sometimes I get it sometimes I don't.'

By now, Aamir had played more of the Frank Capra-esque underdogs. There was the taxi driver of *Raja Hindustani* (1997) for which *Filmfare* called out his name for Best Actor—too late, the actor had decided the film awards had lost their meaning and had become 'too commercialised'. There was Raja, the lowly mechanic of *Ishq* (1998), who is in love with the rich heiress, played by Juhi Chawla. There was Siddhu Marathe, the boxer of *Ghulam* (1998), singing the ultimate mating call of all taporis, '*Aati kya Khandala*'. He was the compulsive flirt-turned-committed-lover of *Mann* in 1999. But it was his role in *Earth* (1998) as the gentle Dilnavaz who becomes mad with rage when his sisters are butchered in Partition-hit Lahore, and as the upstanding ACP Ajay Singh Rathore in *Sarfarosh* (released in April 1999, just before the Kargil War, and chronicling in a most nuanced way, Pakistan's terror tactics in India) which fashioned the next phase of his career. So astoundingly successful was he in the new decade that there was instant amnesia over the resounding failure that *Mela* was, a dated rustic romance that was the first release of the new millennium.

Earth was the first time Aamir played a Muslim—the second and third occasions would be as tourist-guide-turned-terrorist Rehan Khan in *Fanaa* (2006) and in *Dhoom 3* (2013) where he played the twins, Sahir and Samar Khan. In *Sarfarosh*, he was a police officer who has a complicated relationship with a Muslim officer on his team as well as a Mohajir ghazal singer who is actually part of Pakistan's informal terror network. Given that the attack on Kargil in May 1999 was by Pakistani soldiers disguised as Kashmiri militants, the theme of *Sarfarosh* was especially contemporary. In May 2000, in an interview to NDTV, Aamir carefully enunciated his emerging politics, both as an Indian and as a Muslim. This was something the three Khans would have to do repeatedly in a more divided India. In the interview, Aamir said: 'There is a certain section of Muslims in India who do have loyalties towards Pakistan and this film (*Sarfarosh*) tries to tell them that is not right. I believe that is a minority. Equally, it tells that section of Hindus which I believe is a minority that looks at all Muslims with distrust.' He added, thoughtfully: 'Radicals and right-wingers in all communities are having a field day. We need people who are balanced to come out and speak publicly about this.'

Shah Rukh, on the other hand, was more concerned about positioning himself as number one. One of the ways was by constantly proclaiming he was the best. By 1998, riding high on the success of three consecutive films, *Dil To Pagal Hai*, *Pardes* and *Yes Boss*, he was responding with confidence bordering on arrogance to most questions from journalists. A typical exchange can be found in a March 1998 interview published in *India Today*:

India Today: With those brown eyes proclaiming innocence, Tommy Hilfiger clothes, glib tongue, you must be the pinnacle of Bollywood yuppiedom, the style and star of the 90s?

Shah Rukh: The 90s? Make it star of 2010 or maybe 2020.

Shah Rukh was defining his stardom. 'I'm not into becoming the character,' he told *India Today* in 1995. 'I will always be Khan playing the beggar or goonda or villager.' He added: 'I don't believe in acting that doesn't have style.' Yet, underlining

Mahesh Bhatt's comment which described him as a man with a split personality, a man with two people lurking inside, working ceaselessly to fill the emptiness within himself, he was making every effort to stretch his acting muscles, even if they didn't work. Nowhere was this more evident than in the final part of Mani Ratnam's terror trilogy. *Dil Se* (1998) closed the book on *Roja* (1992), which chronicled terror in Kashmir, and *Bombay* (1995), which placed a Hindu-Muslim couple in the heart of riot-torn Mumbai.

In *Dil Se*, Shah Rukh was Amar, an All India Radio reporter with a penchant for telling marginal stories, and Manisha Koirala was Meghna, a mysterious young woman who wants to take revenge on the Indian state for having been raped by Army officers. Her mission: assassinating the prime minister on Republic Day, on the fiftieth anniversary of India's independence—which, in reality, had been celebrated a year earlier. *Dil Se* was a commercial flop in India but spawned many discussions on the nature of terror. '*Chhaiyaan Chhaiyaan*', spectacularly shot atop a moving train, was one of the first few hits from Bollywood that became popular internationally—even featuring as the soundtrack to the opening credits in Spike Lee's *Inside Man*. The song brought global acclaim to the musician behind it, A.R. Rahman, who went on to win an Oscar for Best Original Score for *Slumdog Millionaire* (2009). International offers followed for the choreographer, Farah Khan. She co-choreographed Andrew Lloyd Webber's *Bombay Dreams* for the West End in London (beginning in 2002) and Broadway in New York.

Shah Rukh's political views were also slowly coming to the fore. In 2000, he would star as Amjad Ali Khan, a nationalistic, pacifist Muslim archaeologist in Kamal Haasan's epic *Hey Ram*. Both *Hey Ram* and *Dil Se* questioned the role of the nation state—while the former showed how its creation was mired in blood, the latter with its concertina wires, soldiers with guns and burning villages showed what an imperfect democracy India still was. Was the poster boy of Hindu ritualistic traditions and rampant consumerism in Bollywood rethinking his future? The next year would clarify the question.

In 1997, Salman was turning his life around. He had started speaking to the media about his movies—among others, *Auzaar*, directed by his youngest brother, Sohail Khan. When he turned producer with *Pyaar Kiya To Darna Kya* (1998), directed by Sohail Khan again, and starring his brother, Arbaaz Khan, he gave a series of interviews to the media, during which he swung between being friendly and recalcitrant: '*Main kisi ko maaroon, kisi ke saath soon, yeh mera personal problem hai. Aap meri performance ke baare main likhiye, ki main bura tha ya accha, aap meri picture ke baare main likhiye, ki ghatiya picture thi. Aap meri real life ke baare, personal life ke baare main kyon likhte hain?*' (If I hit someone, or sleep with someone, that's my personal problem. You can say what you want about my performances, or my movie. Why do you have to write about my real life?).[5]

His opinions haven't changed much—twenty years later, in a 2018 interview to *Filmfare* magazine, he said, 'When things are written against you over and over again, somewhere, people begin to feel it's too much. That automatically changes opinion in your favour.' He was also friendly enough with Shah Rukh to participate in a prank at the *Filmfare* awards that year, when Shah Rukh won the best actor award for *Dil To Paagal Hai*. Called on stage by Shah Rukh to share the award 'because he never wins any', Salman went up, cried fake tears, and then walked off with Shah Rukh's trophy.

1997 was a year that Salman Khan would remember because it added a new dimension to his dutiful, lovable, Barjatya-inspired Prem. As the long-lost twins in *Judwaa*, the posh Prem and the street-smart Raja, in a role originally meant for Govinda, Salman was able to extend his repertoire, adding a comic flourish to the character of Raja. Aided by his young producer friend Sajid Nadiadwala, who spared no expense to up its production value, and directed by David Dhawan who had a great sense of comic timing, the film saved Salman's sagging career.

As Dhawan described it, Prem had 'masoomiyat' (innocence) and Raja had 'badmashi' (naughtiness). In an interview on the making of the film, he said Prem was *'acche ghar ka bachcha'* (a child from a good home) and Raja was a 'street ka tapori'. Shooting, according to him, was like a picnic. The film underlined the motto of the Dhawan school of filmmaking: *'Zyaada hasao, thoda rulaao'* (make them laugh, but also make them cry a little).[6] The film established several precedents for a Salman Khan movie: it was his first Eid release, it had catchy songs with simple signature steps, and franchise possibilities (albeit twenty years later, starring the director's son, Varun Dhawan).

1998 was a great year for Salman at the box office. *Pyaar Kiya To Darna Kya* was the first big hit of the year, followed by *Jab Pyar Kisise Hota Hai*, co-starring Twinkle Khanna. *Bandhan*, reported *Filmfare,* had been written off by the trade but was a hit too. It was the same with *Kuch Kuch Hota Hai* where he had a cameo. In March 1999, Dhawan would collaborate with Salman again on *Biwi No. 1*, where he managed to make a two-timing husband seem endearing, by being a devoted son and father. Sanjay Leela Bhansali's *Hum Dil De Chuke Sanam* (June 1999), where he met and romanced Aishwarya Rai, in what would emerge as one of Bollywood's most turbulent romances, was also a hit. In October 1999, he delivered a blockbuster again for the Barjatyas as Prem in *Hum Saath Saath Hain*.

That was his last major hit until *Baghban* in 2003, though there were some sporadic movies that were termed average revenue earners at the box office: *Dulhan Hum Le Jayenge* in March 2000, which reunited Salman with *Judwaa* and *Biwi No.*

1 director David Dhawan and co-star Karisma Kapoor; *Hum Tumhare Hain Sanam* in May 2002 where he again starred with Shah Rukh Khan; and *Tere Naam* in August 2003.

On the personal front, things were turning grim. While Salman was shooting for Sooraj Barjatya's *Hum Saath Saath Hain* in Jodhpur in September–October 1998, he went with Saif Ali Khan, Tabu, Neelam and Sonali Bendre on a hunt and allegedly shot blackbucks and chinkara. This resulted in a long legal tangle. Eventually, everyone in the group of friends, except Salman, returned to Mumbai on bail. A decade later, he was sentenced to five years imprisonment by the Sessions Court in Jodhpur. 'I reminded Salman that a star is watched every moment by a thousand eyes—*kisi ko mauka hi nahin dena chhaahiye,*' Salim Khan said in *Filmfare* in December 1998.

An *India Today* article, reporting from Jodhpur, chronicled the saga, saying the storm in the desert had begun brewing from the day he arrived in Jodhpur. First, Salman had complained that his plush Umaid Palace Hotel room was too small. So what if Sonali, Tabu and Neelam had similar rooms, he demanded better, and the result was that he was given a suite. The hero, said the article, was turning into a swaggering villain. 'He was haughty with the hotel staff. He constantly lost his shirt, literally so, strutting bare-bodied along hotel corridors. And when he and Saif got bored, they lined up soft drink bottles, drew their guns—the police say he carried a revolver in his waistband—and played cowboys.'

As if that was not enough, in late November 1998, a drunk Salman punched director Subhash Ghai in the face at a party to celebrate the wedding anniversary of his old friends, Kailash and Aarti Surendranath. The background was that Ghai had rejected Salman and cast Vivek Mushran instead, in *Saudagar*, and for him to ask Salman to act in his movie now was not correct. The next day, Salman was made to apologise to Ghai by his father and invite him and his wife to dinner as a make-up gesture. A thirty-three-year-old man, a superstar for the world, was still behaving like a man-child and was being treated as such by his domineering father.

As India went into the new millennium with the spectre of terrorism hanging over it and the hijacking of IC 814 bringing horror right into the country's living rooms with 24x7 television coverage, there was, as usual, competing good news. Indian engineers were the great victors of the Y2K crisis, emerging as champions of the re-engineering required for the coding of computerised systems that had been projected to create havoc around the world in the transition from 31 December 1999 to 1 January 2000.

As it happened, year 2000 would be significant for the three Khans as well.

3

2000

The Year of Reset

The new millennium began on a dark note for India. An Indian Airlines Airbus A300 (IC 814) was hijacked by five gunmen on 24 December 1999, on its way from the Tribhuvan International Airport in Kathmandu, Nepal, to Indira Gandhi International Airport in Delhi. The hijackers ordered the aircraft to be flown to a series of locations—Amritsar, Lahore and Dubai (where 27 of the 176 passengers were released)—before forcing the plane to land in Kandahar, Afghanistan, which was controlled by the Taliban at the time. Finally, on 31 December, the hijackers released the passengers, but not before fatally stabbing one and wounding several others.

The hijacking was played out live in TV studios with reporters and commentators covering it from every angle, informing both the government and the desperate relatives, as well as tracking the flight pattern of the hijacked plane. For India, Taliban-controlled Afghanistan was the worst possible place in the world for the hijacked IC 814 to have landed. Not only did the Indian government not recognise the Taliban government—allegedly a creation of Pakistan's ISI—it also considered Afghanistan to be the training ground for terrorists exported to Kashmir. For the Taliban, however, the arrival of the hijacked plane was literally an opportunity to break its isolation and gain respectability in the wake of international sanctions. By condemning the hijackers, the Taliban told the world that it was not a terrorist regime. But the Taliban's track record did not inspire trust, according to the 10 January 2000 issue of *India Today*, quoting an Indian diplomat: 'There can only be two reasons why the hijackers went to Kandahar. Either the Taliban or its mentor, the ISI, had a hand in the hijacking or because it is the only place in the world where terrorists felt safe.'

In order to secure the release of the passengers and the crew aboard IC 814, the BJP-led coalition government had to release in exchange three terrorists, Maulana Masood Azhar, Omar Sheikh and Mushtaq Ahmed Zargar, who had all been arrested for terrorist activities in Kashmir and incarcerated in Indian prisons. The London School of Economics-educated Omar Sheikh went on to finance one of the hijackers of the 9/11 attacks as well as kidnap and behead American journalist Daniel Pearl in Karachi in 2002, in one of the most brutal and telling acts of terror in this part of the world. Maulana Masood Azhar formed the Jaish-e-Mohammed (JeM), and its roster of evil was equally bleak—the JeM carried out the attacks on the Indian Parliament in 2001, the 2016 attacks on the Indian Air Force base in Pathankot, and targeted CRPF jawans in 2019 in Pulwama. Mushtaq Ahmed Zargar was one of the men involved in the abduction of Rubaiya Sayeed, the daughter of then Union home minister, Mufti Mohammed Sayeed, in December 1989—yet another embarrassing capitulation by the Indian state to terror.

Sayeed, then a medical intern at Lal Ded Memorial Women's Hospital, Srinagar, was kidnapped by members of the Jammu Kashmir Liberation Front, a Kashmiri terrorist organisation. The kidnappers (Zargar was one of them) demanded the release of their imprisoned members in exchange for Rubaiya's release. Chief Minister Farooq Abdullah, in conjunction with the central government, accepted their demands and freed five jailed militants. Zargar was later arrested in May 1992.

This was a far cry from the tough victory India had managed against Pakistani irregulars (trained civilians) and soldiers disguised as Kashmiri militants in the Kargil War, earlier in 1999. Much like the seven-day IC 814 hostage crisis, this too was played out on television-screens, relayed into living rooms across India, causing an outpouring of emotional nationalism. There was a sense of betrayal because the stealth war had come on the heels of a grand gesture of peace by Prime Minister Atal Bihari Vajpayee in February 1999, which saw him travelling by bus to Lahore via the Wagah border with an assortment of film stars, politicians and writers. Peace with Pakistan was imminent, it seemed, and India's poet-prime minister was the man who had made it possible.

But now, with Muslims within and outside India being identified or associated with terror attacks, the idea of secularism and treating all faiths as equal in the public domain was increasingly under strain. The division of Indians along religious lines played itself out in every area of popular culture, from sport to cinema. In cricket, Mohammed Azharuddin, the golden boy of Indian cricket, was exposed as a fallen hero, a man who had allowed his natural and untrammeled talent to be tarnished by the corruption of money and fame. From a simple, generous team player, he had slowly morphed into a party boy found in the company of mafia dons and Mumbai's beautiful people. Sacked South African captain Hansie Cronje told a match-fixing inquiry in Cape Town that Azharuddin had introduced him to a bookie, Mukesh Gupta, in 1996. Azharuddin responded by saying he was being victimised and targeted by some ex-cricketers who had personal grudges against him, mainly because he belonged to the minority community.

This was enough to provoke Shiv Sena chief Bal Thackeray to use the opportunity to hit out at the Khans as well, calling them 'puppets of the underworld'.[1] Thackeray was not the only one who was incensed by a light-hearted, if somewhat tasteless gag, in a Pepsi Cola commercial that featured Shah Rukh Khan and made fun of the new movie sensation, Hrithik Roshan. On the heels of the ad's release, the RSS's Hindi newspaper *Panchjanya* ran a cover story, sometime in the second half of 2000, blaming MNCs (Coca-Cola and Pepsi) for sowing 'seeds of bitterness' between the two superstars, Shah Rukh and Hrithik.

The newspaper also ran another story in the same issue with a headline that aimed to second-guess the motivations of the Khans: '... they are not worried about drought victims ... At a stars vs. cricketers match for drought victims, captained by Hrithik Roshan, neither Salman, Shah Rukh, or any other Khan turned up ... along with rivalry, isn't there a communal mindset behind this?'

The *Panchajanya* story also touched upon the connection between the underworld and the film industry, claiming there was 'a conspiracy at an international level, whereby hurdles are put in the way of Hindu film actors in order to prove them unsuccessful so that the film industry would be dominated by Muslim actors and their sponsors in Dubai'.

The rumours associated with *Josh*, Shah Rukh Khan's June 2000 release, that tickets were purchased in bulk, aimed to tell a different story about its success: 'Seeing it would not be a hit, tickets for two weeks were bought in advance (by the underworld) to give the impression of a hit ... Hindu producers are threatened and made to hire the Khans.' And who supported this rather far-fetched claim, as quoted in *Outlook* magazine? BJP general secretary, Narendra Modi, who said: 'Is *Panchajanya* not a paper? Is a *Panchajanya* reporter not a reporter? Whenever any other paper writes something, no one asks for a comment on the article or questions the editor.'[2]

In January 2000, the enormous success of newcomer Hrithik Roshan's debut film, *Kaho Naa ... Pyaar Hai,* directed by his father Rakesh Roshan, was seen as a sign of hope. Though Rakesh Roshan's earlier film *Karan Arjun* had contributed greatly to endearing Shah Rukh Khan and Salman Khan to a mass audience with its powerful subplots of Kali worship, reincarnation, and the references to the Mahabharata, the rumour mills were turning. Sandwiched between Aamir Khan's *Mela*, directed by Dharmesh Darshan and released on 7 January 2000, and Shah Rukh Khan's *Phir Bhi Dil Hai Hindustani*, directed by Aziz Mirza and released on 21 January 2000, Hrithik's film stood out as the big winner of the year.

The 20 March 2000 cover of *India Today* screamed 'Heartthrob Hrithik' (with a symbolic heart in the headline, of which writer Justine Hardy memorably said that it was as if the latest boy band had appeared on the cover of *The Economist* with Bambis hopping around the title words). The cover story proceeded to measure Hrithik against each of the three Khans, which was a stretch given that this was only his first film, and was not an appropriate yardstick to compare the work of over a decade by the 'Y3K', as the magazine called them.

Comparing Hrithik Roshan to the three Khans, the article continued: 'Shah Rukh has great energy and sheer mannerisms with flashes of histrionic ability, but Hrithik is more sophisticated.

Finally you have an actor who is also a star.' Aamir Khan was a 'very intense actor besides being a heartthrob', but Hrithik had 'intelligence and charisma. He can do complex roles and has nuance.' As for Salman Khan, the man who gave Hrithik advice on how to build his body, the magazine said, 'He (Salman) can be good. But what sets him apart is his great body and amazing narcissism ... in comparison, Hrithik's honesty comes through to all people. The camera loves him.'

It is interesting to note that the media in India nearly always had the tendency of comparing every popular newcomer with the reigning stars—it is almost as if a new actor cannot be judged on his own merit and acting skills, but needs to be matched against familiar faces. There is also, always, the hint that the arrival of the fresh face would sound the death knell for established performers.

At this point in the industry, a whole array of other newcomers were about to make a mark. In another cover story titled 'Newcomer Mania', *India Today* wrote, 'Distributors who couldn't see beyond the Khans are saying sagely that it's not the star but the story that clicks. The buzz words are: youth, packaging, presentation, marketing.' It proceeded to list the 'gene pools' that were being tapped; Abhishek Bachchan and Kareena Kapoor were among those named. The Khans and Bollywood's other saleable heroes—Ajay Devgan, Anil Kapoor, Govinda, Sunny Deol, Sanjay Dutt—were clearly beyond the college-boy age. Producer Ratan Jain of Venus told the magazine: 'If I'm making a film with Shah Rukh Khan, I won't make him run around trees anymore. The I-Love-You roles are going to a new generation of actors.'

Adding to the new and very real competition was the revolution in television. After almost a decade of satellite television, the small screen was ready to mirror the reality of India's growing economy and changing society. In an ambitious quiz show for which Star TV licensed the format from Celador, a British TV company, the host asked a series of questions that, through a process of ups and downs, like a game of snakes and ladders led the winning contestant to a prize money of ₹1 crore—a sum that could entirely change the life of the winner. Star TV was then headed by Peter Mukerjea, who had recently arrived from Hong Kong and was still untainted by his later alleged involvement in the bizarre and tragic murder of his second wife's daughter, Sheena Bora. Mukerjea got Sameer Nair on board in 1999 as programming head. Following Rupert Murdoch's visit to India in early 2000, he upped the prize money to ₹1 crore and together with his team, renamed the show: *Kaun Banega Lakhpati* became *Kaun Banega Crorepati*. They knew they had to have a host who was a star and went for Amitabh Bachchan, whose success was not limited to a latest release; he had long attained an iconic status across generations.

Initially, Bachchan was not convinced that he was ready to move to television. It was a visit to London, to the sets of *Who Wants to Be a Millionaire*, that finally persuaded him. It is possible that Bachchan, who was emerging from the debris of ABCL's financial wreckage, and had started work on Aditya Chopra's *Mohabbatein*, knew the financial advantages of being the host of an internationally famous quiz show. *Kaun Banega Crorepati* not only changed the fortunes of the winning contestants, it was also a key vehicle for Bachchan to appear as himself and firmly re-establish his army of fans, who already numbered in the millions. The show naturally broke all records in TV ratings and viewership.

Kaun Banega Crorepati allowed Bachchan to instantly gain the status of an aspirational 'Friend, Philosopher and Guide'. With his sharp suits and sharper Hindi, he shepherded contestants through each episode, allowing middle-class India to live vicariously and fulfill its most loved goal—wealth through wisdom. As Nair described it in Vanita Kohli-Khandekar's *The Making of Star India: The Amazing Story of Rupert Murdoch's India Adventure*, 'KBC's impact was like Michael Jackson's *Thriller*—immediate and overpowering. We were one, two, three, four, all within a week.' (He was speaking about the top of the ratings chart.)

With the consumerist, aspirational aspect taken care of, Star TV soon addressed the incipient insecurity in the Indian middle class: the loss of family values. Long-running shows at that point, such as *Tara* (Zee TV, 1993-1997), focused on contemporary urban women. Extra-marital affairs, broken marriages, the woman claiming emotional and financial independence—television had started to mirror what was happening in the world at large, through soaps such as *Swabhimaan* (1994), *Shanti* (1994) and *Hasratein* (1994), as well as talk shows, including *Purush Kshetra* (1994), hosted by actress Kirron Kher, who was later elected a BJP MP twice over, and *The Priya Tendulkar Show* (1994). Purnima Mankekar believed that these serials and talk shows which suggested the pursuit of 'erotic desire' pushed at the boundaries of conventional Indian womanhood.[3] Mankekar's work, anchored in researching viewers' responses to these portrayals of women, revealed a deep distrust. This was especially so among lower middle-class women, who seemed to believe that financial independence and upward mobility went against a 'fundamental understanding of our culture, of what it means to be Indian, and what it means for a woman to obey her elders, be loyal to her family, and put her family first'. Patriarchy was going to hit back soon.

It did.

Vinta Nanda, the producer of *Tara*, tells it like it was. '*Tara* was the highest rated show when it was yanked off air. It was deliberately done by forces which had entered the channel it was running on and which were dictating terms. The producer and director of the series *Chanakya*, Dr Chandraprakash Dwivedi (CPD) was the new CEO (at Zee). He called me in for a meeting and told me that he was pulling off all my shows at the end of that week. *Tara*, *Raahat* (satellite TV's first daily series), *Ummeed* and *V3Plus*, all of them were capturing eyeballs and doing very well and all the shows in question had strong women protagonists and characters. Dr CPD told me twice that my kind of woman didn't deserve to be given a place in the media and when I spoke back to him and asked him why he thought he could be that audacious towards me, he told me that I should be thrown out of the country. I tried reasoning with him and he called his staff to take me out of the conference room—in other words they kicked me out of the room. That was it. No further discussion, no more explanations, four shows thrown off air overnight and my company Traciname, which I had built brick by brick through my hard work, collapsed overnight.'

A new behemoth was taking shape, headed by another big name. Star TV collaborated with its India-based partner, Balaji Telefilms, run by Ekta Kapoor, the young daughter of actor Jeetendra, and ushered in a new brand of programming with *Kyunki Saas Bhi Kabhi Bahu Thi* and *Kahaani Ghar Ghar Ki* towards the end of 2000. The series, though very popular, and appearing to tread new territory, can be traced back to the old B-grade melodramas in Hindi cinema of the '50s and '60s, in which the young bride enters her husband's home and instead of finding love, discovers she is at the mercy of a cruel and exacting mother-in-law.

Ekta Kapoor's TV dramas put the Indian woman back into 'her natural space', in other words, back into the domestic sphere, and the ensuing drama in the narrative was born from the squabbling and quarrelling between pliant daughters-in-law and nasty mothers-in-law. These hugely popular TV serials made Ekta Kapoor the creator and arbiter of all domestic dramas. Her productions and their screenplays reinforced traditional values and gender identity at a time when they were considered to be under threat. The character of Tulsi in *Kyunki Saas Bhi Kabhi Bahu Thi*, played by Smriti Irani, who would go on to become a leading light in Narendra Modi's government, is a priest's daughter who gets married into an upper-class Gujarati family and eventually becomes its fiercest protector. In *Kahaani Ghar Ghar Ki*, Parvati, played by Sakshi Tanwar, is the ideal daughter-in-law and the moral compass of a Marwari family. It was obvious the families were Hindu and undivided, with several generations living together under one roof—and the duty of the woman and to uphold tradition, toe the line and accept that happiness lies in maintaining the joint family.

Even the mafia was divided along religious lines in this new universe. Chhota Rajan, once a close aide of Dawood Ibrahim, became his biggest enemy. *India Today* magazine reported in a cover story, 'War of the Dons', that Rajan had broken away from Dawood Ibrahim after the Mumbai blasts—although it was known that he had helped Dawood establish his underworld empire. Positioning himself as the 'Hindu don,' Chhota Rajan now formed links with Indian investigating agencies. The magazine said: 'The murder attempt on Chhota Rajan in Bangkok (in September 2000) has actually generated a sort of latent sympathy for Rajan in middle class Mumbai. As a senior police officer points out, "It is perhaps unfortunate but there is a feeling among some youth, and even business people, that a Hindu don is required."' Perhaps more so with the underworld looming large over the film industry.

For a while, during this period, nothing seemed to be going right for the Khans. *Stardust* did a particularly nasty piece on Aamir Khan in January 2000, questioning his nationalist credentials and accused him of giving an interview to a Pakistani radio host in Houston, Texas, (KGOL 1180 AM) in which, as the writer of the article, Prakash Rane said, 'he equated India with Pakistan at a time when the Kargil issue was fresh … It was all because there was a threat from Pakistani-origin Americans to boycott a song and dance show by Aamir Khan in Houston.'

In response to a question from the host of the radio show whether part of the funds collected from the show would be given to victims of the Kargil War, Aamir replied, 'None of the proceeds is going to any fund whatsoever'. But what made *Stardust* throw a hissy fit was a perfectly anodyne remark from Aamir: 'I feel that India and Pakistan have been neighbours for so long and it's sad that there have been conflicts. I don't think that the people of India and Pakistan are happy with the conflict. I feel that it's the common man who can change all that. If the common man indicates to the leadership that they do not like this conflict and they don't want to indulge in this, then in both the countries it would lead to a lot of peace and friendship.' The magazine also made a big story of Aamir's public announcement that he no longer had anything to do with his father Tahir Husain's company, TV Productions.

It's not surprising then, that when filmmaker Rahul Dholakia came to India on a TV Asia assignment in 1999 to interview Nari Hira, the publisher who founded the film magazine *Stardust* in 1971, he remembers being told by one of the writers that the industry was in search of a replacement for the Khans. In recounting the conversation to me, Dholakia, who directed Shah Rukh in *Raees*, which was, by a strange quirk of fate released in 2017, in the same week as Hrithik Roshan's *Kaabil*, said, 'I was also told that Hira said the industry was backing a new Hindu hero, Hrithik Roshan.' Indeed, Hrithik was shooting *Kaho Naa … Pyaar Hai* but had already been cast by Khalid Mohamed in his first film, *Fiza*, and by *Mission Kashmir*'s director Vidhu Vinod Chopra. Both films were released in 2000.

In what can only be described as a further irony, Hrithik played a Muslim terrorist in both *Fiza* and *Mission Kashmir*.

Both movies consolidated the dichotomy of the 'Good Muslim' versus the 'Bad Muslim'. So when Fiza, played by Karisma Kapoor, is told by a local politician: 'The Mughals attacked us and subjugated us yet we forgave them. You people went and created your own separate country, that too we accepted.' She replies: 'You people? The people who created Pakistan went there, and the majority of Muslims stayed here in India. There is no one in this country who wishes to create a Pakistan. We are as much Indian as you are.' In *Mission Kashmir*, the character of Kashmiri Muslim security officer Inayat Khan (played by Sanjay Dutt) echoes this sentiment when he is not allowed to oversee the security arrangements for a prime ministerial visit to Kashmir because he is Muslim. 'My love for this country needs no certificate from a bureaucrat,' says Inayat Khan.

These two films also established the 'terrorist-as-victim' hero, with *Fiza*'s Amaan having been affected by the 1993 Mumbai riots and *Mission Kashmir*'s Altaaf watching his entire family being killed by Inayat Khan in a raid.

Esra Mirze Santesso and James McClung write in *Islam and Postcolonial Discourse: Purity and Hybridity* that the distinction between the cine-patriotic Muslim and the evil jihadi Muslim was taking place in the dynamic conjuncture of what Karen Gabriel and P.K. Vijayan have called 'religious right-wingism' (Hindu nationalism) and 'economic right-wingism (liberalisation-privatisation-globalisation),' which produced a protectionist ideology that increasingly sought to target and brand Muslims.

Meanwhile, Aamir Khan's early 2000 release, *Mela*, proved to be a financial disaster. Writer Jessica Hines candidly stated that if Aamir's acting style was considered naturalistic, then the rest of Bollywood must be populated with hams who would give Messrs. Sinden and Callow a run for their money, referring to the British actors Donald Sinden and Simon Callow's rather operatic style of acting. Hines later helped Aamir with the casting of the British characters in *Lagaan*, and eventually, according to several tabloid reports, had a relationship with him in 2003 after his divorce from Reena, his wife of sixteen years.

From January to June 2000, Aamir was busy shooting *Lagaan* in Bhuj in sync sound under the direction of Ashutosh Gowariker, his friend from Ketan Mehta's *Holi* days. He then went to Sydney for a long shooting spell for Farhan Akhtar's debut film *Dil Chahta Hai*, a film that created the template for a new kind of youth movie about friends with little or no family in sight. There were rumours in film magazines about how he had to reshoot 40 per cent of *Lagaan*, but Aamir pooh-poohed them, saying the movie would be released in June 2001, as planned. It was. *Lagaan* was a big hit with audiences and also won great critical acclaim, including an Oscar nomination for Best Foreign Film.

Incidentally, it was on the sets of *Lagaan* that Aamir was to meet his future wife, Kiran Rao. As a young assistant director on the sets, her job was to handle the actors—eleven Indians, eleven Britons and 1,500 villagers. Their relationship during the film was professional, and it was only later, when Rao was assisting Ashutosh Gowariker on an advertising film that Aamir was acting in, that they became 2 a.m. friends. They started seeing each other in 2004 and by 2005, they were married.

By 2000, Shah Rukh had finally moved his young family into his dream house, Mannat, which stands proudly on one end of Mumbai's Bandstand. Mannat was originally called Villa Vienna, and is a heritage property originally owned by Nariman Dubash, a member of the family of Kekoo Gandhy, a celebrated Indian gallerist whose descendants are now Shah Rukh's next-door neighbours.

In the year that Mannat became his, Shah Rukh started a film company called Dreamz Unlimited with the release of

Phir Bhi Dil Hai Hindustani. The film, directed by his old friend Aziz Mirza, tanked, leaving its three partners, Mirza, actors Juhi Chawla and Shah Rukh, dejected and depressed. In retrospect, *Phir Bhi Dil Hai Hindustani* was ahead of its time, with its storyline of rival networks propping up political parties, anchors who believed they were the best, riots being given a communal colour by manipulative politicians, the involvement of the 'videshi haath' (foreign hand, meaning foreign interference) while the embattled, 'bebas, lachaar aam aadmi' (helpless common man) suffered.

Another interesting movie that Shah Rukh starred in was *Hey Ram*. The film's narrative had honourable intentions, but it didn't fare well. There was also *Josh*, another flop, despite being directed by hit filmmaker Mansoor Khan, Aamir's cousin. The troika behind Dreamz Unlimited nevertheless soldiered on, producing *Asoka*, directed by ace cinematographer Santosh Sivan. The film, it was hoped, would be Shah Rukh's magnum opus and spread the message of peace across the world.

Despite the ups and down of 2000, the year ended on a good note for Shah Rukh with the success of Aditya Chopra's second directorial venture, *Mohabattein*. This coincided with him starting to air his political opinions in print and on TV. No doubt influenced by the narrative of *Phir Bhi Dil Hindustani*, he spoke of the importance of 'genuine nationalism' on Shekhar Suman's talk show, *Movers & Shakers*. In an interview with Karan Thapar on BBC's *Face to Face*, he talked about his family and said his parents were liberals, though they believed in Islam. 'I would read the namaaz and was made to respect it, but it was not mandatory,' he said. If he were to make the same statement today, he would be attacked by both ends of the spectrum—by Hindu right-wingers for bringing religion into the public domain, and by Islamic fundamentalists for not being a strict follower of Islam in every sense.

As for Salman Khan, he was battling self-inflicted demons. In a video interview in 2000 titled 'A Day at Salman Khan's House', the interviewer stands outside his home in Galaxy Apartments in Bandra and says: 'Everyone says he is drinking a lot. Salman Khan *ko pyaar ho gaya hai* (Salman has fallen in love) and is destroying himself.' His relationship with Aishwarya Rai was at its height but it was also extremely volatile. They had met on the sets of Sanjay Leela Bhansali's *Hum Dil De Chuke Sanam* and though he was dating Pakistani actress Somy Ali then, the two became close. Salman even played a bit part in a 2000 film starring Aishwarya Rai and her future husband Abhishek Bachchan, Raj Kanwar's *Dhai Akshar Prem Ke*.

But Salman's films were not doing as well as expected. *Dulhan Hum Le Jayenge* (2000) did average business at the box office, even though it was directed by David Dhawan and starred Karisma Kapoor (his partners from *Judwaa* and *Biwi No. 1*). Salman spent a lot of time in the movie shirtless, and the rest of the time, he was either dancing by the seaside in Mauritius or driving around Switzerland. *Chal Mere Bhai* (also co-starring Karisma Kapoor and directed by Dhawan) was yet another flop *Har Dil Jo Pyaar Karega*, produced by old buddy Sajid Nadiadwala, did average business and was not the hit everyone hoped for, despite a cameo by Shah Rukh Khan. The foot-tapping but silly music by Anu Malik did the film no favours, and then came *Kahin Pyaar Na Ho Jaye,* which wasn't a roaring success either.

Salman's films seemed clones of each other, and it was clear that the formula of comedy/drama/good music and worship of his bare chest was fast getting dated, as was his comic-book-lover-boy image. While his contemporaries were busy trying to explore new stories and push technical boundaries by making *Lagaan* and *Asoka*, Salman was still trying to get by on his charm and good looks. Diminishing returns were setting in and would dog him for pretty much the rest of the decade.

The '90s hero was from everywhere and nowhere, as screenplay writer/lyricist Javed Akhtar said perceptively to Nasreen Munni Kabir (*Talking Movies*). Rahul/Raj for Shah Rukh Khan, Raja for Aamir Khan, and many versions of Prem for Salman Khan were heroes not rooted in any particular geography, nor do we know if they belonged to any particular class or caste, he noted. They were just the grandsons of Shammi Kapoor, who like the hero of *Junglee* in 1961, put all their energy into dance, music, lightheartedness, and winning the girl. With undivided family, big brands emblazoned on his chest, a composite romantic world that often excluded the Indian outdoors with songs shot in exotic locations such as Mauritius and Switzerland, the '90s hero was a product of confused times, the personification, as Akhtar noted, of contemporary morality.

However, by the end of 2000, Shah Rukh and Aamir were on their way to giving their heroes a specific postal address and an unalloyed moral universe. Salman Khan, lurching from allegations of physical abuse to fatal drunk driving to compulsive drinking, would take a little longer to catch up with the other two Khans.

4

2001–2009

Going Global

10 September 2001.

Santosh Sivan remembers walking down Vesey Street in New York after the formal music launch of *Asoka* and telling the late Sanjeev 'Bobby' Chawla, brother of Juhi Chawla, a close friend of Shah Rukh Khan's and long-time production controller on the star's movies, 'What if a plane was to crash into the World Trade Centre?'

Sivan recalls Bobby telling him to stop talking like a terrorist—referring in jest to the director's arthouse hit about a suicide bomber, *The Terrorist*, which was adopted by Hollywood star John Malkovich as a presenter.

The next day, 11 September 2001, at 8.45 a.m., an American Airlines Boeing 767 loaded with 20,000 gallons of jet fuel crashed into the north tower of the World Trade Centre. Eighteen minutes after the first plane hit, a second Boeing 767—United Airlines Flight 175—appeared out of the sky, turned sharply toward the World Trade Centre and ripped into the south tower, near the sixtieth floor.

Asoka, Shah Rukh's film, was to premiere at the Toronto Film Festival two days later, in the Contemporary World Cinema section.

The film prints never left John F. Kennedy Airport.

The screening of *Asoka* in Toronto was to have been Shah Rukh Khan's big debut on the global stage. Sivan had first suggested the idea of the film to Shah Rukh when they were both atop a train, shooting the iconic '*Chhaiyyan Chhaiyyan*' song for Mani Ratnam's *Dil Se* in 1998. Now, in 2001, their film was almost on its way to being shown to film-goers and international critics in Toronto. For the occasion, Shah Rukh, had travelled to New York with co-star Kareena Kapoor and Karan Johar's mother, Hiroo. But 9/11 stopped the world in its tracks and the *Asoka* team had to stay on in New York. Shah Rukh returned to India without screening the film in Toronto. And *Lagaan* stole a march on *Asoka.* It had released to a rapturous response in India in June 2001 and was chosen to represent India at the Oscars.

Thanks to a sustained campaign by its lead star and producer, Aamir Khan, *Lagaan* would end up in the shortlist of 'Best Foreign Language Film'. Aamir knew that getting noticed by the Academy of Motion Picture Arts and Sciences—and being picked among the final five—would not be easy. But he is a methodical man and went about the film's promotion systematically. He got one of the earliest enthusiasts of the film, director Roland Joffe, to recommend it to his friends. Parmeshwar Godrej called her well-placed pals, Steven Spielberg, Richard Gere and Ismail Merchant. Mira Nair, whose *Salaam Bombay* had been nominated in the same category in 1988, wrote to 'friends who are Academy members to see *Lagaan* and vote for it'. Aamir himself did a series of interviews in the US with *USA Today*, *Variety* and *Hollywood Reporter*, among others; and the film's US distributor Sony Pictures Classics issued full-page colour ads in publications such as *Variety* and *Hollywood Reporter*.[1]

Finally, on 24 March 2002, Aamir, who had spent over two months in Los Angeles promoting the film, after it had been bought by Sony Pictures Classic, walked the red carpet of the Kodak Theatre in downtown Los Angeles with wife Reena Dutta and director Ashutosh Gowariker and his wife Sunita. The sports epic he had made was really a film about national honour and Indian pride. It was not only about defeating the colonial rulers at their own game, cricket, but also about trying to storm the bastion of global storytelling with a three-hour-forty-minute drama. Though the movie was replete with song-and-dance, the director refused to edit it or remove any musical scenes so that the film would be more compatible with the Academy's sensibilities. It was felt that the West, having lost its love for the musical, was not that keen on seeing songs pop up in other cinema traditions. This has always been, and to some extent still is, the obstacle for popular Indian cinema in the West.

Shah Rukh, who had for so long been the favourite of the NRI audience and the Indian star who seemed most likely to break out to a larger audience, had been bested. *Asoka* got great reviews though, when it was finally released in the UK in October, with Peter Bradshaw, the respected film critic of *The Guardian*, calling it a 'big, brash and deeply enjoyable Bollywood epic starring Shah Rukh Khan: the Tom Cruise of South Asia. He is Prince Asoka, in self-imposed exile from his kingdom in the third century BC, who falls in love with the mysterious beauty Kaurwaki, played by Kareena Kapoor. This movie's narrative gusto, its intricate, indirect eroticism—no sex, or even kissing—its lavish musical numbers and its sheer self-belief are a treat.'

But Bradshaw had earlier been bowled over by *Lagaan* when he saw it in June 2001. He surmised that 'the most expensive Bollywood musical ever and the first to include British actors, this might just do for the genre what *Crouching Tiger* did for the martial arts romance'. *Lagaan,* added Bradshaw, was a lavish epic, a gorgeous love story, and a rollicking adventure yarn. Larger than life and outrageously enjoyable, he believed that it had a dash of the spaghetti western, a hint of Kurosawa, with a bracing shot of Kipling. The world seemed to agree, with the film winning countless hearts at the world's second oldest film festival, Locarno. Reporting from Locarno for *The Times of India*, Uma da Cunha wrote that, for the first time, a mainstream Indian film screened at the festival's Piazza Grande and was an unqualified success, with the 6,300-strong audience cheering at all the right moments.[2]

Speaking to Asif Kapadia at a screening of the film at the National Theatre in London in October 2002, Aamir recalled: 'That was a really amazing screening and we won the Audience Award. From then on we got invited to a lot of festivals and a lot of distributors wanted to acquire it for mainstream screenings.'[3]

The Oscar experience was profoundly transformative for Aamir. But the change in the actor had its genesis in 2000 when he was making *Lagaan* and *Dil Chahta Hai*. Both films were shot at one go, and the shoot was organised very much in the Hollywood style, working from a bound script, with sync sound, call sheets and professional assistant directors, some of whom were trained abroad, including Apoorva Lakhia, who came on board on the recommendation of Farhan and Zoya Akhtar. Zoya knew him from her days at New York University, when she was studying for a diploma in filmmaking. Lakhia was supposed to have worked as assistant director on Farhan Akhtar's directorial debut, *Dil Chahta Hai*, shot between Mumbai, Goa and Sydney, but he'd had to return to the US to keep his union card. Zoya had taken his place as first assistant director on the film.

When Aamir met Apoorva Lakhia, in a New York hotel towards the end of 1999, he signed him on as first assistant director on *Lagaan*. By then, Lakhia had also worked as an assistant director on *Addicted to Love* (1997).

A few months later, on 6 January 2000, Lakhia found himself on the sets of the film in Bhuj, Gujarat. He instantly won the respect of the cast and crew by taking a tough stand and insisting that the bus would take the cast to the sets without the lead star, Aamir, because he was late. Aamir, also the producer of the film, got the message that this would be a tightly-run ship. He was always on time after that. The other assistants who worked on the film were Reema Kagti, who would go on to become Zoya Akhtar's partner in Tiger Baby Films, the enormously successful production house which has produced shows such as *Made in Heaven* and movies such as *Gold*; Kiran Rao, fresh out of Jamia Millia Islamia, who would go on to renew her acquaintance with Aamir in 2004 and marry him in 2005, and Priyamvada Narayanan. Most of the crew that worked on *Dil Chahta Hai* also worked on *Lagaan*, including the ace sound designer Nakul Kamte. Kiran Rao also made a brief uncredited appearance as a character's friend in Goa. Narayanan went on, in later years, to become a medical practitioner in the US till she realised where her true calling lay. So, ten years after she had first decided to try her hand at filmmaking, she returned to India and became a second unit director for Reema Kagti on her second film, *Talaash*. Subsequently, in 2013, she made her own film, *The Breadfruit Tree*.

Aamir spent a year making *Lagaan*, and then another year promoting it all over the world. But while his professional world was being reinvented, his personal life was collapsing. In

October 2001, Reena had moved out of their home, with their children, Junaid, then nine, and Ira, then four. In December 2002, they filed for divorce by mutual consent in a family court in Mumbai citing 'temperamental differences'. It was a sad end to a youthful romance that had once captivated the nation.

Aamir and Reena were married in April 1986, long before Aamir became a star. A *Star & Style* April 1991 issue chronicled their relationship. Calling Reena level-headed, it quotes Aamir as saying: 'We don't like show or exhibitionism of any kind. We're a very simple couple.' It says their favourite way of spending time together was sitting and just chatting, since they didn't own a TV or a VCR or a tape deck. 'We can't afford these luxuries,' says Aamir, 'since all my money has gone into buying the flat.'

The article also stated that Reena was most unlike the other star wives, who whiled away their time at beauty parlours, hosted kitty parties or attended parties dripping with diamonds. Nor was she interested in setting up a shop with her husband's money like Zarine (Sanjay) Khan or Shobha (Jeetendra) Kapoor. 'I would never have married anyone like that,' says the proud husband. Interestingly, the article quotes a famous astrologer (without mentioning his name) who believed that Aamir would marry again. 'Was that really predicted?' asks Aamir, amused at the very idea. 'No way ...' he says, 'I'm a one-woman man.' But he hastens to add that he is not conservative. 'I wouldn't hold on to my marriage if it was against all odds. I don't believe it is binding for keeps if it doesn't bring happiness, compatibility, understanding and togetherness for the couple. If two individuals cannot live together they should part ways instead of living in hell under one roof.' He was twenty-five then.

By January 2003, Aamir was in a relationship with English writer Jessica Hines, who wrote a brilliant biography of Amitabh

Bachchan, titled *Looking for Big B*. A piece in *Outlook* from that time talks of the writer running into Hines at Jogger's Park in Bandra, a Mumbai suburb, before she jumped into a waiting chauffeur-driven car belonging to Aamir.[4] Hines was then living with Aamir and would do so for another six months before her pregnancy drove them apart. In September 2005, *Stardust* would carry a cover story with the title '2-year-old Jaan: The Child Aamir Khan Abandoned!'

The reference was to Jaan, born to Jessica in September 2003. The then editor of *Stardust,* Sonali Jaffer, released the following statement, after Jessica Hines accused the magazine's journalists of intruding on her privacy: 'We are very certain about the authenticity of this. If he (Aamir) wants, he can ask for the DNA test. We were very confident about what we were covering. There was no point in getting into fake denials. But when we thought wounds were healed and the time was right, we published the pictures. As you see, she (Jessica) is not very remorseful, she is not vindictive or anything towards Aamir Khan. I think she was accepting about it and his stance. Everything should be directed to Aamir Khan from now onwards. We have said what we have to through articles and now he should go ahead and clear his stance. Why should we justify what we have written? It is upto him to justify. If he has to deny, let him deny.'[5] Many years later, *Stardust* founder Nari Hira would refer to the story in an interview to a former editor, Piyush Roy, as one of his best scoops.[6]

While the paternity of the baby was questioned by Aamir, the usually effervescent Hines remained enigmatically silent about it. There is no doubt that they had a close relationship. Among other things, they shared a love of books. The first book Hines got him was Elizabeth Smart's 1945 novel *By Grand Central Station I Sat Down and Wept*, inspired by the author's passionate affair with British poet George Barker. Aamir wrote her a furious letter in response, which she still has somewhere, accusing her of flirting with him. Hines spent years trying to convince him that she had shared it with him because she thought it was the most beautiful piece of prose poetry. She also introduced him to *The Confederacy of Dunces*, the American writer John Kennedy Toole's novel published eleven years after his suicide, and to the work of Grit Lit icon Harry Crews, with whom they even stayed for a week in Florida.

Despite this, it was a traumatic time for Aamir Khan, who had spent sixteen years with Reena, all the while weathering rumours of affairs with co-stars. As he admitted in an interview to me in 2010, after he had separated from Reena, he drank a bottle of Bacardi every day for a year-and-half, except for the six hours a week and every alternative weekend when he would see his children.[7] He says it was his mother who brought him to his senses one day, telling him he was soon going to look like Adnan Sami, in the days when the singer was overweight.

His cousin, Nuzhat Khan, who is a psychoanalyst and has been close to him since he was ten and she fifteen, was also there for him. I remember talking to her about Aamir. She told me he was fastidious about honesty and that he simply could not tell a lie. That, and the level of professionalism in his work, where each person was given due respect, was reflected in his personal life as well. He was not superhuman, she said. He did make mistakes and hurt himself. But he was totally open to learning and feeling new things, which she believed was an act of courage.[8] A former girlfriend was less charitable. 'He is very literal. He has no grey areas,' she told me, on condition of anonymity. 'It's his way or the highway. No ability to really connect and have dialogue outside his own received reality.'

Aamir has talked about this difficult time on *Koffee with Karan*, saying that for a year-and-a-half, he stayed locked up in his house. Drinking brought him close to Salman again. He was on a downslide and happened to bump into Salman, who invited himself over to his home. Recalls Aamir: 'He came over and we began drinking. Something connected there. Then it grew. We began spending a lot more time together.'

Emerging from those dark days was difficult, but Aamir was helped enormously by initial conversations, and an eventual friendship and relationship, with Kiran Rao. They met again on the sets of a commercial with Ashutosh Gowariker in 2003. A chat with her on the phone around this time led Aamir to say that he had finally found someone he was happy talking to. In Kiran's words, they hung out a lot and became 2 a.m. friends.[9] They started dating in 2004, then lived together for a year.

He was on his way back, emotionally and professionally.

Plans were afoot for his next film, *The Rising: Mangal Pandey*, which Ketan Mehta had wanted to make since the 1980s. In November 2003, Prince Charles played clapper boy for the traditional muhurat shot—for a film that celebrated the First War of Independence against the East India Company. The war had ended with India becoming part of the British Empire, ruled by Queen Victoria, Charles's great-great-great-grandmother. The film further established the Aamir Khan way of working, throwing himself completely into a project, changing his physical appearance and getting under the skin of the character. One can almost say that Aamir lives from film to film, living, breathing and working towards perfecting the character he will play, or throwing himself into the details of his next production. He spent a year-and-a-half growing his hair long, nurturing a huge moustache, and soaking himself in the period.[10] Back then, this kind of approach was seen as 'Aamir playing the perfectionist'. And the 'perfectionist' was not a compliment.

The casting for *The Rising* was not without its controversies. After Aishwarya Rai's debut at Cannes Film Festival with *Devdas* in 2002, she had become a global name. Her inclusion was an important part of *The Rising*'s international allure, with Toby Stephens of *Die Another Day* already cast in a prominent role as Mangal Pandey's unlikely British ally. *Devdas* had made Rai an international name to reckon with, especially since Harvey Weinstein, then at the peak of his power, had shown interest in her.

Today, the world knows what that interest means. In a comment posted in response to a news story by *Variety*, veteran talent manager and owner of the California-based Canyon Entertainment, Simone Sheffield, wrote: 'I used to manage Indian actress Aishwarya Rai. While dealing with Harvey, I found it comical how hard he tried to get Aishwarya alone.' Of Weinstein, Sheffield adds: 'When we were leaving Mr Weinstein's office, he cornered me and said, what do I have to do to get her alone? When Aishwarya and I returned to our hotel, I sent Harvey a steel pig trough filled with Diet Coke as a thank you gift for the meeting. Yes, we did do business and yes, he eventually threatened me. Told me I'd never work in this business, blah blah blah. What I said to him I can't print. But you can be sure, I never gave him the opportunity to even breathe on my client,' Sheffield wrote. She and Rai went their separate ways in 2011.[11]

Rai's Hollywood agent, William Morris, was handling her contract for *The Rising*. When they wanted to renegotiate her fee for the movie, the producer, Bobby Bedi, decided to drop her. Rai, busy shooting what she thought would be her breakout film, Gurinder Chadha's *Bride and Prejudice* (2004), never spoke about this incident in public—but as a consequence, her supporter, Subrata Roy's Sahara Entertainment, withdrew its investment in Manmohan Shetty's Entertainment One, on the grounds that the company was funding *The Rising*. Shetty then pulled out, having invested ₹5 crore, leaving *The Rising* struggling for finance.

At that time, *The Rising* was being hyped as Bollywood's biggest film yet and an attempt to make the first international film out of India in a Bollywood idiom—though it must be noted that Sanjay Leela Bhansali's *Devdas*, starring Shah Rukh Khan and Rai, was vying for the same title.[12]

On the face of it, the idea of *The Rising* seemed perfect. Bobby Bedi was the producer of *Bandit Queen*, the film that gave director Shekhar Kapur an international career; he went on to make the Oscar-winning *Elizabeth*. Stephens, the son of Dame Maggie Smith, was a rising British star. Rai had wowed Cannes a year ago. And Aamir was fresh off an Oscar nomination. The ingredients for success seemed right but the global reception to the film was underwhelming. Released on Independence Day in 2005, without Rai, it was the country's fourth-highest grossing movie.

Aamir was in a good place again, professionally and personally. He had started *Fanaa* for Yash Raj Films, with Kajol, who was starring in her first film after motherhood. Taking four days off during the shooting of *Fanaa*, Aamir married Kiran Rao on 28 December 2005. The marriage was formally registered in Mumbai under the Special Marriage Act, 1954. The couple later had a private function for friends and family in Panchgani, at a house he later bought from director Homi Adajania.

If Aamir was trying to put Indian cinema on the world map, so was Shah Rukh. *Asoka* could not make it to the Toronto Film Festival but it premiered at the prestigious Venice Film Festival in September 2001. In his review of it, *Variety*'s David Rooney said the 'ambling nature of Indian storytelling makes crossover business unlikely in this case', though 'some degree of arthouse attention appears indicated'. Coming on the heels of *Lagaan*, *Asoka* provided further evidence that Bollywood was poised for wider commercial impact beyond its already substantial, established niche.

Shah Rukh had been working extraordinarily hard, doing three shifts a day for a while, acting in *Asoka*, *Kabhi Khushi Kabhie Gham*, and then *Devdas* at night (all at different locations within Mumbai's Film City), sometimes turning up drunk on set to keep in character. *Devdas* took an enormous toll on everyone, especially on Sanjay Leela Bhansali, with the film's 260 shooting shifts over two-and-a-half years, seven months of night shifts for the lead stars, the death of two crew members in accidents, sixteen months of jail for producer Bharat Shah, and even a stint of borrowing from close friends to keep the film going.[13]

However, the screening of *Devdas*, at the Cannes Film Festival in May 2002, a year after *Lagaan* made it to the Oscars, seemed to suggest that Indian movies had arrived on the world stage. The Cannes experience was heady for Shah Rukh. He attended the festival with Karan Johar. I remember talking to him on the phone from Delhi—he could barely control his excitement at meeting heavyweight producers such as Weinstein. There was a bit of good-natured self-deprecation too—how the Hollywood big daddies assumed that as a big star in India, he would have his own private plane and yacht.

But the one who truly benefited from the appearance at Cannes was Aishwarya Rai, who became a regular at the red carpet as a jury member, and then as a brand ambassador of L'Oreal Paris.

Shah Rukh had ended 2001 with *Kabhi Khushi Kabhie Gham* (K3G), where he played the older, adopted son of the Raichand family. The movie, directed by Karan Johar, was a casting coup, with Amitabh Bachchan playing his father and Hrithik Roshan, the actor who was said to be the one to most likely replace him, playing his younger brother. Shah Rukh was on familiar territory here, with the second half of the movie based in England. Cast as a rich businessman with a mansion in Hampstead, he is married to Anjali (Kajol), whose heart still beats for India and for her roots in Chandni Chowk. There were two unforgettable moments in the film, which was designed to make NRIs weep into their Gucci scarves and Burberry mufflers. One, in which Jaya Bachchan, the mother separated from her son and daughter-in-law, talks of sending the sargi, the traditional offering during Karva Chauth, to her in London. The other is when Anjali's son sings the Indian national anthem during a function in a British school, uninhibited by the fact they are on alien soil in a very English environment. Nationalism was given a religious angle and any guilt the NRI may have felt about leaving behind his homeland was assuaged by Hrithik Roshan dancing to Vande Mataram with 'goras' dressed in the colours of the Indian flag, alongside him in the heart of London's Leicester Square.

Consumerism was celebrated in not-so-subtle ways—a helicopter drops Shah Rukh close to his mansion, so he can run in slow motion to his mother, who has come bearing a traditional welcome thali, and a private plane brings the Raichands to London to meet their son. And what could be more fitting than the climactic meeting between Rahul and his father being set in the upmarket Bluewater shopping mall in Kent.

By the end of 2002, Shah Rukh could afford to feel somewhat compensated for the failure of *Asoka*. K3G was a blockbuster. Perhaps slightly disaffected by the failure of *Asoka*, he went back to the romantic drama template and decided *Chalte Chalte* would be Dreamz's next production.

While they were shooting *Chalte Chalte,* Shah Rukh met Amol Palekar, an actor he had grown up watching. He had come to narrate the story of *Paheli* to Rani Mukerji, to ask her to play the role of a woman in love with the ghost of her husband. The film, based on Vijaydan Detha's novel, had first been adapted to the screen by Mani Kaul as *Duvidha* (1973) and Amol Palekar was keen to do a remake. 'He had come to narrate the script to

Rani when we were shooting. I heard the story and offered to do it,' says Shah Rukh. He also produced the film.

I remember meeting Shah Rukh on the sets of *Paheli* in Film City, when they were shooting the song *Phir Raat Kati*. It had taken over a hundred trucks of sand to create a mini-Rajasthan on top of a hill. The afternoon sun was beating down as Shah Rukh, clad in an angarakhi and ready-made dhoti, and Rani Mukherji, in a brocade choli and lehnga, pretended to be puppets. Cinematographer Ravi K. Chandran took aim with his camera and choreographer Farah Khan hollered into the mike. 'Has your camel bitten you?' she asked a dancer clad in Rajasthani regalia, who was being lax. 'Or has he died?' Everyone, including the unfortunate dancer, cracked up.

Shah Rukh was in a philosophical mood, as he talked about how proud he was to be known as a woman's hero. 'All the women in my movies, whether it was *Dilwale Dulhaniya Le Jayenge* or *Kuch Kuch Hota Hai*, have been very strong. That's what I like personally too, not the bra-burning feminist but the resilient woman who takes it on the chin and moves forward. That's what I liked about this story. It's about a woman's right to choose a man.'

It was clear that he wasn't an enormous fan of director Amol Palekar and his screenplay writer-wife Sandhya Gokhale, but *Paheli* was nominated as India's entry to the Oscars in the Best Foreign Picture category. It was selected for major screenings—for the Hollywood Foreign Press Association (for the Golden Globes), at the Palm Springs and Sundance festivals. The PR firm Rogers and Cowan were hired to promote the film in the US, and while Shah Rukh was in New York for three months, till the end of December 2005 shooting for Karan Johar's *Kabhi Alvida Na Kehna* (KANK), he tried his best to push the film. He gave a string of interviews where he spoke about the movie's strong feminist core, as well as the idea, tongue-in-cheek, as he would put it: that for a woman, the perfect man is only an illusion. He also emphasised that the film was based on a folktale and was culturally rich, just like '*Devdas* and *Asoka*'.

Palekar stayed in Los Angeles till the end of January 2006, when the nominees for the Best Foreign Language Film were announced. *Paheli* did not figure in the list.

While Aamir and Shah Rukh were trying to take Indian cinema to the West, Salman was digging a deeper hole for himself. By 2002, his relationship with Aishwarya Rai had become toxic. In November 2001, he spent an entire night banging on the door of her seventeenth-floor apartment in Lokhandwala, demanding to be let in. Incensed, her father reported the incident to the police. A month later, in December 2001, he landed up on the sets of Rohan Sippy's *Kuch Na Kaho* (KNK) to object to her acting with Abhishek Bachchan (ironically, the two were not dating then, but would go on to marry in 2007). For good measure, Salman rammed his car into hers.

On 12 February 2002, Salman took the unprecedented step of speaking to *The Times of India*—not to a film journalist, but to senior reporter S. Balakrishnan. In the interview, he talked of his love for Aishwarya: 'I've been through one too many people but this time, it's not obsession, but love and only love.' When the interviewer asked what it was about Aishwarya that attracted him, he said: 'The person, her balance, she's a typical middle-class Indian girl. She's had the right kind of upbringing.'

On 16 February 2002, Aishwarya Rai made an appearance at the Filmfare Awards with her arm in a sling and dark glasses, saying she had slipped and fallen. The rumour mills went into overdrive, claiming Salman had assaulted her. When the rumours refused to die down, she gave an interview to *Filmfare* in May 2002. She said, 'For some perverse reason, no one wants to believe that I fell down the stairs. First, the media calls me the woman of the millennium, a woman of substance. Then how can the same media make me out to be such a doormat? I'm a self-respecting woman, I don't take nonsense from anyone. No one tries caveman tactics on me. Even Arnold Schwarzenegger can fall and get hurt, so why should I be any different? If I had been accosted or physically beaten, I'd have reacted violently. If there has been no reaction from my side, it means there's no truth in those stories about me. My silence fanned the rumours. I don't react to mudslinging.'

Later in the same year, Salman disrupted the shoot of Aziz Mirza's *Chalte Chalte*, where Shah Rukh was shooting a song with Aishwarya. Set members from that time recall that Salman was uncontrollable for four-and-a-half hours, forcing Mirza to cancel the entire schedule. It not only cost Aishwarya the film (she was replaced by Rani Mukerji), but she was also not cast in *Main Hoon Na* and *Veer Zaara*, which also starred Shah Rukh.

On 27 September 2002, Aishwarya finally put an end to all rumours in a powerful interview to Afsana Ahmed and Smrity Sharma, which appeared on the front page of *Bombay Times*: 'Salman and I broke up last March, but he isn't able to come to terms with it.' She revealed that she had broken up with Salman only when he indirectly confessed to cheating on her. She also alleged that Salman suspected her of having affairs with her co-stars Abhishek and Shah Rukh Khan, and had even physically abused her, but 'luckily without leaving any marks'.[14] Later that same night, Salman's Landcruiser ran over people sleeping on the pavement in suburban Bandra, in front of the American Express Bakery, tragically killing one person and injuring four.

It would be thirteen years before the Bombay High Court acquitted Salman of all charges in the 2002 hit-and-run case. The court, in its judgment, said that the prosecution had failed to establish its case beyond a reasonable doubt. Salman's family would forever try to link Aishwarya's interview to Salman's troubled state of mind. His only film in 2001, *Chori*

Chori Chupke Chupke (CCCC), directed by Abbas Mustan, also attracted controversy when its prints were seized by the CBI because the film had been funded by underworld don Chhota Shakeel. Nazim Rizvi, the producer of the film, was held for having links with the underworld, and its financier, diamond merchant Bharat Shah, was arrested by the Crime Branch in January 2001 for aiding and abetting Chhota Shakeel under the Maharashtra Control of Organised Crime Act (MCOCA)—an event that would cast a shadow on Bhansali's *Devdas* and cause it to nearly miss its Cannes deadline. The last shot of the film was completed only on 29 April for the 23 May premiere. CCCC did average business, but the next three films that Salman did—*Yeh Hai Jalwa, Tumko Naa Bhool Payenge* and *Hum Tumhare Hain Sanam* (the last helmed by Tamil director K.S. Adhiyaman and co-starring Shah Rukh had taken five years to complete)—did not do very well, either critically or commercially.

Still wounded by the very public dumping by Aishwarya, and facing the twin legal complications of the hit-and-run case and the black buck shooting from 1998, Salman put his heart and soul into *Tere Naam*, which was the ultimate exercise in narcissism and didn't leave much to the imagination with its tag line, 'Unfortunately a true love story'.

The film, released on 15 August 2003, had enormous resonance in the days before toxic masculinity became an issue in the era of #MeToo and stalking the heroine as a way of expressing love became a sore point with critics. In the film, Salman plays Radhe, a small-town college student who falls in love with the temple priest's daughter (Bhumika Chawla). He ends up kidnapping her when she doesn't reciprocate his feelings. Among other acts of violence, he ties her to a chair, gags her, and at various points, threatens to beat her up, kill her and kill himself. 'I used to be so happy before I met you,' he says in the film, 'If I die, you'll be widowed.' When a brawl ends with him becoming mentally unstable, he is admitted into a mental institution. And when the love of his life commits suicide rather than agreeing to marry the person chosen by her family (because, of course, women love psychotic men according to Bollywood), Radhe accepts his madness and lives on to become an old man who keeps her memory alive. Directed by Satish Kaushik, based on Tamil director Bala Palanisamy's *Sethu* (1999)—the director claimed it was based on a friend's life—and written along with veteran potboiler writer Jainendra Jain, the film was a huge hit.

Even as far away as Kashmir, its soundtrack and pirated VCDs made the film so popular that Basharat Peer wrote in *Curfewed Night* that 'every other youngster was getting his hair done like Salman'. The much-imitated haircut was the star's own idea, as was the way he flipped his hair. In Shopian in Kashmir, a nineteen-year-old Pakistani militant, a member of the Jaish-e-Mohammed, apparently bought a copy of the video and hovered around the local women's college, pining for the girl he had fallen for. He wanted to marry her and take her back to Pakistan, but her parents were against it. He even got his hair cut in the *Tere Naam* style, causing the entire town to call him 'Tere Naam'. Such was Salman's popularity in the Valley that when Vishal Bharadwaj made *Haider* (his interpretation of *Hamlet*), the twin owners of a pirated video store, meant to play Rosencrantz and Guildenstern, were dressed as Prem from *Hum Aapke Hain Kaun*. Salman made another entry in *Haider*. Indian Army soldiers are shown sitting in Faraz cinema, watching his 1994 film *Sangdil Sanam*, when a line of prisoners are marched up to the screen to be identified as informers.

The *Tere Naam* tale of unrequited love had a great impact on young men, not merely in the Kashmir Valley. Here was an actor who was still rooted to the melodrama of old Bollywood, who was not bothered about global ambition or about taking

India to the West. He was content to speak to small-town India about love across caste, class and reason. And yet, he was a big star, showing his wounds on-screen and dressed, as academic Kaushik Bhaumik described it to me, 'mostly in a ganji and kachcha throughout the movie'.

Salman's relationship with Aishwarya Rai continued to make headlines well into 2005. In July of that year, when the *Hindustan Times* launched an edition in Mumbai, it did so with a splash, publishing transcripts of an old argument between Salman and Aishwarya, which the police had apparently tapped as part of their surveillance of Bollywood and the underworld. Salman was overheard bullying Aishwarya into performing for a show funded by underworld don Abu Salem and boasting about his connections. The tapes were declared to be false in 2006 by a national forensic lab. In an interview to *Tehelka* in 2005, though, Chhota Rajan said he had seen Salman lunching with Dawood Ibrahim in Dubai.

In the case of Aishwarya Rai, Shah Rukh hadn't covered himself in glory either, announcing in September 2002, that she had been replaced in *Chalte Chalte* (2003) after Salman's tantrum. Released in June 2003, *Chalte Chalte* was a commercial success, but Shah Rukh had already taken off for London's Wellington Hospital in March for a much-publicised spinal surgery that involved surgeons opening vertebrae six and seven, removing a herniated disc, and inserting a new one made of titanium. Accompanying him were wife Gauri and friends Karan Johar, Aditya Chopra, Kajal Anand, Juhi Chawla and husband Jai Mehta. It would be one of nine surgeries which he claims has made him quite well-educated on the subject of medicine. Coupled with four honorary doctorates from La Trobe University in Melbourne; University of Law, London; University of Bedfordshire in England; and University of Edinburgh, Scotland, they have made him a doctor, he jokes, and he can hold forth on the protocol for the use of ventilators with as much fluency as the interplay of muscles in the shoulder.

Shah Rukh had just completed four days of shooting *Kal Ho Na Ho*, which was finally released in November 2003. Advertised as 'The Story of a Lifetime ... In a Heartbeat', the film was about an MBA student in New York, Naina Katherine Kapoor (Preity Zinta), who falls in love with her neighbour Aman Mathur (Shah Rukh Khan), who is terminally ill. Though Aman has strong feelings for her, he wants Naina and her friend Rohit Patel (Saif Ali Khan) to fall in love with each other because he fears she will grieve for him when he passes away. The film, with its simple message of living in the moment, was a hit, and debuted a refreshed version of Shah Rukh Khan as the elder statesman, too old to be the romantic lover, but perfect to play the problem solver, the people pleaser, and everyone's best friend. For Johar, *Kal Ho Na Ho* was deeply personal because his father Yash Johar was being treated in New York for cancer during the shooting of the film. In June 2004, Yash Johar died of a chest infection related to the cancer.

As Aamir was re-building his personal life and making *The Rising* and Shah Rukh was re-engineering his romantic image to suit his age, Salman was trying to find his way back, professionally and personally. He met Katrina Kaif around the time she had made her debut in Kaizad Gustad's disastrous *Boom* in 2003, in which much was made of her intimate scenes with Gulshan Grover. She was eighteen and Salman later recalled how he first met her. 'It was at a small get-together. She had come home for a party and I thought she was one of the sweetest girls ever. She knew my sister and all my friends, but she didn't know me,' he said in an interview in 2017.

Salman's career was also looking up. His fifth collaboration with David Dhawan and fourth with Sajid Nadiadwala (*Mujhse Shaadi Karogi*, 2004) was being talked about for its construction of a huge set resembling a Goan village in Film City. The Director of Photography was using a new motion capture camera for this film, a camera that had been used in the production of the Hollywood blockbuster, *The Matrix*. With the addition of Akshay Kumar as the wicked Sunny, Priyanka Chopra as the sultry Rani, Salman Khan did very well as Sameer, the man who has anger management issues.

The highlight of *Mujhse Shaadi Karogi* for adoring Salman fans were scenes where his shiny, hairless, bare chest was on display, although this was not the first time he had taken off his shirt. *Veergati* in 1995 had a dour Salman fighting a battery of villains clad in nothing but his jeans. But the first time his shirtlessness was noticed widely was in the song '*O O Jaane Jaana*' in the 1998 film *Pyaar Kiya To Darna Kya*, where Salman was the perfect example of what Paromita Vohra has called the 'real man' capable of supporting a woman by using his body to survive in the world. 'It was like the reverse-migration of the Indian metropolitan film hero, from the world of the mind and spirit, and urban material prosperity to the hinterland,' she wrote.[15]

Salman Khan, Vohra notes, was also playing out a parallel narrative in real life—his training and body building were often talked about and written about in the popular media. It is as though the on-screen persona and real-life personality came together to become one in *Pyaar Kiya To Darna Kya*, creating a powerful symbol of the physical man hitherto not taken seriously. The built body presented the idea that there was, apparently, no natural order of things. The natural—the body—could be converted into the appropriate ideal for a new version of India taking shape in the post-globalisation years.

A year later, in 2005, Salman reunited with Dhawan for *Maine Pyaar Kyun Kiya*, where he played a womanising doctor (again called Sameer, like his man-child character in *Hum Dil De Chuke Sanam* and *Mujhse Shaadi Karogi*) who falls in love with Katrina Kaif's character, only to have her show him how his heart really beats for his gorgeous nurse (Sushmita Sen). Kaif (who was by then Salman's real-life girlfriend), marries the character played by Sohail Khan (Salman's real-life brother). The same year, Salman played another philanderer, Prem, in Anees Bazmee's *No Entry*, produced by Boney Kapoor. It was a remake of the Tamil film *Charlie Chaplin*, directed by Sakthi Chidambaram, and was the year's biggest hit. It was every middling, middle-aged man's dream: Mauritius resorts, beautiful bodies, sand and endless partying. If only life were like that! Bazmee, who wrote Dhawan's *Aankhen* and *Mujhse Shaadi Karogi*, was an old hand at the screwball comedy of manners involving extra-marital affairs, and in *No Entry*, he didn't disappoint. Neither did Salman, whose first appearance in the film was predictably shirtless and surrounded by bikini-clad beauties. An *India Today* review from that time said: 'He doesn't even pretend to act anymore. He plays himself: a Bollywood rock star.'[16]

But Salman's decisions were still largely driven by personal emotions. He did *No Entry* because he could sense that Boney Kapoor was going through a rough patch financially. It was an ensemble film and Boney needed someone other than brother Anil to market the film. When he got in touch with Salman, he suggested a ridiculous amount as a fee to him. Anil Kapoor then called Salman, who promptly came over to his Juhu home. Anil told him there were two roles on offer: that of Kishen, which required fifty days of shooting and the other of Prem, requiring ten days. Salman quickly chose the latter.[17] Later, in an interview, Anil Kapoor said that when they went to South Africa for the shoot, they booked Salman in a suite in a luxury hotel befitting his star status. The rest of the cast was in more modest digs. When Salman found out, he promptly changed his accommodation.

There are other examples of Salman's generosity towards those he likes. When he found out that no one was willing to play a supporting role in Revathy's *Phir Milenge* opposite Shilpa Shetty (they were working together on another film, *Garv: Pride and Honour*, in Rajasthan), he immediately said he would do it. 'It's such a nice subject, why wouldn't I do it?' he asked.

Salman's working style is famously erratic. Anil Kapoor remembers having to go to his hotel room and wait for him while he ordered breakfast and had his coffee, to ensure he would come to the sets for shooting to begin. Professionally, 2005 would be his last good year for some time—though there was a bright spot with *Partner* in 2007, which reunited him with director David Dhawan. But none of his work drew much attention, while the other two Khans were performing consistently during this period.

Having recovered from surgery, Shah Rukh had a banner year in 2004, highlighting a strategy that would serve him well over the next few years. Choose one film for art and another for commerce. In 2004, he appeared in *Swades*, but he also kept one eye firmly fixed on the box office with Yash Chopra's epic India-Pakistan romance, *Veer Zaara*, and Farah Khan's *Main Hoon Na*. It was a year in which he narrowly, and controversially, missed the National Award which was given instead to Saif Ali Khan for *Hum Tum*, a surprising choice given that it was a romantic comedy and coincided with his mother, Sharmila Tagore, being chairperson of the Central Board of Film Certification. The chairman of the feature film jury, independent filmmaker Sudhir Mishra, added to the controversy when he said that the 'quivering of lips'—no doubt referring to Shah Rukh—usually passes for great acting in Bollywood.

In *Swades*, directed by *Lagaan*'s Ashutosh Gowariker, Shah Rukh plays Mohan Bhargava, a project manager at NASA, who is haunted by his inability to help the woman who raised him, Kaveri Amma. He returns to the Indian village where she now lives, Charanpur, in Uttar Pradesh, in order to bring her back to America. But once he arrives in India, he finds himself examining his own values—in his mind, his material success is pitted against the enormous deprivation he sees around him. Overcome by sadness at the plight of a tenant in a neighbouring village, he decides to build a hydroelectric plant to provide water and electricity to the village before returning to the US. And when he does return, he cannot stop thinking back about what he has left behind in that deprived village. Like a more famous Mahatma before him, he returns to India forever, to work for change.

The movie was inspired by the life of Aravinda Pillalamarri and Ravi Kuchimanchi, an NRI couple who returned to India and developed a pedal power generator to light up remote, off-the-grid village schools in the Narmada Valley. Made at a time when 'India Shining' was being questioned in a wave that saw the BJP-led NDA being defeated in the elections and a Congress-led coalition coming to power, it had a radical idea at its heart: *'Main nahin maanta hamaara desh duniya ka sabse mahaan desh hai ... lekin yeh zaroor manta hoon ... ki hum mein kabliyat hai, taqat hai, apne desh ko mahaan banane ki.'* (I do not think India is the greatest country in the world, but I do believe that we [Indians] have the potential, the strength to make our nation great.)

To show the character's journey into the soul of India, Gowariker has Shah Rukh sitting in a plane, a train, a bus, a boat, on a scooter sandwiched between two villagers, and even in a trailer van, underlining the pro-poor political consciousness of the day that was soon to translate into the 'aam aadmi' philosophy of the first UPA government which passed historic enabling legislations such as the Right to Information Act (2005) and the National Rural Employment Guarantee Act, also known as the Right to Work (2005). Both were the result of the UPA government working closely, even if grudgingly, with the National Advisory Council, a group of civil society activists and technocrats assembled by then Congress party president Sonia Gandhi. Gandhi had declined to take over as prime minister and appointed Manmohan Singh, one of the architects of the 1991 liberalisation (as finance minister), in her place.

At a time when dissent and debate were not seen as anti-national, Mohan Bhargava sings a song written by Javed Akhtar set to music by A.R. Rahman and speaks of another radical idea: Where does Ram reside?

Raam hi toh karuna mein hai, shaanti mein raam hai
Raam hi hai ekta mein, pragati mein raam hai
Raam bas bhakton nahin shatru ke beech chintan hai
Dekh taj ke paap Raavan, Raam tere mann mein hai
Raam tere mann mein hai, Raam mere mann mein hai
Raam toh ghar ghar mein har, Raam har aangan mein hai
Mann se Raavan jo nikaale, Raam uske mann mein hai
Raam toh ghar ghar mein har, Raam har aangan mein hai
Mann se Raavan jo nikaale, raam uske mann mein hai

That Ram resides in people's hearts, and not in any particular place, was a healing message after the cataclysmic Gujarat riots. *Swades* did not do well at the box office, perhaps it was overlong and came across as somewhat preachy, but even now, when Shah Rukh talks about the film, he gets emotional. In 2013, on its ninth anniversary, he posted on Twitter: 'Making *Swades* was such an emotionally overwhelming experience that I never saw the finished product. Didn't want the feeling to end.' He also thanked Ashutosh for changing his life.

Slowly, Shah Rukh's own politics was finding an echo in his movies. Earlier in the year, Farah Khan's *Main Hoon Na* (the first production of Red Chillies Entertainment, which he had set up in 2003 with wife Gauri Khan) had a Hindu fanatic as the villain (played by Suniel Shetty). It was a deliberate decision for Farah. She didn't want the villain to be a Muslim and deliberately chose the name 'Khan' for Suniel Shetty's right-hand man who eventually realises that he was being misled.

This was against the backdrop of the 2002 Gujarat riots, three days of communal clashes which had shaken the confidence of Muslims in the state and left a deep divide between Hindus and Muslims. Triggered by the burning of a train in Godhra that was carrying Hindu kar sevaks home from Ayodhya, causing the death of 58 people, the riots ended with over 1,000 dead, over 200 missing, and 2,500 injured. Of the dead, 790 were Muslim and 254 Hindu. The Concerned Citizens Tribunal Report estimated that as many as 1,926 may have been killed, while other sources estimated the death toll to be in excess of 2,000.

The chief minister of Gujarat, Narendra Modi, was accused of standing by as the brutality raged and it was not until 2012 that the cloud of suspicion was lifted when he was cleared of complicity by the Special Investigation Team (SIT) appointed by the Supreme Court of India. In April 2014, a month before Modi was elected as prime minister of the country with a clear majority, the Supreme Court expressed satisfaction over the SIT's investigations in nine cases related to the violence, and rejected as 'baseless' a plea contesting the SIT report. Modi had by then been transformed from Master Divider, as *India Today* described him in its January 2003 issue, to a hardline nationalist and economic reformer, whose promise of 'acche din' (good days) had energised the electorate into voting overwhelmingly for change. He had become The Conqueror, as the *India Today* issue after the 2014 general elections called him.

But it was still 2004 and nationalism could be nuanced. In Shah Rukh's Diwali release, *Veer Zaara*, he played an Indian fighter pilot in love with a Pakistani girl, played by Preity Zinta. In a duet that Preity Zinta sang with Shah Rukh, she spelt out the philosophy of the movie: '*Yahan bhi wahi shaam hai/ wahi savera/aisa hi des hai mera/jaisa des hai tera.*' (Our dawn and our dusk are the same. My nation is like yours.) It was, as Javed Akhtar noted, a more sophisticated patriotism for a more complex era: where the enemy was starvation, disease and deprivation, not Pakistan.

Sociologist Shiv Visvanathan thought it was a most exciting time for Bollywood as it fashioned a whole new definition of unity in diversity.[18] This was not a homogenous one-size-fits-all straitjacket, forcing linguistic, religious or even social conformity on its people. A new identity was emerging, balancing call centres and cows on the street, India's confidence and Pakistan's fears, the Raj's legacy (as evident in *The Rising*, which was being made at this time) and independent India's aspirations, as seen through the eyes of Mohan Bhargava in *Swades*.

Perhaps to tap into this zeitgeist, Aditya Chopra advised his father to make an 'Indian' movie, even though Yash Chopra was all set to make a 'mature' love story partly set in the West. Like many of his generation from Punjab, Chopra had lived through the Partition and witnessed several riots, but he thought of Islam not so much as a religion as a way of life that had spawned Urdu, the language of his beloved poetry. It was his late best friend Sahir Ludhianvi's anti-war poem, *Parchhaiyan*, that inspired *Veer Zaara*.

Shah Rukh went on to star in another big movie, *Kabhi Alvida Na Kehna* or KANK, as it came to be known. The movie was made collaboratively, with all the stars, including Amitabh Bachchan and his son Abhishek, staying together in New York. The days were long, mostly beginning at six and ending just in time for dinner. Shah Rukh would often step in to direct the action scenes, the football sequence with his on-screen son, for instance. He was so involved in the shoot that he would turn up for scenes even if he didn't feature in them.

A report in *rediff.com* at the time quoted a junior artist on the set, Jen, as saying: 'They all get along very well.'[19] Jen adds,

'I saw Karan give Shah Rukh and Rani (Mukerji, who played his lover in the movie) a hug the first day. I saw Abhishek massaging (co-star) Preity Zinta's shoulders at one time. It was like a family. They really care about each other.' Another guest artiste, Virginia Kelley's nicest memory was from the end of the wedding-day shoot. As she stepped out in the early hours of the morning, she saw Shah Rukh on a bench, eating a pizza. 'I am sure his bodyguards were nearby,' she says. 'But I am sure he did that just to give a glimpse to the people who had been there the whole day. He let people take pictures and get his autograph.'

But as Shah Rukh himself would say about playing Dev, the cynical, wry, ex-football star, for the first time, he experienced 'some discomfort in a Karan Johar film'. And why not? Far from being the dimpled, loveable, romantic, Dev is a man plagued by insecurities and resentments, trapped in a marriage to a woman who adores him but is too busy making a good living for them both. The man-child who wants to be nurtured and nourished by his woman is played by the younger actor, Abhishek Bachchan. Shah Rukh was free to play a more adult version of his romantic self. Much later, in *Ae Dil Hai Mushkil* (2016), Johar underlined this theme further when he positioned Shah Rukh as the older rival whose wife is dating a younger man. Playing a well-known artist, Shah Rukh puts Ranbir Kapoor's man-child in his place by dismissing his loud talk of keeping Aishwarya Rai Bachchan's character (Saba) awake all night. Shah Rukh stops him by saying he should allow her some sleep so he can visit her in her dreams.

Released in August 2006, KANK did very well internationally. It allowed Shah Rukh to age gracefully and realistically. It also prepared the audience for his next film, *Don*, a remake of the 1978 Amitabh Bachchan starrer. Shah Rukh shot over 80 per cent of the film in Kuala Lumpur and Langkawi in Malaysia, a country in which he is enormously popular.

The next year, 2007, was important for Shah Rukh. He replaced Amitabh Bachchan as the host of Star Plus's *Kaun Banega Crorepati* in January—continuing a long tradition of going head to head with the actor, his idol whom he wanted to equal or perhaps even replace. As Roshmila Bhattacharya writes in *Matinee Men: A Journey Through Bollywood*, Shah Rukh told her he dreamt of being like Babu, the *Satte Pe Satta* (1982) guy with the light eyes; of lighting dynamite with a beedi and coolly sauntering away even as it exploded a few feet away from him like Vijay in *Trishul* (1978); and of locking the door, putting the key in his pocket, and turning to the villains to say quietly: 'Only one of us is going to get out of here unhurt,' like another Vijay in *Deewar* (1975).

This time the memory was less than savoury. Shah Rukh also had a very public rift with Amar Singh over the seating given to the politician and his 'bade bhai' Amitabh Bachchan at a Zee TV awards show in Dubai in 2004. Three years later, in 2007, as the host of the Filmfare Awards, Shah Rukh said he saw 'darindagi' (evil intent) in Amar Singh's eyes. It was enough for a group of agitators to turn up at Shah Rukh's Mumbai house. And enough to ignite Shah Rukh's temper: 'If you scare me by saying that you will harm me, I will be scared, because if I die, who will look after my kids? But if you threaten my children, I will not be in self-preservation mode.'[20]

In 2007, Shah Rukh got a chance to explore his twin identities, of a liberal Muslim and a feminist man, which were being reshaped by his choice of films. In *Chak De! India*, he explored an updated version of the Nehruvian nationalist Indian who was emerging post *Swades*. This nationalist lived in India and was a Muslim—Kabir Khan, former captain of the Indian hockey team, who famously misses a penalty goal in a match against Pakistan and is accused of doing so purposely. Like Mohan Bhargava though, he sees an India beyond caste and community when it comes to working for the common good. The difference is that he is as much a victim as some in his team, which includes people from Jharkhand and Manipur. There's a telling scene, when his friend tells him, '*Ek galti toh sabko maaf hoti hai*' (Everyone is allowed to make one mistake) when referring to his missing the penalty shot, and Shah Rukh's Kabir Khan asks, with a bitter smile and a raised eyebrow, '*Sabko*?' (Everyone?).

There's a public outcry that follows the defeat against Pakistan, and Kabir Khan is accused of being a traitor and told to 'go to 'Pakistan'. It was a precursor of the social media lynching that would happen to Shah Rukh, beginning with his remark about how humiliating it was that none of the Pakistani players was picked up to play in the Indian Premier League, while promoting *My Name is Khan* (2010), and then again, when he spoke about the rising intolerance in the country. Written by Jaideep Sahni, who was inspired by the victory of the Indian women's hockey team in 2002, and directed by Shimit Amin, an editor trained in the US, who had directed the thriller *Ek Hasina Thi* in 2004 with Saif Ali Khan, the film cast Kabir Khan as a man who had taken some hard knocks in life and yet was not a 'diljala' (burnout); good-natured, but not necessarily polite.

The film, released around 15 August 2007, touched a deep chord of patriotism among viewers, and blended themes which became a recurrent theme in later Hindi cinema: strong sports dramas, with a powerful feminist core. The cynical hockey administrator played by Anjan Srivastava says to Kabir Khan, who wants to become the coach of the Indian women's team, '*Yeh chakla belan chalane wali Bhartiya nariyan hain, kahan yeh knicker-vikkar pehenkar daudegi*?' (Indian women are meant for the kitchen, not to wear shorts and run around the hockey field). Kabir Khan and his team respond by playing good hockey, but not without squabbles over regions, religions, and egos. At the end of *Chak De! India*, in a stinging comment on media-orchestrated public outrages, Kabir Khan is lauded as *'India ki jaan/desh ki shaan'* (India's life, country's pride) and a 'saccha Hindustani' (true Indian).

In his second release of 2007, *Om Shanti Om*, directed by his friend and choreographer-turned-director Farah Khan, Shah Rukh explored the idea of masculinity. For long, he had considered himself a weakling in the industry compared to actors such as Salman Khan, but for *Om Shanti Om*, he was made to work out and acquire a six-pack. He also performed an entire song virtually shirtless. The star he played in the movie, Om Kapoor, was not a nice man to know, brash, entitled, all too aware of his stardom, and like Dev of KANK, short-tempered. But as in *Chak De! India*, in the second half, he realises that he cannot succeed unless the woman/women around him commit to hard work. In that sense, from the quintessential lover, he moves effortlessly into the role of mentor, whether it is to the hockey team in *Chak De! India* or to Sandy in *Om Shanti Om*, who has to recreate Shantipriya to bring the villain Mike Mehra to justice.

In such a role, and with a more masculine body, Farah Khan completed his identification with the middle class, says academic Michiel Baas. A muscular body, till then, was seen more as a working-class production, embodied by the favourite of blue collar cinema-goers, Salman Khan. As the middle class itself became fitness conscious, trying to erase the traditional image of prosperity—the potbellied Indian man—Shah Rukh struck a chord. *'Dard-e-Disco'* was a performance meant to appeal to other men, rather than to women, who were big fans anyway. They always regarded him as the one star who was in touch with his feminine side and not afraid to explore it, with his respectful touches (no kissing, except on the side of the neck, first seen in *Dil to Pagal Hai*, 1997) and his roles as an enabler of women to find their true potential.

The song *'Deewangi Deewangi'* extended his stardom in other ways, with Farah getting almost every major actor, male or female, to make a walk-on appearance, in an unprecedented show of solidarity. This camaraderie of stars was only seen some decades earlier in Manmohan Desai's *Naseeb*, in which the Bachchan song *'John Jaani Janardhan'* had all the top names of the previous and current era joining in. Shot over six days, *'Deewangi Deewangi'* had stars from the previous generation such as Dharmendra, Jeetendra, Rekha and Shabana Azmi, practically all the women who had acted with Shah Rukh, and all the top male stars of the current generation, with the exception of Aamir Khan. They all got huge gift hampers from Shah Rukh for their efforts, including a Tag Heur watch and a Blackberry, plus keepsake costumes by Manish Malhotra for the women. Those who didn't appear in the song (Amitabh Bachchan and Akshay Kumar), did so in a faux Filmfare Awards function. The underlying message of the film, which was like a love letter to Hindi cinema, was this: Shah Rukh Khan was the undisputed king of Hindi cinema. Salman Khan's presence in the song underlined this status.

There had been bad blood between Shah Rukh and Salman since the time Salman had disrupted the *Chalte Chalte* shoot. But when common friend Farah Khan got married in 2004 to *Main Hoon Na*'s editor, Shirish Kunder, the two men had an emotional reunion at one of the wedding functions. Salman even made an appearance with Katrina Kaif as a gesture of friendship in the grand finale of *Kaun Banega Crorepati* (Season 3), hosted by Shah Rukh. But the truce didn't last long and in July 2008, the two stars almost came to blows at a party at Mumbai's swish Olive restaurant where Katrina Kaif was celebrating her birthday. Old resentments had surfaced—about Aishwarya Rai, and about Shah Rukh not reciprocating Salman's cameo in the *Om Shanti Om* song with a cameo in Salman's *Main Aurr Mrs Khanna* (2009), produced by his brother Sohail Khan and Ronnie Screwvala. Later, in a 2010 interview, Shah Rukh said, 'Sometimes two people run parallelly to each other and parallels don't meet. We don't have any common ground. I've spent some really good times with him and his family has been really kind to me and I know deep inside my heart he will never wish me ill.'[21] Salman wrote in a blog in 2008: '*Main sher hoon aur koi bandar sher ka shikaar nahi kar sakta* (I am a tiger and no monkey can hunt me).' In 2014, he said in an interview: 'He thinks my thinking is wrong, I think his thinking is wrong. I'm hurt, I've always loved Shah Rukh as a younger brother. I've shared an amazing time with Shah Rukh.'[22]

At the core of the 2008 fight was a proposal by Salman that the three Khans, who were seated at one table at Katrina's party, do a stage show for charity. Trouble began when Shah Rukh hesitated. Salman then launched into a rant about how how much his family had done for Shah Rukh when he began in the industry and how Shah Rukh had always undermined his intelligence. Many ugly things were said by both that evening but the deal-breaker came with Salman saying Shah Rukh was not capable of even being called a man, to which the latter retaliated: 'Why don't you ask your ex about it?' That was it.

Karan Johar and Gauri Khan were called to help and Gauri had to pull Shah Rukh out of the restaurant. Pictures from that day show her virtually dragging Shah Rukh to the car, as a weeping Katrina emerged at the entrance with an enraged Salman. The next evening, after a sleepless night that left both Katrina and Salman agitated, the latter went to his farmhouse in Panvel. Over a three-hour conversation frequently interrupted because of poor connectivity, he vowed to a close friend how he would show Shah Rukh his place in the industry. 'He thinks I am an ass. You wait, I will finish him.'

Words spoken in anger but somewhat prophetic, given that Shah Rukh has always known he may be a bigger star globally but Salman is beloved as the eternal 'bhai' in the domestic market.

This was an echo, if the December 1991 issue of *Stardust* is to be believed, of Salman's behaviour after the unexpected success of *Maine Pyaar Kiya* at the beginning of his career. 'Two years ago, he was a gawky, gum-chewing, pint-sized young boy' who hoped to one day show his 'smilingly sarcastic father' and his 'supercilious girlfriend' Sangeeta Bijlani that he was 'not an idle layabout, that he could stand on his own two little feet'. It talked about how Salman had been transformed by the illusion of fame, showing hitherto unseen traits of 'arrogance, ruthlessness, indifference, intolerable conceit'. The article talks of his long string of affairs, his 'way of getting back at Bijlani for all the humiliation she had heaped on him in his underdog days'.

The article said that when Salman had told his father he wanted to be an actor, the ace scriptwriter let out a hoot of laughter. 'Have you seen your face in the mirror?' it quoted Salim Khan as saying. 'You can never become an actor so please don't embarrass your family by making your ambition public.' The article stated that Salman hated his father for that remark. Indeed, he had hated him all his life. Don't you be deceived by the happy facade put up by the ménage-à-trois, wrote *Stardust*, adding 'Salman has never forgiven his father for bringing Helen into the family. Yet today father and son are the best of buddies.'

His relationship with Shah Rukh had the same love-hate quality. The contrasting reactions to their stints on TV highlighted their other differences.

After his stint on *Kaun Banega Crorepati*, Shah Rukh hosted the only season of *Kya Aap Paanchvi Pass Se Tez Hai* for Star Plus in 2008. Sony, meanwhile, convinced Salman Khan to host *10 Ka Dum*, which the actor believes began his journey back to stardom. As he said in an interview, 'In 2008, when it came to me, I had a very negative image in the public. And I was indeed scared to project my original personality. But then I made my debut, and from then on I realised that it is the most powerful medium.'[23] His father had pushed him to accept the offer. 'I was scared and so I asked my father whether I should do it because there will be the common man. I was scared of being me. He told me, "Who do you want to be then? If people accept you, it is good. If not, you will need to change yourself." That's when I decided to do this show.'

The first season of the show set the tone, with Salman joking, dancing and bonding with celebrity guests, ranging from his brothers to cricketers Yuvraj Singh and Harbhajan Singh. He showcased his ability to laugh at himself ('*Bahar niklo tum dono*'—You two, step outside please—he told the cricketers when they said Katrina Kaif was their favourite actress). He also had just the right kind of attitude to ask questions that ranged from the inane to the risqué. The show's format was borrowed from *Power of Ten* and had contestants guessing answers to questions in percentage, which would then be compared to the studio percentage. The winner could potentially take home ₹10 crore for questions such as this: What percentage of Indian men scratch themselves inappropriately in public? What percentage of Indians believe that *mard ko dard nahin hota* (men don't feel pain)? What percentage of Indian men believe they are more intelligent than women?

The episode with friend Aamir Khan, who came to the show in the middle of shooting *Ghajini*, with a freshly shaved head, is a delight to watch even now. Salman counts the numbers between fifty-one and sixty-one in one go and looks at himself approvingly. 'Who says film stars are not educated?' Aamir, relaxed as if he were sitting around in Salman's Galaxy Apartments, talks of how he pranked his co-stars by spitting in their palms while ostensibly reading them. Salman, in a bantering mood—while referring to a question on how many Indians believe stars are beautiful even when they wake up—talks of how his girlfriends leave for their shoots by the time he wakes up, so he can't tell. He also pokes fun at Aamir's habit of insisting on multiple retakes. Both recall their work together on *Andaz Apna Apna*. And both agree that '*Hindustani mard darpok hote hain.*' (Indian men are cowards).

The show revealed Salman at his uncensored best. Siddhartha Basu, who was then the director of the show, remembers meeting Salman at Film City with Shah Rukh (with whom Basu was shooting *Kya Aap Paanchvi Paas Se Tez Hain*?). 'It was a hot day. He was sitting out in the sun. The food was laid out. And I remember him taking me aside and asking me: "Do I have to read?" He didn't like reading, so the teleprompter was of no use. And he didn't like to memorise dialogues. Wireless prompts had just come in and we would prompt him line by line, until he would just take off, and then it would be difficult to bring him back to earth.' His strength, says Basu, was that he connected with ordinary people, in a batty, entertaining way. Suddenly, the angry Salman people had read about, the one who shot black bucks, ran over poor people sleeping on pavements and assaulted defenceless women was gone. In his place was a teddy bear with rippling muscles.

10 Ka Dum came at a time when Shah Rukh had also invested in friend Lalit Modi's Indian Premier League, buying Kolkata Knight Riders with long-time friend and colleague Juhi Chawla and her husband Jay Mehta. Its first season in April 2008 showcased a marriage of big business, entertainment and cricket which was unique at the time, with owners such as Nita Ambani, Preity Zinta and Jeh Wadia, Vijay Mallya and G.M. Rao. With its mix of svelte on-screen hostesses like Mandira Bedi, foreign cheerleaders, hectic after-match parties, and on-ground scandals like Harbhajan Singh slapping S. Sreesanth, it became the byword for a new kind of gilt-edged celebrity culture. Shah Rukh Khan was no longer just an actor, he was a celebrity businessman as well, quite a contrast from Salman's backslapping, relatable, working-class persona.

But Shah Rukh's friends had been working on his on-screen persona to reinvent it for the new decade. His tweaked image from *Om Shanti Om*, as an older romantic hero, was underlined further in Aditya Chopra's third directorial venture, *Rab Ne Bana Di Jodi* (2008). There was also a song which saw Shah Rukh stepping into the shoes of superstars through the years—Raj Kapoor, Dev Anand, Shammi Kapoor, Rajesh Khanna and Rishi Kapoor—which was meant to display the beauty of love and romance, Hindi film style. In a way, it harked back to what Farah Khan had done just a year ago in *Om Shanti Om* in the song *Dhoom Taana*, with Shah Rukh replacing (thanks to technology) Sunil Dutt, Rajesh Khanna and Jeetendra, thereby establishing himself as their natural successor.

Rab Ne Bana Di Jodi also trod the now-familiar path of redefining masculinity in popular culture, with Shah Rukh as the great mentor of women. This was a clever way of making the middle class man, increasingly faced with images of hypermasculinity, comfortable with the idea of the nondescript, regular sort of guy getting the girl. When his friend, played by Vinay Pathak, explains that girls like macho, manly men, Shah Rukh evolves his own philosophy—no one likes a bodyguard for a boyfriend, he says, every girl just wants someone who loves her madly.

The film was also a way of making audiences comfortable with the idea of an ageing Shah Rukh working with a new generation of heroines without it looking creepy. At forty-two, Shah Rukh was exactly double the age of his leading lady, Deepika Padukone, when *Om Shanti Om* was released. When *Rab Ne Bana De Jodi* was released, he was forty-three to

Anushka Sharma's twenty. These were young women who had been in school when Shah Rukh was doing some of his most iconic roles, so public discomfort had to be reckoned with, and eliminated, for India's poster boy to be able to romance them.

Meanwhile, Salman's film career seemed to be muddling along. There was quantity but no quality. In *Saawariya*, the film that launched Ranbir Kapoor and Sonam Kapoor, he was reduced to a showpiece, playing a Muslim character called Imaan, all dark eyeliner and even darker, brooding looks. *Salaam-e-Ishq*, directed by Nikkhil Advani, was beautifully shot and Salman had an interesting role in this desi version of *Love Actually*, but the movie didn't do well. Salman experimented with an English film, with Willard Carroll directing him in *Marigold*, which starred American actress Ali Larter. But that didn't work either. It was left to David Dhawan to rescue him in yet another comedy, *Partner*, where he was paired with Govinda, whose career, too, was in a trough.

2008 was no better. Subhash Ghai, who had clearly lost his once-golden touch at the box office, cast him with Katrina Kaif in a film set in the world of music. No expense was spared in the making of *Yuvraj*, which featured some all-too-real romantic scenes with Katrina Kaif. But it tanked. *God Tussi Great Ho*, co-starring Amitabh Bachchan and Priyanka Chopra, was a critical and commercial failure. A cameo in *Hello*, produced by brother Sohail Khan and adapted from Chetan Bhagat's *One Night at the Call Centre*, and another in Samir Karnik's *Heroes*, didn't help the films or Salman.

In 2009, Salman finally found his groove with the Eid release, *Wanted*. Produced by Boney Kapoor, it was a remake of the Telugu blockbuster, *Pokiri*, directed by Prabhudeva, who would become a dependable ally in his reinvention. *Wanted* cast Salman as a mysterious gangster called Radhe (recalling his character in *Tere Naam*), who was rough with his girl and soft with his friends. When the movie was released, he told interviewers he liked the film because it was on heroism and involved hard work. *'Ek mehnat karne ka jazba tha, to kiya. Agar nahin chalegi to phir mehnat karna chhod denge kyunki woh* better *hai hamare liye.'* (I wanted to work hard. If it works, I will continue to do so, otherwise I won't because that seems to be better for me.)' The film with its memorable one-liner, *'Ek baar jo maine commitment kar di to phir main apne aap ki bhi nahin sunta'* (Once I've made a commitment, I don't listen even to myself); its tough action scenes; and his soon-to-be-trademark pelvic gyrations in danceable songs such as *'Love Me Love Me'* and *'Le Le Mazaa Le'* won over audiences. It also had him articulating certain principles in life: he did not hit women and children, and he did not approve of smoking.

Boney Kapoor, the producer of the film, was quite candid when he said the film was important for both his 'izzat' (honour) and his 'jeb' (bank balance), for despite the success of *No Entry*, he had still not recovered from the bad patch induced by his other high-spending failures. The film was followed by two failures in October for Salman—Prem Soni's *Main Aur Mrs Khanna* with Sohail Khan and Vipul Shah's *London Dreams* with Ajay Devgan. But by this time, he had evolved his own box office formula, the epitome of which was *Dabanng*, a year later.

Aamir Khan, by now, was marching to his own tune. In 2006, he made up for his absence of four years from the screen with two films, *Rang De Basanti* and *Fanaa*. Both films questioned the state and, coupled with an extremely strong critique of Narendra Modi's record on the riots in Gujarat in 2002, cast him as the thinking person's Bollywood actor. Suddenly, he made himself available for television and print interviews where he articulated ideas about the nation and humanity.

Speaking to Shekhar Gupta for *Walk the Talk* in 2005, he was critical of Narendra Modi, then chief minister in Gujarat. 'He

(Modi) and his people are responsible for the killing and high trauma of thousands of Indians and in my opinion, people who do this are unpatriotic. They damage the idea of humanity. And yet nothing is being done about it. I have complete faith in the people of India.'[24]

Released around Republic Day in 2006, *Rang De Basanti* was a huge success, commercially and critically. The plot revolves around a documentary being shot by an Englishwoman, Sue McKinley (played by Alice Patten), whose grandfather had been the jailor of Bhagat Singh. She shoots it with a group of five Delhi University students, among whom is DJ, a 'mature' student who falls in love with her. The group is friends with a MIG pilot whose plane crashes due to substandard machinery; political kickbacks are part of the backstory. The group of students goes on a candlelight march to India Gate, peacefully, demanding the truth from the government. When that is not forthcoming, they shoot the defence minister and take over a radio station to broadcast the truth to the country.

This second revolution the movie talked of was critical in fostering several civil society movements, most notably the re-investigation of the Jessica Lal murder case from 1999 and the Priyadarshini Matoo rape case from 1996. In her thesis at the University of Amherst, Meghana Dilip proved with the use of social media exactly how 'a commodified cinematic product like *Rang De Basanti* helped revitalise citizenship among the youth and brought about an expansion of the public sphere in India'.[25]

In *Fanaa*, directed by Kunal Kohli, Aamir played a tour guide who was actually a terrorist fighting for Kashmiri freedom. As Rehan, his mission is to bring to his grandfather, also his boss, the trigger that will allow them to acquire a functioning nuclear device. His character believes totally in the Kashmiri cause, not even stopping to rethink after he falls in love with Zooni, who becomes the mother of his child.

Around this time, BJP workers in Gujarat professed to be deeply upset by Aamir's off-screen actions. He had, for instance, surprised a group of people protesting against the Narmada Dam, under the leadership of Medha Patkar, by joining them at Jantar Mantar in New Delhi to lend his support. Though the government of Gujarat demanded an apology from him, he refused to oblige. 'I am saying exactly what the Supreme Court has said. I only asked for rehabilitation of poor farmers. I never spoke against the construction of the dam. I will not apologise for my comments on the issue,' he said.[26] Following this, there was an unofficial ban of *Fanaa* in the entire state of Gujarat. There were protests against the film, including the burning of posters of the star in effigy. As a result, several multiplex owners stated that they could not provide security to audiences. Theatre owners in Gujarat refused to screen the movie. Aamir went on several platforms, such as NDTV, saying he would not allow himself to be bullied.[27]

For a Hindi film hero, Aamir's Rehan was a complicated character—an enemy of the Indian state from within, without any obvious history of trauma, just deep ideological indoctrination by his grandfather. Like *Kurbaan* (2009) and *New York* (also 2009), *Fanaa* explored the trope of the Good Muslim (in this case, Zooni, who performs at the Republic Day parade and salutes the tricolour) and the Bad Muslim (Rehan) in the context of a post-9/11 world. In all these three films, the Muslim terrorist is shown as urbane, sophisticated, even charming—he is not bearded or salwar-kurta-clad, or reading the namaaz. As Fareed Kazmi and Sanjeev Kumar note: 'To be politically correct this bad Muslim is counterpoised against the "good Muslim" or some righteous soul who either liquidates him or shows the right path by sermonising on the true meaning of Islam. Even when there is only the "good Muslim" as in *My Name is Khan* (2010), throughout the film, he has to keep on proving that he is not a terrorist. But that is precisely the point. The vileness of the present discourse is such that it has Muslims being forever on the defensive, which is precisely the agenda of Hindutva and all such forms of authoritarian ideologies.'[28]

By this time, Aamir was reading scripts and listening to narrations, sometimes even announcing films before dropping out. He was meant to start *Lajjo*, co-starring Kareena Kapoor, with Mani Ratnam and producer Bobby Bedi. An adaptation of a short story by Ismat Chugtai, it was about a debauched bachelor, who is forced to hire a prostitute from a brothel he frequents, as his maid. The film was set in Rajasthan, and Bedi and Ratnam wanted to shoot it around winter on a non-stop schedule. The shoot was expected to begin in mid-October 2007 and the screenplay was ready, but Ratnam was not willing to let Aamir vet it.

Aamir then dropped out of the project and settled for *Taare Zameen Par* instead, a script brought to him by his college friend, Amole Gupte. The film dealt with a dyslexic child (Ishaan, played by Darsheel Zafary) who could not fit in academically because no one understood his condition. Until an art teacher, Ram Shankar Nikhumb (played by Aamir), diagnoses his condition and helps him come to terms with it by involving him in art therapy. The film was received with great warmth and moved many parents and children affected by the condition. Aamir's own son, Junaid, is dyslexic, but he did not reveal this during the film's promotions, saying it would be his son's personal choice to speak about it when he wished to.

But the film left a somewhat unpleasant taste as well, with Amol Gupte claiming that Aamir had snatched the director's credit from him. According to Aamir, though, the first week's rushes were a great disappointment, and he lost faith in Gupte's ability to direct. On the verge of withdrawing his participation in the film because of these 'creative differences', he was requested by Gupte to stay on. Gupte remained on set, 'guiding and, at times, even correcting' Aamir, but the actor was clear that the latter would not be the director.[29]

As the director, Aamir spent considerable time getting things right, including having artist Samir Mondal instruct him on a painter's typical mannerisms and movements and recruiting four life guards for a shot of children playing near a well when he realised how deep it was. He also had many previews for friends, after which he took feedback from them.

I still remember the screening he held for friends at PVR Director's Cut in Delhi. Nervous and yet curious, he asked each member of the invited audience what they thought of the film. As was becoming a habit with Aamir's films, there was a message wrapped in the movie and it sparked a conversation in public about dyslexia among parents, schools, activists and policymakers. The film, only ten days after its debut, influenced the Central Board of Secondary Education to provide extra time to special children—including the visually impaired, physically challenged and dyslexic—during exams.

In 2008, Mumbai's civic body opened twelve classrooms for autistic students. In Chandigarh, the education department started a course to educate teachers on how to deal with children with learning disabilities.[30] Around this time. Aamir also hired a professional publicity firm, Spice PR, for the first time, replacing the old-fashioned individual publicists he had worked with previously. They gave him an edge in retelling his story, as a superstar who combined commercial success with critical appreciation. For so long, he had abstained from the discourse around the Badshah and the Shahenshah, or even around who among the Khans was the most saleable, but he now seemed to enter it with a sense of mischief. As he wrote in a much-quoted blog in 2008: 'We are in the middle of one of our favourite board games "Settlers Of Catan". Shahrukh is licking my feet and I am feeding him biscuits every now and then. What more can I ask for? Now, before you jump to any conclusions let me add that Shahrukh is the name of our dog. And before you jump to any further conclusions let me add that I had nothing to do with naming him. In fact, Shahrukh is the dog of the caretakers of our house. When I bought this house it came with the caretakers and their dog!'[31]

Taare Zameen Par, his own production, also began the Aamir tradition of releasing films around Christmas. His next, *Ghajini*, released on Christmas Day in 2008, was a thriller for which he famously working on his body for over a year, the last of the three Khans to do so. He also shaved his head, adding to the legend that he would go to any lengths to transform himself for his movies. Adapted from the Tamil original, the film was helmed by the same director, A.R. Murugadoss.

Set in Mumbai, *Ghajini* tells the story of Sanjay Singhania, a businessman who develops anterograde amnesia after an encounter in which his love interest is killed. He tries to avenge the murder, committed by the gangster Ghajini, with the aid of photographs and the permanent tattoos on his body. The movie was ripped off from the 2000 Christopher Nolan movie, *Memento,* starring Guy Pearce, but neither the Tamil nor the Hindi version acknowledged this. It made ₹225 crore at the box office (worldwide), a record that was broken the next year by *3 Idiots*, another Christmas release and another film which entertained as much as it enlightened viewers about the rigidity of the education system and the need to allow students to excel in fields of their own choice rather than that of their parents.

Aamir was also building his reputation as a 'marketing genius'. If he acted as a barber and gave free Ghajini haircuts for a day to promote the film, for *3 Idiots*, he went on a countrywide roadshow in disguise, doling out prizes to those who recognised him. Two years before that, he was strategically placing 'butt chairs' at multiplex chains for his nephew Imran Khan's debut film, *Jaane Tu … Ya Jaane Na* (2007), which he co-produced with Mansoor Khan, Imran's other uncle and director of *Qayamat Se Qayamat Tak* and *Jo Jeeta Wohi Sikander*.

Directed by Rajkumar Hirani, who was coming off the dual hits, *Munnabhai M.B.B.S.* (2003) and *Lage Raho Munnabhai* (2006), *3 Idiots* is possibly Aamir's most beloved film, though *Lagaan* may have been more seminal. As Ranchhoddas 'Rancho' Shamaldas Chanchad aka Phunsukh Wangdu, a mysterious young man who loves science, he is one of three friends (and one 'enemy') at the fictional Imperial College of Engineering. He is forever coming into conflict with the principal of the college, played by Boman Irani, who is a strict disciplinarian and not so lovingly called Virus by his students (his name being Viru Sahasrabudhe). The movie changed common perceptions about knowledge versus degrees, raised awareness about pressure on students, and emphasised the value of hands-on, practical learning. As with all Aamir movies, it had its share of controversies. Chetan Bhagat insisted that the film was inspired by his book, *Five Point Someone*, and that he was not given due credit. Sonam Wangchuk, the inspiration for Aamir's character, was also not appropriately credited.

The film made Aamir a star in China, mostly due to the widespread distribution of pirated DVDs. By 2013, China grew to become the world's second-largest film market (after the United States), paving the way for Aamir's stupendous Chinese box office success, with *Dhoom 3* (2013), *PK* (2016) and *Secret Superstar* (2017). With its anthem 'All is Well' and a delightful performance by Aamir, *3 Idiots* was again the highest-grossing Hindi film of the year.

In contrast, Shah Rukh had the worst year among the three Khans in 2009. *Billu*, co-starring Irrfan Khan as the eponymous barber, was a pallid film directed by Priyadarshan. What was interesting about *Billu* was Shah Rukh's role as superstar Sahir Khan, shades of which would be evident in one of his most ambitious films, *Fan* (2016). Whether it was his view of politicians who create problems for filmmakers by stoking controversies or the security he had to have ('I am the only movie star with more men around me than women'), Shah Rukh played a version of himself. It was both highly intelligent, allowing the audience a peek into what the life of a mega star could be, as well as emotional, as it underlined the reel star's humble origins while mirroring the real star's incredible journey.

The film was again made in service of Shah Rukh's stardom, with vignettes from his actual films, and repeated shots of devoted fans waving photographs and magazine covers. With posters declaring him King Khan, presidential-style motorcades, helicopter landings and cameos from three of the top female stars of the time, Kareena Kapoor, Priyanka Chopra and Deepika Padukone, it was not so much a film as an advertisement for Shah Rukh, punctuated by Irrfan's soulful helplessness.

As Aamir increasingly picked characters that he could immerse himself in, and Salman started playing various kinds of working-class superheroes, Shah Rukh began a journey where his screen persona would come closer to the superstar image he had created for himself off-screen. This image would now articulate Shah Rukh's real-life concerns and ambitions. It would also make him increasingly and worryingly self-reverential.

The actors were set for a fascinating comeback, a sustained and stable career, and one spectacular flameout.

5

2010–2019

Revenge, Retribution and Self-Reverence

I remember meeting Salman Khan in September 2010, almost immediately after *Dabanng* had met with thunderous success. The film, in which Salman played a crooked and cheeky police officer, Chulbul 'Robin Hood' Pandey, was set in the fictional town of Laalgunj in Uttar Pradesh. We met at a restaurant run by Farhan Azmi, the husband of his *Wanted* co-star, Ayesha Takia. Accompanying Salman was Rohini Iyer, his friend and unofficial publicist at that point. After a few minutes, during which I suppose Salman assessed, through an exchange of monosyllables, whether talking to me was worth his while, I was invited to his ground-floor flat at Galaxy Apartments. Opting for self-preservation, I followed his SUV in my battered hired taxi, negotiating the usual crowd of a hundred-odd fans waiting at the gate for a glimpse of their hero. Salman has been known to pay for the medical treatment of those who cannot afford it—and every morning, opposite Galaxy Apartments, where his whole family lives, a crowd lines up on Bandstand, clutching their medical bills in their hands. A man appointed by Salman hands out money and collects applications as well as petitions for various admissions/tests/jobs. These are usually handed over to his sister, Alvira Agnihotri, who handles the work of the Being Human Foundation. A charitable trust registered in 2007, it works, through partners such as the Max Foundation and the Akshara High School, in the area of education and healthcare, financing surgeries and funding scholarships.

Once inside, Salman parked himself on his favourite leather couch, looked at himself in a mirrored wall conveniently adjacent to the sofa, asked for a steaming cup of black coffee, and insisted I take notes rather than record the conversation.

From his record-breaking turn in *Dabanng* to his proclamation that his body was in the best possible shape, from his sleep patterns (three hours a day) to sometimes waking up weeping, dreaming of his days at the Scindia School, Gwalior, he was surprisingly candid. And also comfortable with his renewed success.

From the outside, it seemed that not much had changed about his life. Even in late 2010, after *Dabanng* had stormed the box office, and he had reclaimed the hearts of India's under-served working classes, he continued to live in his one-bedroom apartment; despite his huge earnings over the years, he did not move into a bigger place. He remained in awe of his father, Salim Khan, and continued to play big brother to his immediate family and to those who sought his help.

The beginning of 2010 had affirmed his stardom, his version of old-fashioned screen heroism, and much like another personality who would rise in this decade, Narendra Modi, he was able to channel his message directly to his adoring fans, bypassing the intermediary of critics, who he believed did not respect his work in any case and were only interested in digging up dirt on his private life. He was also, despite being a Bollywood insider, able to convince his fans of his 'ordinary' (I am one of you) identity. He did not own a flashy mansion like Shah Rukh Khan or hold legendary parties. Salman's wealth was subdued, used for the good of many and mostly out of sight. His farmhouse in Panvel is where signs of wealth are on display—it is set in a 150-acre plot, with a swimming pool, three bungalows, and a state-of-the-art gym.

There has never been intellectual cachet attached to Salman, like with Aamir Khan, who almost always had a thoughtful and socially-sensitive response to events, whether it was the riots in Gujarat in 2002 or protests by the Narmada Bachao Andolan in 2006. Salman was all muscle; a bachelor, a devoted brother to four siblings, a troubled but affectionate son, and always conscious of playing the hero. He perfectly fit the 'celibate warrior model', as Paromita Vohra said to me. Salman underlined this when he announced, tongue-in-cheek, on *Koffee With Karan* (Season 4, 2013) that he was still a virgin.

When I met him in 2011, Salman talked about his kind of cinema. This was on the heels of his success in *Ready* (June 2011) and *Bodyguard* (August 2011). A film, according to him, had to have the following: good music, which he usually chooses himself (he picked the lyricist and composer); a girl in peril; a villain who is bigger than him so it is fun to beat him up in the climax, simple clothes that any small-town tailor can copy, iconic names that recall previous avatars, cool accessories, such as his turquoise bracelet or dark glasses (*Dabanng)*, easy-to-copy dance steps that any uncle-ji can perform even when drunk, such as the belt dance in *Dabanng*; comic lines which he sometimes pens himself; and of course, a generous show of his bare chest and rippling muscles. As for kissing on-screen, no way. 'Why mix business with pleasure?' he asked.[1]

Biceps with a diameter of 17-and-a-half inches, a 30-inch waist and a 42-inch chest aren't easy to maintain but Khan knows the audience wants to see the shirt coming off. And what they want, they deserve to get, even if he has to have a physiotherapist on the set, ever-ready to work on his increasingly creaky knees. He is proud of his physique. As he told me once, 'The only fat I have is under my eyes.'

The prototype of the Salman kind of hero was set by Sooraj Barjatya in Salman's very first blockbuster in 1989, *Maine Pyaar Kiya*. As Prem, he was the good son, and as the years passed, Salman saw no reason to break that image. 'Parents have to want you as their son, youngsters have to think they can be like you, children have to idolise you,' he says. He had strayed from the formula, as when he played the talented drug-addicted singer of Vipul Shah's *London Dreams* (2009), or the somewhat vengeful brother of Subhash Ghai's *Yuvraaj* (2008), the movie was a resounding failure. Even after *Wanted*, he had not arrived at the winning formula. Between *Wanted* in 2009 and *Dabangg* in 2010 were three bloopers—*Main Aur Mrs Khanna, London Dreams* and the colossal flop, *Veer*.

Salman's appeal is a certain kind of virile masculinity that Indian males aspire to achieve. He is single but has a string of beautiful girlfriends. He combines rural mobility with urban ideas, something that Govinda or Mithun Chakraborty, also working-class heroes, were never able to do. The dichotomy comes from Salman's small-town roots (he was born in Indore and spent every summer there until he was old enough for regular school) and his status as the son of one of Bollywood's most successful screenwriters. As more people migrate to cities from villages, there is a greater idealisation of the rural and small-town life, says sociologist Sanjay Srivastava. They feel a kinship with Salman because of where he was born and who he plays on-screen. Yet, he is an aspirational figure for the kind of man he appears to be—one who helps his family, friends, and those in need.

Nowhere is this more in evidence than in the 2014 documentary *Being Bhaijaan* directed by Samreen Farooqui and Shabani Hassanwalia which follows the lives of three Salman fans, Shan Ghosh, Balram and Bhaskar. Of them, Ghosh, from Chhindwara, Madhya Pradesh, is the most intriguing. Having worked on a slight resemblance to the actor, he has developed his body and perfected his cloning to such an extent that he now makes a living by performing as Junior Salman. The film explores all the themes that make Salman so popular with young men in small towns. One of them is that they believe he is a virgin (because he announced it on Karan Johar's *Koffee With Karan* Season 4). At one point, Balram who works as a salesman in a clothes store, calls him an avatar of Vishnu who is balancing the world on his finger. 'If Bhai gets married,' he says, '3-4 crore of his fans will marry too, produce children within a year, and then the global population will be out of whack.' They admire him for not kissing (though they'd be disappointed to see him giving Disha Patani a peck his new movie, *Radhe: Your Most Wanted Bhai*, albeit she has, for all sorts of reasons, got a tape on her mouth). Shan compares Salman to Narendra Modi and Atal Behari Vajpayee, echoing Vohra's celibate warrior model, and explains their abstinence as the reason for their 'stamina' and 'power'.

Shan also makes an appearance in Snigdha Poonam's acclaimed book *Dreamers: How Young Indians are Changing their World*, having moved to Mumbai for stage shows. Like Bhai, he is stiill umarried. As Shan says in Being Bhaijaan, '*Duniya* modern *hoti jaa rahi hai, lekin mera* traditional *se* modern *hone ka* process *thoda* slow *hai … uss* way *mein main Bhai ke jaisa hoon. Unhone bhi shaadi nahin ki kyunki unko apni maa ke tarah ek ladki chahiye. Lekin vaisi ladkiyan to* market *se khatam ho rahi hain…*' (The world is becoming modern but my process of transition from tradition to modernity is slow … in this way I am like Bhai. He didn't marry because he wants a woman like his mother. But such women are becoming increasingly rare in the market.)

Increasingly, Salman is the only thing that stands between life and death for young men in small towns. In his sharply observed movie, *Sandeep Aur Pinky Faraar*, Dibakar Banerjee creates the character of Munna who, according to his father, knows only three things in life: 'naach' (dancing), 'kheti' (farming), and Facebook. Munna wants to build a body like Bhai and asks Pinky (a suspended constable in Haryana Police, played by Arjun Kapoor) for advice when he recognises a fellow Salman fan by the famous turquoise bracelet—which Salman has copied from the one his father wears and which has now become a trademark of his stardom.

Salman Khan is the working-class hero who has captured the imagination of audiences with his new brand of irreverence. He can seamlessly break into comedy in the middle of an intense action scene—the shovel used to attack an opponent becomes a back scratcher in *Bodyguard*, and the rival goon is merrily allowed to take a call from his mother before Salman thrashes him in *Dabangg*. Salman observes the people around him and remembers simple things: he picked up the *Bodyguard* walk from the way people strut about when they have just joined the gym and he imitated the bicep dance, also for *Bodyguard*, of one of the cameramen on the Patiala shoot. 'Most things I do are improvised from what I see in real life … there's nothing original.'

Dabanng is where tapping into an emerging vernacular cosmopolitanism began, as described by Harvard scholar Homi

Bhabha. It is a term that indicates that it is sometimes the working class who display more openness and cultural hybridity—than the so-called elite—a case in point is how Salman's character uses the term 'Robin Hood' Pandey to describe himself in the film.

Using the small-town space that became popular in Bollywood's imagination in movies like *Haasil* (Tigmanshu Dhulia, 2003), *Gangajal* (Prakash Jha, 2003), *Omkara* (Vishal Bhardwaj, 2006) and *Gulaal* (Anurag Kashyap, 2009), *Dabanng* brought what film scholar Hrishikesh Ingle calls 'regionalist' cinema to the front and centre of Bollywood's experience. This was hitherto occupied by the diaspora and the new middle class in India. Ingle argues in *Salaam Bollywood: Representations and Interpretations,* that *Dabanng* was a 'pivotal moment' in Bollywood's consumerist appropriation of the small-town cultural experience.[2] It also took care to underline Salman Khan's identity politics. Though he plays an upper-caste police officer, the song '*Mast Mast Nain*', sung in the Sufi tradition by Rahat Fateh Ali Khan, is placed in a clearly Muslim-dominated neighbourhood where shops sell rehamat ittar (perfume) and surma (kohl) and shopkeepers wear skullcaps.

The Salman Khan persona, as Ingle notes, is renegotiated with a hint of *Sholay* and a touch of Rajinikanth's iconicity (the trick with the dark glasses and back collar for instance). As Avijit Ghosh pointed out in a review of *Dabanng,* 'When did we last see a mainstream superstar drinking water from a tap clad in a lungi and ganji?' This would be appropriated by Shah Rukh Khan in Rohit Shetty's *Chennai Express* (2013), referencing Rajinikanth, talking national unity and promoting gender equity, in what was clearly a panicked reaction to Salman's return to stardom.

A renewed Salman Khan, with a new publicity agency, the highly rated Matrix, run by Reshma Shetty, and a better work ethic, was now doing one movie at a time. He also had a corrective surgery in the US for trigeminal neuralgia, a persistent condition originating from the trigeminal nerve, which carries sensation from the face to the brain and is responsible for most facial sensations. In 2011, he delivered two back-to-back hits, *Ready*, the remake of a Telugu film, and the remake of a Malayalam film (released, as was now the convention with Salman Khan movies, on Eid).

Ready, directed by Anees Bazmee (director of *No Entry)*, was criticised for its lack of plot and too much reliance on Salman's tricks, but it was a crowd pleaser. Salman attributed this to his new-found ability to 'take more interest not only in my work but also in the entire film'. But he was also realistic enough to attribute it to 'a wave, a time, since *Wanted*'. 'Suddenly times are good,' he said in an interview to *Bollywood Hungama* where he spoke about the re-shooting of two key songs in the film, '*Character Dheela*' and '*Dhinka Chika*', because he was not satisfied with the way they were filmed.

Ready was all about Salman and his charisma. When he grabs the mike in the middle of a dinner scene and starts singing '*Chaudhry ka chand ho, ya aftaab ho*' (the hosts' surname is Chaudhry), one can sense that it was totally unscripted. As are several other scenes in the film, with lines like: '*Yeh hilla hilla ke life hell banaa degi.*' (almost untranslatable into English since it is a play on the similar-sounding 'hilla', meaning shaking or moving, and 'hell') or '*jisko family support ho, usko koi deport nahin kar sakta*' (anyone who has family support cannot be deported—again a play on similar-sounding words).

Then there was Salman peeing on a haystack to announce a pee break, meaning the interval. In another scene, we see him shaking his pelvis in a most indecent fashion in a song that goes '*Dhinka Chika Dhinka Chika*'. In *Bodyguard*, he updated his formula: inventive dance steps flexing his biceps and twisting his calves; jokes in rhyme ('I'm not a fool/You think I'm in nursery school?'); a signature ring tone; and a pre-fight ritual—in this case, the act of taking off his watch. And, of course, a cleavage to rival the heroine's, in the song '*Teri Meri Prem Kahani*'.

'I don't live a star's life. I will go for a run on the roads sometimes early in the morning, sometimes late at night. I will ride my motorcycle, sometimes I will drive. I say what I believe in, not what is politically correct,' said Salman in a *Bollywood Hungama* interview when asked to evaluate his rising popularity. If any further proof was needed of his re-established stardom, Shah Rukh's favourite production house, Yash Raj Films (YRF), led by long-time friend Aditya Chopra, announced a collaboration with Salman on one of their biggest movies yet: *Ek Tha Tiger*. Directed by Kabir Khan, who had earlier directed Katrina Kaif in *New York* (2009), the movie cast Salman as a RAW agent and Katrina as an ISI operative. Salman's mission: to ensure an Indian scientist's research did not fall into the hands of the rival agency.

Salman's RAW agent was an ordinary man, who woke up in the morning to greet the doodhwala (milkman), cooked his famous daal for his boss, to be shared over a drink, and carried a briefcase to work. He was no superhero, just an ordinary civil servant with a superhero's job. So, when he rounded off 2012 with a reprisal of Chulbul Pandey in a sequel to *Dabanng*, it didn't feel as if Salman was descending from Tiger's global canvas to the local. It was clear that Tiger may have found himself in exotic destinations, but his heart stayed doggedly middle class.

Ironically, Tiger was a role that Shah Rukh Khan had rejected in 2010, just as he had said no to *3 Idiots*. The shoot of *Ek Tha Tiger* was stormy, with the director and the actor not always on the same page. This was Salman's new, assertive style of working; he felt his creative inputs made a critical difference. This was even more evident in *Dabanng 2* (released in December

2012). The sequel had no involvement from Abhinav Kashyap, the director of the original *Dabanng*. In 2020, Kashyap wrote a scathing Facebook post about how he had been obliterated from the franchise by 'the Salman Khan family' whom he described as the venomous head of a serpent. He alleged that they cleverly used 'their ill-gotten money, political clout and connections with the underworld to intimidate anyone and everyone'.[3] The other side of the story I heard was that Abhinav Kashyap had said he was not interested in directing the sequel and had conveyed the same to Arbaaz Khan, the producer, in an SMS.

Dabanng 2 was entirely self-referential, down to the shirt flying off Salman's chest. There was a belt dance, with the belt dancing on its own this time; an item song by Salman's sister-in-law, Malaika Arora (then wife of Arbaaz Khan); and even a product placement, this time, not of Zandu Balm, but of Fevicol. Clearly, audiences loved the familiarity of the embrace. They endorsed it, and Salman had yet another hit on his hands.

The next two years saw more of the same. *Jai Ho*, a film directed by brother Sohail Khan, and *Kick*, a film produced (and directed, for the first time) by friend Sajid Nadiadwala hit the screens. Both were remakes, *Jai Ho* of a Telugu film and *Kick* of a Tamil movie. By 2014, it was clear that Salman Khan was becoming the pre-eminent Khan at the box office, even though there was an element of cynicism from viewers and critics alike about him following an unoriginal blueprint.

The other Khans were not inactive during this period. Shah Rukh had embarked on one of the most ambitious films of his career, to which he devoted over a year: *My Name is Khan* (2010). The film was Shah Rukh's instinctive response to his rising stature as a global Muslim icon. I remember being at the Berlin Film Festival a day after *My Name is Khan* was premiered on 12 February 2010. Gigantic posters of Shah Rukh and co-star Kajol dotted the ice-laden streets leading to the Berlinale.

Crowds, distracted by Martin Scorsese and Leonardo DiCaprio promoting *Shutter Island*, were still talking of people waiting outside patiently to catch a glimpse of Shah Rukh, who had an enormous following in Germany since the screening of *Kabhi Khushi Kabhie Gham* (*In Guten Wie in Shweren Tagen* in German) on Channel RTL II in 2004. It was the first Bollywood movie to be dubbed and shown on German television and got an audience share of over 12.3 per cent among the target group of 14- to 49-year-olds, setting off a trend. Dorothee Wenner, curator of Asian cinema at the Berlin film festival since 1990, featured *Om Shanti Om* at the festival in 2008 and in 2010, a packed audience turned up to watch *My Name is Khan*.

I remember talking to Shah Rukh, who was in Mumbai by then, on the phone from inside the Palast in Berlin. He was excited by the success of the film in Berlin though, ironically, in his own adopted city, the Shiv Sena was protesting against his remarks on how humiliating it was to see no Pakistani players being selected for the IPL. His posters had been defaced, his effigies burnt, and his patriotism questioned. The Sena's viciousness manifested in a *Saamna* editorial asking him to 'go to Karachi and Islamabad to play cricket with the Pakistanis' and to Uddhav Thackeray comparing him to Ajmal Kasab: 'Kasab and Shah Rukh are the most secure people in Mumbai'.[4]

Kasab was a member of the Lashkar-e-Taiba and one among ten militants who attacked Mumbai across twelve locations and over four days in November 2008—the horrifying period acquired its own short-form nomenclature, with most people referring to it simply as 26/11, mirroring the 9/11 reference to attacks on the World Trade Centre in New York in 2001. At least 174 people died in 26/11, including nine of the attackers, and more than 300 were wounded. Kasab, alongside fellow Lashkar-e-Taiba recruit Ismail Khan, is said to have killed 72 people, most of them at the historic Chhatrapati Shivaji Terminus railway station. As with the bomb blasts of 12 March 1993 in Mumbai, the intention was to paralyse work and life in India's commercial centre. Kasab was held at the Arthur Road jail in Mumbai and was finally hanged in 2012 after a trial court found him guilty of eighty offences, including murder, waging war against India and possessing explosives. Clearly, the comparison with Kasab was poisonous and intended to question Shah Rukh's nationalist credentials.

In *My Name is Khan,* Shah Rukh is Rizvan Khan, a cosmetics-salesman-cum-repairman who suffers from Asperger's, and whose life changes dramatically after 9/11. He turns into a Forrest Gump-like folk hero and journeys across the States, attempting to make America see the errors of stereotyping Islam. Rizvan's travels take him from the 30,000-strong town of Banville in California to the 204-strong village of Wilhelmina in Georgia, where he helps residents battle a hurricane.

Shah Rukh prepared for the role with the zeal of a struggling new actor. He read books, watched documentaries, met two youngsters suffering from Asperger's, recorded himself talking in character, then watched himself on-screen in his bathroom-cum-video projection room, and even followed a man with the disorder around San Francisco for two days. It was a role without any of the crutches of stardom. There was no star gaze, because Rizvan has trouble looking people in the eye. There was no flamboyant walk, as his character tends to hop like a penguin. There were certainly no outstretched arms, the signature Shah Rukh gesture seen in countless songs. It was also a film that tackled a difficult issue, even if in a somewhat naive manner.

Shah Rukh has always taken pride in being a deeply secular Indian as well as a good Muslim. His religion may be something he embraces with cosmopolitan ease, but it is certainly one reason why he is greeted so warmly in the Middle East, Indonesia and Malaysia. For Johar, it was a film he felt he was finally capable of making, something his late, Lahore-born father would have been proud of. For Shah Rukh, it was a chance to break the shackles of stardom and call on his skills as an actor, like he had done in *Swades* and *Chak De! India*. The eighty-day shoot in the US and the subsequent twenty days in India gave him an opportunity to exist in the 'true world of the film' and become Rizvan.

More than that, it was a film that squarely centrestaged Shah Rukh's identity as an Indian and as a Muslim. In show after show, conference after conference, from London to New York, where he promoted the film, he was asked about being Indian. When I asked him the same question, he said to me: 'But it defines who I am. My father would always tell me, "Your mother may have given you birth, but I gave you India".' His father's freedom fighter's tamrapatra, Shah Rukh told me, was lying in a trunk with his papers, with relatives in Bangalore, and he intended to reclaim it soon.[5]

The controversy caused by the Shiv Sena captured the national imagination and was consumed like a daily reality show, making minor celebrities of people such as Sena spokesperson Neelam Gorhe, who emphatically said that support 'does not only mean giving shelter to terrorists, it can also be given in terms of moral backing'. Shah Rukh took to Twitter, addressing his audience directly, sometimes apologising to fans for 'disturbing sentiments', at other times saying how tired he was of 'interpretations of this whole undesired and sad affair'. All through this time, the film industry remained largely silent, having often suffered in the past at the Shiv Sena's hands. Only a few spoke up, like Kabir Khan, whose *New York* had sparked off the 9/11 theme as the big new Bollywood idea. He said: 'When an icon like Shah Rukh decides to take a principled stand on something, people rally around him which was proved last

Friday when Mumbai stepped out in such huge numbers to watch the film (*My Name is Khan*) despite the threats.'

Contrast this with the silence that enveloped the industry in 2015 when Shah Rukh was attacked for saying there was 'extreme intolerance' in India. In an interview to Rajdeep Sardesai on *India Today TV* on his fiftieth birthday, he said: 'It is stupid ... It is stupid to be intolerant and this is our biggest issue, not just an issue ... Religious intolerance and not being secular in this country is the worst kind of crime that you can do as a patriot.'

Yogi Adityanath, then an MP, accused him of 'treason' and compared him with Pakistani terrorist Hafiz Saeed. BJP General Secretary Kailash Vijayvargiva said that though Shah Rukh lived in India, his soul was in Pakistan. Uncharacteristically, Shah Rukh apologised for his remarks, perhaps because his film *Dilwale* was to release in December. The other Khan, Aamir, had faced a similar situation when he spoke at the Ramnath Goenka Excellence in Journalism Awards in Delhi in 2015 against rising intolerance and said his wife Kiran felt very unsafe in the country. Aamir, too, apologised for his comments.

In 2010, India was still a country where you could speak your mind without being heckled. And even if you were heckled or viciously trolled, as Shah Rukh was, you could still stand up for what you believed in.

My Name is Khan's release was bookended by two events, which highlighted the Muslim problem at home and abroad. Shah Rukh, while on a trip to the US, was detained by Homeland Security in the Newark airport and questioned for about two hours, because his name, Khan, was found on a 'no-fly' list at the airport. In Mumbai, as we have seen, the Shiv Sena threatened the opening of the film.

In the words of scholar Kathleen Erndl, the film was an attempt to dispel stereotypes about Muslims for a Western, primarily North American, audience.[6] Equally important was a message for the Indian audience, of national unity, inter-religious harmony and co-operation in the wake of 26/11. The film also attempted to celebrate the religious identities of both Muslims and Hindus. It did not shy away from Muslim images, practices and beliefs. Daily public prayers and the wearing of prayer caps, hijabs for women, giving of alms, and the story of Abraham and Ishmael formed part of the narrative.

My Name is Khan, while navigating a minefield of problematic representations and cultural stereotypes, presents an identity that is at once Muslim and Indian, and at the same time, promotes a vision of universal humanity. It reaffirmed Shah Rukh's identity as a multicultural citizen. Not only does Shah Rukh challenge the fundamentalist Dr Faisal Rehman's hateful speech in the film, he also reports the doctor to the FBI. In fact, it is specifically because Shah Rukh helps the FBI locate Dr Rehman that he is released from a detention facility where he has been incarcerated and tortured after trying naively to meet the president of the United States. In spite of the persecution he has undergone, Shah Rukh's loyalty to the nation (in this case, America), is reaffirmed through his naming of the doctor as a terrorist—and therefore a bad Muslim—and through the doctor's follower stabbing him in revenge. Significantly, it is through these actions that Shah Rukh is redeemed as the film's hero.

The film was also an attempt to redress the picture perfect image that Johar and Shah Rukh had worked so assiduously to build over the years—the Indian diaspora as a 'successful', 'integrated' yet 'connected to its roots' community, which enjoys the full rewards of the American dream. As film scholar Nadia Kanani has noted, such romanticised representations of the diaspora failed to take into account the systemic racism and impoverishment experienced by racialised immigrants.[7] After the film released, Shah Rukh began to be seen, even if accidentally, as the embodiment of the 'good Muslim'. It accomplished this by not only making Shah Rukh relatable to the audience as a respectable, multicultural citizen, but also by domesticating him. He is portrayed as having no knowledge of sex and no previous sexual experience (in one scene, we see him learning about sex from a manual), which, notes Kanani, distances him from representations of the degenerate and sexually perverse terrorist. In addition, by using Shah Rukh's disclosures of sexual desire as moments of comedic relief in the film, his sexuality is rendered more or less impotent.

Shah Rukh's next film was also planned on an international scale. It was the fruition of a long-held dream—of making a big-budget superhero spectacle in India. It was an idea that director Anubhav Sinha had brought to him two years earlier, and after dropping initial plans to shoot in the US because of high costs, they filmed it in England.

The film, *Ra.One*, possibly one of the most marketed of Shah Rukh's career, is also possibly one of his least loved. In its inception, it was ambitious, re-imagining the world as one where Britain was a deracinated international zone in which only those with money, whatever their nationality, had power. The final battle would be between an Indian superhero and a Chinese villain, played by Chinese-British martial arts star Tom Wu in a part originally planned for Jackie Chan, played out at Battersea Power Station, an abandoned relic of London's extinct power.

In a clever nod to the Ramayana, the villain from the video game who escapes into the real world is called Ra.One (a homonym of Raavan), played by Arjun Rampal, and the man who must annihilate him, the video game's creator, is G.One (a homonym of Jeevan), played by Shah Rukh. When the action shifts to India, Mumbai's iconic railway station, Chhatrapati Shivaji Terminus (formerly known as Victoria Terminus, designed by British colonial architect Frederick William Stevens, and the site of 52 killings during 26/11) is destroyed by a train crash. The message of *Ra.One* is clear: the history of British colonisation has no relevance in contemporary India's self-image as a powerful nation.[8]

But the film, it appears in hindsight, was overmarketed. Anubhav Sinha says the problem was that both he and Shah Rukh were new to the genre and had to take decisions as they went along. To make matters worse, Bobby Chawla—Juhi's brother, Shah Rukh's production genie, and the CEO of Red Chillies—fell into a coma following a brain haemmorhage, post the first schedule, in April 2010 (he died in 2014).

Sinha says he is still pained by the failure of the film and feels he let down Shah Rukh. 'It was so courageous of him to go ahead with me even after my film *Cash* had flopped,' he adds. He says they were in the bubble of making the film, shooting in London, looking at Excel sheets, examining the numbers, but outside, there was a 'strange energy that wanted Shah Rukh to fail ... He had become invincible and human beings love nothing more than a ruin.' He recalls an article that appeared in *Mid-Day* after the film's 30-second teaser came out; it said that every scene in it had already appeared in a film before, whether it was *Iron Man 2*, *Robot* or *Krrish*. Shah Rukh worked very hard on making and promoting the film—he would fly every morning to a new city, and return home late at night and then go on to another day. He wanted *Ra.One* to play on every screen in the country.

The country's reaction, however, was underwhelming. Sinha had given *Ra.One* six years of his life. When the film did not do as well as they had imagined, he took it personally, hitting an all-time low in confidence and self-esteem. As a result, he did not direct another film for the next five years until he was so broke that he asked Bhushan Kumar for work and directed *Tum*

Bin 2 (2016) for him. He had first met Shah Rukh while working as chief assistant director for two weeks on Ketan Mehta's *O Darling Yeh Hai India*. Shah Rukh was on the sets of *Chak De! India* when Anubhav messaged him to say he had a story and it couldn't be made without him.

In interviews he gave at the time, Shah Rukh insisted the film was 'one of its kind' and would take the Indian film industry forward, laughing off repeated questions about its lack of originality: 'Why should America be the only country in the world to have its own cinematic superheroes? ... We're the largest film producing nation in the world, and if we don't have it, who will?' The film had premieres in Dubai, London and Toronto, and everywhere he went, there were screaming fans, Indian and foreign—a demonstration of how much his fandom had grown. The film exhibited an unprecedented 900 prints abroad and made at least ₹70 crore. But wasn't quite the success it aspired to be.

Within a few months, Shah Rukh followed up with *Don 2*, another 'macho' film as he described it, shot mostly in Berlin, a city that had become beloved to him. It had him reprising his role from *Don* (2006)—this time he played an Asian underlord who becomes the boss of organised crime in Europe. The film has its share of sophisticated financial shenanigans and illegal shipments. His next screen appearance returned him to familiar territory, in the film that would be Yash Chopra's last: *Jab Tak Hai Jaan*. Then followed *Chennai Express* (2013), a comedy directed by Rohit Shetty.

Politically, India was going through an enormous change at this point. Institutions once considered above reproach seemed to be crumbling against a rising tide of activism of a country empowered by new laws such as the Right to Information Act (2005). Leaked conversations taped by the Income Tax department in 2008–09 allegedly exposed misuse of privileged political and business information by journalists in what came to be known as the Niira Radia case. It underlined how this network of relationships between the powerful lobbyist, important ministers in Manmohan Singh's cabinet, and industrialists as respected as Ratan Tata had led a notional loss to the exchequer of ₹1.76 lakh crore in the allocation of 2G licences. This came on the heels of the Commonwealth Games scam of 2010 where the main accused was Congress politician Suresh Kalmadi, chairman of the Organising Committee of the Commonwealth Games, which was said to have involved a siphoning off of nearly ₹70,000 crore having been. The India Against Corruption movement that began in 2011 stoked a nationwide revulsion against such corruption and old ways of doing business, ably aided by hectoring television anchors in studios who questioned the government of the day through almost wall-to-wall coverage of social reformer Anna Hazare fasting at Ramlila Grounds, Delhi.

As if this turmoil was not enough, in December 2012, there were angry protests across the country over the rape of a young woman, whom the media christened as Nirbhaya, when she was returning one night with a friend after watching a movie, *The Life of Pi*, at a multiplex in the capital. The brutal and heinous gang rape and Nirbhaya's fight for her life captured a grieving nation's imagination. Nirbhaya's courage in testifying against the rapists led to their subsequent arrests, and her eventual tragic death, in a Singapore hospital over two weeks later, shook the nation. Manmohan Singh's government seemed effete, out of control, and in a state of paralysis even as Narendra Modi swept the assembly elections in Gujarat in 2013 and began what many declared was the march to Delhi.

A new India was emerging, where the Nehru-Gandhi dynasty was being equated with entitlement, latent communalism was being repositioned as proud Hindutva; liberal values and the advantages of birth were being reinterpreted as the established elite keeping forces of meritocracy and egalitarianism at bay. The rise of social media was bringing down barriers between the rulers and those they were meant to rule, between the media and those they were meant to inform, and criticism was amplified to often become campaigns against celebrities.

Everyone appeared to be using social media. Superstar Amitabh Bachchan broke the news of the birth of his granddaughter 'Beti B' on Twitter. Former Union minister of state for external affairs Shashi Tharoor lost his job after a controversial tweet triggered protests. As prime ministerial candidate for the BJP in 2014, Modi used social media to set the agenda for news channels, communicate directly with voters, and routinely mock his opponents. Amplified by armies of trolls employed by the IT cell of his party, he completely outclassed the Congress, sweeping the general elections of 2014 and ushering in an India where, for the first time, saffron-clad sadhus sat in the front row as the Union cabinet took oath of office in the foreground of Rashtrapati Bhavan, a 340-room imperial palace designed to house the Viceroy of India.

During this time, Aamir Khan kept a low profile, having redefined his stardom in the last decade. In 2011, he acted in wife Kiran Rao's understated *Dhobi Ghat* as a sensitive painter in a film that captured the multiplicity of experiences within Mumbai, as it delved into the lives of a rat catcher, a young wife, an artist, and a photographer looking for the perfect frame. Aamir also willingly played the fool in *Delhi Belly* (2011). Unusually, he was seen in an 'item number' shaking his pelvis with never-before-seen vigour, dressed as a desi Elvis, in the raucous urban comedy he produced for his nephew Imran Khan.

In 2012, Aamir reunited with Farhan Akhtar and Ritesh Sidhwani to play a grieving police officer in the crime thriller *Taalash*, directed by Reema Kagti. This was also the year he launched his ambitious TV series that doubled as a social service programme, *Satyameva Jayate,* which aired simultaneously every Sunday morning on Doordarshan and Star Plus. With stories from real-life survivors of rape, alcoholism, domestic violence, child sexual abuse, it created a new genre on Indian television—what I call 'Socially Useful Productive Work' (SUPW) television. With every tear carefully positioned and every reaction carefully choreographed, Aamir Khan was the star of the show, a problem solver, a shoulder to cry on, and a master healer. This persona was a far cry from his friend Salman Khan's playful avatars as the host of *10 Ka Dum* and *Bigg Boss*, then in its fourth season.

Aamir then took a completely different turn and decided to play the main antagonist in Yash Raj Films' *Dhoom* in 2013. As circus artistes and twins, Sahir and Samar, Aamir's role involved a considerable amount of wirework. He prepared for it with his customary singlemindedness, learning ballet, aerobatics and parkour. He shot for the film for three months in Chicago in 2012, and then for the climax in Switzerland the following year. When it released, it beat almost every record set previously by Shah Rukh's *Chennai Express*, whether it was the number of prints released in the domestic and international markets or the global box office revenue.

In 2014, as an alien in Rajkumar Hirani's *PK*, Aamir broke his own box office record. What is now popularly known as the ₹100 crore club was something that Aamir Khan established with *Ghajini* in 2008. He also starred in the first film to cross ₹200 crore at the domestic box office (*3 Idiots* in 2009), ₹250 crore with *Dhoom 3* in 2013, *PK* with ₹300 crore in 2014, and ₹350 crore with *Dangal* in 2016. Salman Khan, though, is the king of the domestic box office through sheer volume. Not only does he have the highest number of ₹100 crore hits, but also in two years, 2010-11 as well as 2015-16, he has managed to score a hat-trick of ₹100 crore movies. Aamir's *PK* was a coruscating attack on organised religion but was roundly criticised by Hindutva warriors, who felt that as a Muslim, Aamir had taken undue liberties with Hindu gods. The film was accused of 'hurting Hindu sentiments' by various religious outfits who sought to ban it.[9] At the time of its release, the issue of forced religious conversion was in the news, along with news reports of prominent gurus being arrested on charges of murder and rape. There were conversations around 'ghar wapsi' (forced re-conversion to Hinduism by Hindu extremists), 'love jihad' (the marriage or relationship between a Muslim boy and a Hindu girl) and *'Bahu lao, Beti bachao'*, where Bajrang Dal, the youth wing of Vishva Hindu Parishad was encouraging Hindu men to marry non-Hindu girls. The new right-wing government at the centre was, in many ways, the product of the very mindset that was disturbed by *PK*'s truth-telling.

Other changes were in the air too. Women had increasingly started to tell their own stories or at least act in movies where they were central characters. Interesting examples are Vidya Balan's trifecta of films, *Ishqiya* (2010), *The Dirty Picture* (2011) and *Kahaani* (2012). In 2014, Kangana Ranaut fronted a feel-good comedy about a woman who is jilted at the altar, which became a sleeper hit. *Queen* set the stage for *Tanu Weds Manu Returns* in 2015, which made over ₹100 crore, riding on the charisma of its heroine in a double role. Suddenly, it seemed it was not necessary for actresses to settle for item songs and brief romantic scenes in movies shouldered by male heroes when they could be the stars of their own stories. With *Piku* in 2015, Deepika Padukone joined the club of women who were powering their way to the box office without the trappings of male-dominated blockbusters. Ably supported by winning performances from Amitabh Bachchan and Irrfan Khan, Padukone pushed *Piku* to box office success with a quiet performance that underlined the emancipated woman who was not afraid of being sexually active or remaining single.

The financial aspects of movie-making were also changing. The excessive spending by studios was winding down, but not before reaching absurd heights. In 2008, PVR Pictures green-lit Ashutosh Gowariker's *Khelein Hum Jee Jaan Sey* without reading the script, and at an unheard price of ₹46 crore for a film starring Abhishek Bachchan. When the Bijlis, who own PVR, realised what they had got into, they met Gowariker during the shoot and tried to negotiate the price to ₹28 crore; it was settled at ₹35 crore. The film had a return of only ₹5 crore and was one of the biggest flops of the year.[10]

In 2009, after Sanjay Leela Bhansali had delivered a flop with *Saawariya*, Sony Pictures India still made him an offer. But then UTV came into the picture and offered him a director's fee of ₹35 crore, an amount that was unheard of in Bollywood. It made no sense at all as he had just delivered a huge flop with a big Hollywood studio and Sony shut shop in India soon after that.

In 2013, Phantom Films was shopping around for ₹55 crore, to finance the movie *Bombay Velvet*. Fox Star Studios backed the film to the tune of ₹95 crore and it turned out to be one of the biggest flops in recent years, nearly causing director Anurag Kashyap to break down and claim he was leaving Bollywood for good. In 2015, Reliance Big Pictures released Vibhu Puri's *Hawaizaada*, which was also a colossal flop. Made on a budget of ₹35 crore, it could not even make ₹10 crore. The film starred Ayushmann Khurrana along with a new actress, Pallavi Sharda. This was the last nail in the coffin for Reliance Entertainment. Sanjeev Lamba, the CEO, was asked to step down along with the senior management team, and further movie production under the banner was stopped. By 2018, Walt Disney Company, one of the biggest studios in the world, closed their production division in India, and Siddarth Roy Kapur, the managing director, parted ways with it.[11]

Something changed around 2015 when the alliance between independent filmmakers and big studios which produced movies such as *Bombay Velvet* stopped working. The industry fell back increasingly on tried-and-tested producers such as Yash Raj Films, Dharma Productions and Sajid Nadiadwala, and the power of insider networking intensified. Just one example sums it up: in 2015, just a few months after *Hawaizaada* crash-landed, Yash Raj Films released another film starring Ayushmann Khurrana, this time with Bhumi Pednekar—*Dum Laga Ke Haisha*. Made on a budget of under ₹10 crore, it went on to make ₹30 crore at the box office, got huge critical acclaim, and bagged a bunch of national awards. Everyone in the industry had warned Yash Raj Films that they shouldn't release another Ayushmann Khurrana-starrer just after *Hawaizaada*. But Aditya Chopra proved them all wrong. The movie, with its independent-minded, believable young woman, retro music, and the small-town boy-man next door, proved to be a success, relaunching Khurrana, whose star had dimmed after *Vicky Donor* (2012).

2015 was also the year *Baahubali: The Beginning* was released. The epic was directed by S.S. Rajamouli, produced by Shobu Yarlagadda and Prasad Devineni, and shot in Telugu and Tamil. Dubbed into Malayalam, Odia and Hindi, the film was the first of two cinematic parts, and followed Shivudu/Shiva, an adventurous young man who helps his love, Avanthika, rescue Devasena, the former queen of Mahishmati, when she is taken prisoner by the tyrant king Bhallaladeva. Made on a budget of ₹180 crore, it was the most expensive Indian film ever. With worldwide box office revenues of ₹600 crore, it became the highest-grossing film in India, the highest-grossing Indian film worldwide, and the highest-grossing south Indian film. Its magical mix of myth and special effects cast a spell over audiences. It also showed up Bollywood with its scale, ambition and originality. A broken Bollywood 1.0 ended around

2015 when big studio money started drying up and it was no longer feasible for the film industry to remain open to new ideas with the same intensity as before. This is how 34-year-old actor Sushant Singh Rajput's death in 2020 became inextricably linked with a moment in history, becoming emblematic of the debate around insiders and outsiders as well as about the alleged stranglehold of dynasty children on the industry.

Suddenly, there was a feeling that star children had a claustrophobic hold on the industry, at least, that is how social media users seemed to see it. Having watched the advent of star children like Shraddha Kapoor in 2010, Varun Dhawan and Alia Bhatt in 2012, Tiger Shroff in 2014, Jahnvi Kapoor in 2018 and Ananya Panday in 2019, the public felt self-righteous about 'outsider' talent not being given a chance. This had been underlined many times in the past, with the much-hyped release of *Student of the Year* in 2012, directed by Karan Johar and starring director David Dhawan's son Varun, director Mahesh Bhatt's daughter Alia and Delhi model-turned-assistant-director Sidharth Malhotra, being a case in point.

This feeling of being 'excluded' and 'not being given a chance' was very much on the minds of a majority of people, who felt that all power was in the hands of the elite and the only way the powerful could be kept in check was by insisting that merit be given a chance.

In 2015, *Detective Byomkesh Bakshy!* starring Sushant Singh Rajput and produced by Yash Raj Films failed and Aditya Chopra's three-film deal with director Dibakar Banerjee went cold, with the third film, *Sandeep Aur Pinky Faraar*, taking its time to be made and released. Aditya Chopra also pulled out of Shekhar Kapur's *Paani*, which was to star Sushant. In 2020, after Sushant's death stirred anger against Bollywood's big-boy producers who were seen as preventing new talent from surviving and thriving, Aditya Chopra had to give a statement to Mumbai Police explaining why *Paani* was shelved.[12]

Clearly, the Mumbai film industry was terribly out of touch with the outside world—and the world of young people. The power of star kids increased precisely because the industry wanted to produce youthful cinema but did not know how to do so. They tried a conservative version of it by capitalising on the star child's value, built up through Instagram posts and paparazzi coverage. What academic Kaushik Bhaumik describes as years of conservative cinema enforced by public morality actually destroyed the industry's capacity to work with transgression. Even the kids of 'traditional' India, fed on a rising diet of streaming services which were increasingly making edgier Indian content such as *Sacred Games* (which premiered on Netflix in 2018) apart from showcasing the best from the West, wanted racy entertainment. They were no longer happy with retreads of *Dilwale Dulhaniya Le Jayenge*. The very film families that built Mumbai cinema were becoming an obstacle to innovation. The new star kid phenomenon was proof, not of some diabolical plot to keep the outsider out, but an admission that the old idea of Mumbai cinema is, perhaps, dead.

One man, though, kept the flag of old-style cinema flying.

2015 was a defining year for Salman Khan. Like the other Khans, he was turning fifty, and by accident or design, his image was recrafted at this critical juncture. In May, Salman's long and much-reported trial for driving over pavement dwellers in a drunken state in September 2002 and killing one, finally arrived at endgame as the Sessions Court prepared to deliver its verdict. For years, the actor's lawyers had argued that he had not been driving the car. Before the court's verdict, the Khans' driver Ashok Singh had claimed responsibility, insisting he had been at the wheel of the SUV and that Salman was just a passenger. On 6 May, the court found the actor guilty of culpable homicide not amounting to murder and sentenced him to five years in jail. In the judgment, the court also dismissed Ashok Singh's claim, saying that he had clearly come forward at the behest of Salman's father, Salim Khan. Even as the case went into appeal, social media cheered, Bollywood closed ranks.

In July, *Bajrangi Bhaijaan* released a day before Eid, retooled Salman's image. Directed by Kabir Khan, it sought to recast India in the Nehruvian image of a secular nation while also reinventing Salman as a devout Hanuman bhakt, a vegetarian, the son of an RSS shakha pramukh. Kabir had worked with Salman on *Ek Tha Tiger* and though they had had their tussles during its making, Salman was smart enough to see the potential of *Bajrangi Bhaijaan*.

The son of a nominated Rajya Sabha MP, Rasheeduddin Khan, Kabir had spent much of his life in Lutyens' Delhi, playing Hanuman in the local Ramlila and celebrating every festival. In an interview, Kabir said he had hoped to reverse the rising intolerance spurred on by the new government in Delhi. He said: 'Why can't a Muslim say Jai Shri Ram? Or why can't a Hindu say Assalamualaykum? I will not become a lesser Muslim if I say Jai Shri Ram. We can harp on about progress and development but if the secular fabric of our country gets damaged, then nothing can sustain us. I wanted to discuss the Hindu-Muslim issue and in order to bring it all out in the mainstream consciousness, I needed Salman's superstardom. He also feels strongly about secularism and instantly agreed to the film.'

It wasn't easy, and it wasn't only about negotiating Salman's habitual late arrival on the set. The Vishwa Hindu Parishad (VHP) sent Kabir letters saying that they wouldn't tolerate *Bajrangi Bhaijaan* as a title. 'I fought for this title. I knew the baggage Bajrangi carries. Today, the first image that comes to mind is Babu Bajrangi. [A leader of the Gujarat wing of the Bajrang Dal. A central figure during the 2002 violence, he was sentenced to life imprisonment by a special court for his role in masterminding the Naroda Patiya massacre in which 97 Muslims were murdered, including 36 women, 26 men and 35 children, but the Supreme Court of India granted him bail on medical grounds in March 2019]. It's the most negative association you can have with the film. I wanted Bajrangi to stand for what he is—the most fun god. I was not going to let the right-wingers appropriate Lord Hanuman as their own. Hanuman doesn't belong to only one community. Bajrangi is a symbol of our ethos. And the way the audience has taken to the film, it proves that he belongs to entire India,' said Khan.

In *Bajrangi Bhaijaan,* Salman as a Hanuman bhakt does a 'pranam' to any monkey that crosses his path. He is a vegetarian, he doesn't enter a mosque unless it is absolutely essential, he assumes everyone who is fair and lovely is a Brahmin, wears Modi kurtas in fine linen and pastel shades and reforms only when his girlfriend tells him that she loves him because he has a clean heart and doesn't believe in 'paraya dharam' ('other' faiths) and 'alag log' ('other' people).

The movie had one song designed to please each faith—if you cut open my heart, you will find Ram, goes one, while the other praises the virtues of eating chicken (remember this was the time of the beef ban). It had other potent symbols too. The girl gets lost in Kurukshetra (yes, where the Mahabharata was fought) and the film ends with Salman looking like Dev Anand from *Guide* and people calling him 'khuda ka banda' (a child of God). Salman even got rid of his turquoise bracelet and wore a small Hanuman mace around his neck.

Both Kabir and Salman ignored the protests. Salman told the media: 'If they are a religious group then the basic thing they should know is that every religion respects the other person's religion. Every religion preaches only one thing: "to follow your religion and to be respectful and to respect the other person's beliefs and religion". I don't think anyone can protest about this.'[13]

On Diwali, Salman had another release that burnished his Hindutva credentials, *Prem Ratan Dhan Paayo*, which reunited him with the director of his first blockbuster, *Maine Pyaar Kiya*. Here he played twin roles, one of a feudal inheritor and the other of Prem Dilwale, from Ayodhya, who runs a popular Ramlila, is a vegetarian, and collects money for good causes. Yet again, Prem is a duffer with a heart of gold, falling stupidly in love with princess Maithili, whom he first glimpses stepping down from a helicopter. As a concession to modernity, Sooraj Barjatya makes the man do the cooking, unlike the scene in *Hum Aapke Hain Kaun* where Salman carries Madhuri Dixit from the kitchen and plants her on a pool table (woman as subject and then as plaything?), ensures that girls play football as well as or better than the boys, and sees to it that the woman makes the first move. But *Prem Ratan* was a film in tune with the idea of a new India where all you needed to succeed in life was native intelligence, an unfettered heart, and a loose connection with Lord Ram. Education, a good career, some learning—that was for rich people!

On 10 December 2015, a few days before his milestone birthday, Salman was acquitted of all charges in the hit-and-run case by the Bombay High Court. The verdict said he could not be convicted on the basis of the evidence produced by the prosecution. As the judge read out the order, the actor broke down in court, surrounded by his family. His fans and followers, of whom there were many in the industry, including those whose films depended on him, were relieved. It was the end of case that had surfaced on and off over the last decade and a half.

In his next film, *Sultan* (2016), Salman continued his Hanuman worship, even though he played a Muslim, an aspect of his identity that was hinted at by him praying at a dargah and waving a green flag rather than being underlined and lit up in neon. He played a man-child, an idler who spends his time flying kites and installing cable TV in homes, becoming a wrestler only to win the woman he loves. The setting being Haryana (and this being Salman), he was allowed to be at his regressive worst when it came to women. From referring to the woman he loves as 'saali masterni' and 'sasuri' (a slang word meaning 'damned'), to thinking nothing of making her give up her dream of becoming an Olympic gold–winning wrestler by getting her pregnant, he plays the bhai next door, one who is not afraid of showing his vulnerabilities on-screen. In a particularly affecting sequence, a washed-up Sultan, after winning an Olympic gold, tries to train for a Mixed Martial Arts tournament, only to break down when he sees his paunch in the mirror. This was Shirtless Salman, not so much as the 'Big Bhai' but as the 'Bechara Bhai' or 'Underwhelming Uncle'. Of course, he trains well enough to win the tournament and the love of his life, and together, they walk into the sunset to produce wrestling champions for the state and the nation—a female champ, mind you.

The film, directed by Kirori Mal College graduate Ali Abbas Zafar, was well-received and reiterated his working-class appeal. But the actor's remark that training for *Sultan* made him feel like he was being raped meant trouble for him again. This comment outraged many and required his father to come to his rescue once again, re-interpreting Salman's words for the world. That a fifty-something superstar whose films routinely broke box office records was still being defended by his father struck no one as being odd or awkward. Is this part of Salman's appeal? The good-bad son who still stands to attention when his father calls, who still fears being slapped by him, and who still needs him to talk him out of trouble?

Salman does not have the ability to mesmerise people with his words, which Shah Rukh has, and which helped him win fans internationally. Salman and Aamir's stardom has come from the Indian market—the infamous 100 crore film club—

while Shah Rukh has opened up the rest of the world for mainstream Indian cinema. His stardom is unique, especially amongst Western women and, in general, women outside of India. Fatima Bhutto speaks of this in her book, *New Kings of the World: The Rise and Rise of Eastern Pop Culture* (2019). Calling him an icon of a vast cultural movement emerging from the Global South, she explains how he, along with Turkish soaps and South Korean boy bands, has become one of the biggest challengers to the United States monopoly of soft power. Khan has fans all over the world, she writes including a coterie of eight to ten elderly German women who have followed him everywhere he went for the last twenty years, watching him lovingly from the sidelines.

However, Shah Rukh's dream to make that one Indian film—or be part of that one Indian film—which is watched by the world remains unfulfilled. As he told Bhutto, he's considered stories from the Hindu epics, the Mahabharata and the Ramayana, but feels that for such a film to go global, it would have to have cutting-edge FX, fewer songs, no interval, and not be longer than an hour and a half. That's why *Ra.One* was so important to him. He was going the animation spectacle route, like Hollywood. Its failure was a setback.

The pressures of keeping his box office status alive in India, especially vis-a-vis the other Khans, saw him making mediocre movies such as *Chennai Express, Happy New Year* (2014) and *Dilwale* (2015). Even then, he delivered unusual films like *Fan* (2016), *Raees* (2017) and *Zero* (2018). Shah Rukh nurtured the dream that Red Chillies would become the Disney of Bollywood, but that did not happen. Scale is a major problem for Bollywood because it just does not have the money and the work ethic for it.

Both *Fan* and *Zero*, despite their flaws, are meta-commentaries on how Hindi cinema works. *Fan* is autobiographical spec-fic—

where the fan is Shah Rukh himself: young, star-struck, totally effete, with a strange voice and stammer. It is almost like Shah Rukh's past as the fan boy is catching up with him as his own fan now. The subtext, according to Kaushik Bhaumik, is that Shah Rukh has become something much bigger than the world he came from, in becoming the star that he has become.[14] But today's fans remain stuck at the level of the fan boy he was and can't understand the scale of his stardom. The meaning? Fan boys of today cannot be Shah Rukh because that needs a new kind of fan, not the old fan boy that Shah Rukh was in the 1980s. The audience is still stuck in the old world that made Shah Rukh. Yet, like Aryan Khanna, the star of *Fan*, Shah Rukh knows that '*Agar mere* fans *nahin toh main kuch nahin.*' (I am nothing without my fans.) He also knows the fan can turn mean, like the obnoxious Bhutiani, whose daughter's wedding he dances at, and who demands his money's worth, saying, 'After all, I've spent a bomb on you.' After twenty-five years of entertaining fans with relentless work, you could call it a justification or a tantrum in the actor's continuing search for honesty and relevance.

Privately, Shah Rukh would say Fan was his *Kaagaz ke Phool*, referring to Guru Dutt's 1959 classic about a famous filmmaker who is recognised only after his death. This was Dutt's final film as director and many believed its commercial failure drove him to deep depression, which eventually led to his death, either by suicide or an accidental overdose, in 1964. Shah Rukh was sure *Fan* would be considered a world classic, just like *Kaagaz ke Phool* is.

As for *Zero,* it is probably one of the most moving films about cinema ever imagined, says Bhaumik. 'What a fantastically candid film it is about the energies of Indian cinema, just as *Fan* is candid about the star. Shah Rukh, the film fan, is at one point made equal to the ape which the film fan is—a brute thing driven by primeval attractions of colour and glamour.' The film also captures what Bhaumik calls the primitive and wild real cinema fandom in noisy ramshackle cinema halls in cities like Meerut, something one rarely sees in big city movies these days.[15]

In *Fan* (2016), *Dear Zindagi* (2016), *Raees* (2017) and *Jab Harry Met Sejal* (2017), Shah Rukh was retooling his image, searching for a new form of storytelling with a new group of filmmakers who were always armed with stories for him. *Fan*'s director Maneesh Sharma narrated the story to Shah Rukh soon after he graduated from the California Institute of the Arts (CalArts). Gauri Shinde couldn't imagine casting anyone else as the quirky Dr Jehangir Khan, mentor, counsellor and avuncular friend in *Dear Zindagi*, reinventing his charisma for a whole new generation of young women fans. Rahul Dholakia waited patiently through the star's surgery and other schedules and the changing political environment to complete *Raees*, which starred Pakistani actress Mahira Khan. You can spot the compromises in the film from a mile off—the Ram Janmabhoomi demolition and the Mumbai blasts have been changed and made suitably vague, the characters of Dawood Ibrahim and Abdul Latif altered—perhaps to ward off the kind of unwelcome attention *Ae Dil Hai Mushkil* got for casting Pakistani actor Fawad Khan (forcing director Karan Johar to change Anushka's city of origin from Lahore to Lucknow). The main character is a Muslim, but Shia rather than Sunni, unlike Shah Rukh, but more than that, he is defined by his business: '*Baniye ka dimaag aur miyanbhai ki* daring'. (The brains of a bania and the courage of a Muslim, echoing Swami Vivekananda's dream of a new India with a Vedanta brain and 'Islam' body[16] was the one line of the narration that held Shah Rukh's interest, and it is also the one line that possibly defines him best. Shah Rukh understands Islam at an intellectual level, says Dholakia, who spent some time with him during the extended shoot. The star is well-versed with Islamic texts, adds Dholakia, but is not fanatical.

In *Jab Harry Met Sejal*, as a weary but respectful tour guide to busloads of Indian tourists, Shah Rukh is almost a metaphor for himself. Much like Harry, who takes people around the sites of Amsterdam, Prague, Budapest and Vienna, and organises for their every need, from airplane tickets to sanitary napkins, Shah Rukh, the star, has been sharing bits and pieces of his soul with the world. Had he, like Harry, become cynical? Did he suddenly feel under-appreciated compared to his compatriots? Were we, as an audience, ready to see him as vulnerable, close to tears, often crude, using women as his playthings? A man who had always prided himself on being a feminist on-screen and off it, who had on Women's Day in 2013 pledged to always have the leading lady's name before his in the credits, beginning with *Chennai Express*?

As the ultimate romantic hero, one who had always abided by convention, it was a tricky place to be in. Add to this the sight of Shah Rukh cuddling, canoodling and even kissing Anushka Sharma, and his fans were clearly not amused. How could the Great Romantic turn into the Cheap Lecher? Even the number of times Shah Rukh had to say to Anushka, '*main ganda hoon*' (I am dirty), was not enough to convince audiences that he was, indeed, dirty, leery and lascivious. As the actor, playing himself in Zoya Akhtar's *Luck By Chance* (2009), says: 'An actor's work, apart from acting, is really to choose the right kind of roles.' He may have faltered occasionally while doing so in cinema, but there is no doubt that Shah Rukh was far more sure-footed when it came to alliances off-screen. When TED Talks, a series of inspirational global talks by heroes from across the world, curated by former *Wired* editor Chris Anderson, wanted a home in India in 2017, they chose Star India as their platform and Shah Rukh as the host of *TED Talks India: Nayi Soch*. It connected with Shah Rukh's own hyperintelligent persona, his emphasis on education, and his inspirational status as an outsider who gatecrashed into Bollywood. When Netflix wanted to ally with an Indian star to increase its popularity in 2017, it too chose Shah Rukh, aligning with Red Chillies Entertainment for a slate of new series as well as all his films, old and new.

Salman Khan, meanwhile, was doing more of the same when it came to his film choices, wisely keeping both Kabir Khan and Ali Abbas Zafar close to him. Kabir's *Tubelight* (2017), a sort of China update on *Bajrangi Bhaijaan*, did not do very well at the box office, but that may well have been because China as India's main villain doesn't work as well as Pakistan—therefore, neither does potential peace. In *Tubelight*, Salman plays yet another version of Bajrangi/Prem Dilwale/Sultan, a simple-minded, not-so-young young man who lives in the idyllic Jagatpur in Kumaon in 1962 and spreads the message of 'yakeen' (trust) and 'pyaar' (love). Named Lakshman Bisht in this movie, he is a latter-day Gandhian who believes that an eye for an eye will make the whole world blind. He tries very hard to get into the Army when it becomes clear that Pandit Nehru's belief in China's peace-loving nature is about to implode. But then, his brother, played by Sohail, his brother in real life, joins the war to fight against the Chinese, who are clearly outnumbering the Indians and outsmarting them as well.

There is a detailed and repeated reference to the inadequate shoes of the Indian soldiers, which is part of the 'Nehru-was-evil-he-lost-the-1962-war' lesson we have been handed down. So there is Bhaijaan, left behind to be captain of the Jagatpur civil brigade and defend the village/town against the Chinese. Naturally, a young widow and her child, born to Chinese parents but in India, choose to present themselves in Jagatpur. And the whole question of who is an Indian starts cropping up—A person who is born in India? One who shouts 'Bharat Mata ki Jai' louder than others? Looks 'Indian'? Can speak Hindi? Perhaps most of India was not in the mood to confront such questions, which might explain its relative failure.

In *Tiger Zinda Hai* (2017), which was directed by Zafar, who was Kabir Khan's assistant in *New York*, the RAW spy returns as a Bhagat Singh-reading patriot who can tackle polar bears and save his son as easily as he can whip up breakfast for the woman he loves. In *Bharat* (2019), Salman plays a character named Bharat, who embodies the nation—the moffusil, marginalised, peripheral Bharat, and not the India of Lutyens' Delhi and Malabar Hill, Mumbai. *'Tujh main poora Bharat hai beta'* (All of India is in you), says his father to a young Salman in the film. He asks him to take care of his family, and Bharat does precisely that, over seventy years of change in India—watching over events from Jawaharlal Nehru's death to the liberalisation of the Indian economy and its 'asli' (original) hero, Manmohan Singh.

In the film, Salman plays an oil rig worker who fights with his American supervisor over the quality of food. His younger version is an orphan in a refugee camp in 1947, who refuses to go to Pakistan though he is a Muslim—because his father fought for India's freedom. From playing the classic underdog in *Sultan*, fighting his internal demons, Salman had moved on to *Tiger Zinda Hai*, where he took on an enemy who was threatening to destroy the world with his evil ideology and who could be fought only by uniting the forces of India and Pakistan, to *Bharat*, where he played a man focused on keeping his family together.

Much of the philosophy of the characters he played derived from his director's life and background. Zafar's father had moved from the Border Roads Organisation to the Oil and Natural Gas Corporation (ONGC), and his mother taught English and Urdu at a government school. Zafar left his home in Dehradun at sixteen to study biochemistry at Delhi's Kirori Mal College, but survived on a diet of Saadat Hasan Manto, Premchand and Shakespeare.

The idea for *Bharat* came from Salman, says Zafar. He loved the South Korean film, *Ode to my Father* (2014), and wanted Zafar to adapt it. 'I think what appealed to Salman was the idea of one man looking out for his family,' says Zafar. Salman's tendency to take care of friends and be everyone's big brother was in evidence in his 2018 film, *Race 3*, the third part of the Abbas-Mustan franchise, which ensured the comeback of old friend Bobby Deol, and the casting of *Jai Ho* heroine Daisy Shah. It was evident again in *Dabanng 3*, his return as Chulbul Pandey, where he acted opposite the daughter of one of his close friends, Mahesh Manjrekar. Despite a sense of diminishing returns, Salman has played innumerable self-referential versions of his own self, a trend he seems intent on continuing with *Radhe: Your Most Wanted Bhai* (2021). As an action star, he was able to handle ageing better than Shah Rukh, whose predominant image remains that of the 'Eternal Lover', even though his body of work, over 100 films, indicates a vast diversity.

While these two Khans were locked in mortal combat, the third was marching to his own tune as always, making movies with complete conviction and immersion. In *Dangal* (2016), to which Aamir brought his customary body morphing, he was, as usual, in consonance with the times, making a deeply feminist film in a year where there was a parade of women-centric films, from *Pink* to *Dear Zindagi*. As Mahavir Singh Phogat, he created the ultimate feminist film based on the real-life wrestler and father of champion wrestlers, Babita and Geeta Phogat. Though his character is painted as a strict disciplinarian and a proud patriarch, the film made the valid point—that *'gold to gold hota hai, chori lave ya chora'* (a gold medal is a gold medal, whether it is won by a boy or a girl). In a deeply misogynistic society riven by khap panchayats, this was a powerful message, and Aamir played it for all it was worth. Even audiences familiar with the sight of women's bodies on-screen in various stages of undress, designed to titillate and excite, were made to wonder at his screen daughters' athleticism, their perfectly proportioned figures, so well suited to the arduous and enthralling sport of wrestling.

Dangal is as much a work of art and entertainment as it is a social statement. Like Aamir Khan himself, it is both generous and good-spirited, but also measured. When the national anthem plays during the movie, it does not require a Supreme Court diktat to get everyone in the audience on their feet with tears streaming down their faces. When a Muslim butcher's daughter gets prasad for Geeta-didi to help her perform well at the Commonwealth Games, it does not require a secular party's mandate to make us acknowledge the moment. And when a podgy official devours Mahavir Singh's laddoos but refuses to support his cause—buying wrestling mats for his daughters—you do not need to know the pathetic state of sport in India to feel the rage. Aamir's triumph as an actor and filmmaker has always been his self-belief. Though *Chak De! India* had explored reclaiming women's bodies for sport rather than sex, and *Sultan* had flirted with the idea of two wrestlers creating the perfect champion, Aamir made the movie with blinkers on, as if nothing had come before it. In fact, once he heard *Sultan*'s story and realised it was more of a romantic tale, he knew *Dangal*, at its heart a father-daughter narative, was very different.

Almost every custom that holds women back in Haryana (and indeed in most other states) finds a mention in *Dangal*, but not in a heavy-handed way. Child marriage, female foeticide, poor diets, 'appropriate' clothing. 'Knicker *aur* T-shirt *pehenkar aaya* cyclone' (the cyclone has arrived wearing shorts and a T-shirt) goes one of the songs, referring to the woman wrestlers.

With their carefree gait (not often seen in women in Hindi cinema, where they usually stand with their heads tilted, breasts out, stomachs in, and butts out) and their direct gaze (again, Hindi cinema women are urged to cast their eyes down in order to look bashful), the girls run through the opposition with a smile and a laugh. '*Dangal jeetne se pehle, darr se jeetna padta hai*' (Before conquering the wrestling ring, it is necessary to conquer fear), says Aamir Khan's Mahavir Singh. It works as a motto for life as much as for sport. The movie touched hearts and minds, further cementing Aamir's reputation as someone who tries to be better than his previous best.

There was quite a bit of flag-waving feminism in *Dangal*—'*Choriyan choron se kam nahin, chulhe chauke, byaah, bacche paalne ke liye nahin banayi gayi hain*' (Girls aren't any less than boys and haven't been created to cook, marry and produce babies)—and it continued in *Secret Superstar* (2017) where Aamir plays a seemingly slimy but good-hearted music producer who gives a break to a young Muslim girl who wants to sing. While the film belonged to Zaira Wasim, who also played the young Geeta in *Dangal*, it was an Aamir Khan production, directed by his former manager, Advait Chandan. Perfectly executed to tug at your heartstrings, *Secret Superstar* is also inspiring. '*Sapne dekhna sabko* allowed *hai*,' (You are allowed to dream) says Insia, the fifteen-year-old secret superstar who studies in a Vadodara school and has been singing since the age of six when her mother handed her a guitar despite opposition from her father.

At some level, Aamir was also answering his critics, who had accused him of one-sided criticism of Hindu fundamentalism and obscurantism. In *Secret Superstar*, he highlights the oppression faced by Muslim women trapped in bad marriages. For Aamir to bankroll such a film required courage—unlike what some would like to believe, if he is critical of some of the indignities in Hinduism, he is equally critical of his own faith.

For those blinded by their religion, it is difficult to accept or even understand such secularism.

He also managed to take potshots at a few of his pet peeves—awards shows (all rigged, all rigged), *Bombay Times* front page (easily bought), and TV news channels (*Shakti Kumar ki shaadi toh toot gayi, Salman ki shaadi kab hogi*—Shakti Kumar's marriage has broken up, when will Salman get married—asks an anchor.)

His charming performance as Shakti Kumar (a cross between music director Anu Malik and actor Shakti Kapoor) made his next mis-step a particularly unhappy one. *Thugs of Hindostan* by Vijay Krishna Acharya, *Dhoom 3*'s director, was originally intended as a fictionalised story of thug Feringhea and thug-hunter and British officer William Sleeman, but it ended up as a Diwali whimper. Intended to be a critique of the East India Company, the movie was based in a period that had long fascinated Aamir, as evidenced by *Lagaan* (2000) and *Mangal Pandey: The Rising* (2005). With the added attraction of Amitabh Bachchan, playing Khudabaksh, a warrior-protector who has to return Raunakpur to the princess, the film could have been exciting. Unfortunately, despite an evil English villain, item songs by Katrina Kaif, and some suspense about whether Feringhea is a traitor or a patriot, the movie was a misfire. So much so that Aamir had to apologise to his fans. 'I take full responsibility for *Thugs* not working with the audience. I think we went wrong but I would like to take full responsibility for that. You can be sure we tried our level best. We didn't leave any stone unturned but somewhere we went wrong. There are some people who liked the film, and we would like to thank them but they are in a minority. The majority didn't like it and we realise this,' he said.[17] That didn't stop him from beginning another epic, the shooting of which was interrupted by the pandemic, a remake of *Forrest Gump* called *Laal Singh Chadha*, directed by *Secret Superstar*'s Advait Chandan.

Meanwhile, Shah Rukh, the steadiest of them all so far, seemed to be flailing a little in his personal life. While promoting *Don 2*, he and co-star Priyanka Chopra spent a lot of time together. Their closeness became the subject of tabloid speculation, though it is difficult to tell whether they had a more intimate relationship or not. Shah Rukh did say this in a 2012 interview on TV: 'To me what is most disturbing is the fact that a lady who has worked with me has been questioned and somewhere down the line not been shown the kind of respect I show her or all the women I've worked with. It's a little disrespectful. I am extremely sorry about that not because of anything I've done directly, but the fact that she is my friend, she is one of the closest friends and always will be. I just feel sometimes when things are said I needed to step back from it because I find it very banal, very small and it just tends to spoil relationships that people have while working together. And she's a little girl who started her Miss India crowning with me or Miss World crowning with me, I don't remember. We've shared some of the nicest moments on-screen and off-screen as friends and it's unfortunate that a friendship gets a little soiled.'[18]

Shah Rukh continued to speak about Priyanka unselfconsciously. I remember, when I had gone to Karjat near Mumbai, for the shoot of *Happy New Year* in 2014, he was talking about the 'cool girls' in the industry. Priyanka was one of the names he mentioned—the others being his co-star in *Happy New Year*, Deepika Padukone, and Katrina Kaif, with whom he acted in *Jab Tak Hai Jaan*. By that time, Gauri and he had had a third child, through surrogacy, in 2013. Called AbRam, he was born in the 34th week and weighed a mere 1.5 kg. Once he got better, Shah Rukh talked about him often, shared pictures, and took him to press conferences. As his friend Farah Khan told me: 'It is like Aryan Part Two. I remember how Shah Rukh would take Aryan with him to every party, carrying him and dancing the night away, whether it was Goa or Bangkok.'

Being a father is one of Shah Rukh's greatest joys. He is particular about the education of his children and has often said they should complete it before attempting to join the film industry.[19] He also shares their interests, whether it is football, music or TV. He watched *Breaking Bad* with Aryan, who was at school at Sevenoaks, London, and then went on to college at the University of Southern California, Los Angeles. He's played soccer with him, tried to understand why he doesn't want to learn driving, and complained good-naturedly about him being obsessed with Minecraft, a video game. He is as particular about his daughter's education, though he did gift her a cover on *Vogue* magazine on her eighteenth birthday, an event that triggered many unkind jokes and memes.[20]

Gauri, meanwhile, has evolved from a shy wife to one of the most influential women in the city. Not only is she a great hostess but she has also parlayed her interest in interior design into a business, Gauri Khan Designs, which she launched in 2013. According to *Architectural Digest India*, she has extended her design philosophy from residential interiors to include commercial spaces such as retail outlets, restaurants, spas, hotels and turnkey projects. The brand is a culmination of Gauri's long-standing passion for envisioning spaces. It offers a range of curated pieces in the sphere of flooring, décor, accessories, and rugs, as well as the occasional features from Paris and New York City.[21] She has also designed spaces for Bollywood celebrities—and close pals—such as Karan Johar, Jacqueline Fernandez and Sidharth Malhotra. Not only does she endorse brands with her husband now, such as the home furnishings label, D'Decor, and Airbnb, but she also lends her name to other style brands. She is also co-founder and co-chairperson of Red Chillies Entertainment and its subsidiaries.

But her biggest impact comes from her being the unofficial queen of the Bollywood Wives club. Her status was officially unveiled in the 2021 Netflix series, *Fabulous Lives of Bollywood Wives,* made by Dharma Productions, which is run by her friend, Karan Johar. The show tracks the lives and loves of four Bollywood friends, Maheep Kapoor, Bhavana Pandey, Seema Khan and Neelam Kothari, all wives of actors. Season one ends with Gauri hosting a party at her Mumbai store, Gauri Khan Designs, and presiding over a long chat with her friends, during the course of which Shah Rukh makes an appearance. Much of the conversation is naturally in praise of them both.

Over the years, Shah Rukh and Gauri have emerged as a powerful couple, not merely financially, with interests in movies and cricket, but also socially, throwing and attending parties. I remember Shah Rukh telling me, on the sidelines of the India Today Conclave in 2017, about how their identity as parents was paramount after so many years of marriage and how the children now dominate much of the conversation.

Some of the couple's friends have fallen by the wayside, prime among them being Arjun Rampal, who was questioned by Narcotics Control Bureau (NCB) officials in the drug probe being carried out by the agency after actor Sushant Singh Rajput's death. Rampal was once a staple in Shah Rukh's movies and at his parties, and it is not clear why they are no longer close. Was it Rampal's alleged role as a party boy with all kinds of facilitators on speed dial or the dynamics of his breakup with his wife, model Mehr Jessia, caused by a rumoured relationship with Suzanne Khan Roshan, once Gauri Khan's best friend?[22]

In the complicated lives and loves of Bollywood A-listers, Karan Johar has been a fairly constant friend, except for a brief interregnum when they seem to have had a misunderstanding. Johar has written about it in his autobiography *An Unsuitable Boy* (2017). 'Shah Rukh is a very possessive friend. I think I may have hurt him when I made a film without him (*Ae Dil Hai Mushkil*, 2016). And I think I got hurt because when I did, I felt he didn't give me that paternal or fraternal feeling that I had from him otherwise. I think we were two hurt friends for no reason.' He goes on to write about how the 'simmering silent distance' between them went out of the window when they met at the success party of Shoojt Sircar's *Piku*. 'I hugged him instinctively and said, "I've missed you." And he said, "You've no idea how much I've missed you." We had this moment.' He added, 'when the origin of the friendship is so strong, it just cannot die.'

Johar has always described Shah Rukh as an 'older brother', and adores his children, Aryan, Suhana and AbRam. As he writes in *An Unsuitable Boy*, before he had his twins, Yash and Roohi, through surrogacy in 2017, 'I go to Gauri's house now to play with AbRam. Even if Gauri is not there, I go and sit with him. And he comes and spends time with my mum all the time. My mum loves him. He is like a toy that you want to own. He came to the office the other day and the entire staff came out to see him. Everyone was behaving as if Brad Pitt had arrived. He was delighted with all the attention.'

Shah Rukh has also been a good brother, taking care of his elder sister Shehnaz Lalarukh, who lives with the family, and who is called 'Lala Madam' by paparazzi used to taking pictures of the family. Shehnaz fell into depression after the death of their father and hasn't really recovered since. But go to their home and you'll find that she is very much at every party and sometimes even drops in on Shah Rukh's interviews if they are conducted in his home office.

An unwell sibling is also a part of Aamir's life. Though Faisal Khan was his co-star in the ill-fated *Mela* in 2000, the relationship between the brothers has been strained. In a September 2020 interview, Faisal said the family felt he was depressed and had paranoid schizophrenia. He told *Bollywood Hungama* that they kept him under house arrest for a year and forced medication on him. 'It is illegal but I was taking all this quietly because I thought that the family will realise at some point, that if I am mad, I will show it in some way. I thought I should be patient till they come to their senses that they are troubling me for no reason,' he said.

In the same interview, Faisal said that when he was asked by his family to give up his signatory rights, he decided to 'safeguard' himself and left the house. He fought the case legally, and after several months, the Bandra metropolitan magistrate's court ruled that he need not be in anyone's custody and could live anywhere he wanted to. In 2007, both Aamir and his father filed separate petitions for Faisal's custody. According to Aamir, his brother was suffering from schizophrenia. However, Tahir Hussain claimed that he was suffering from depression and had no other issues.[23]

In 2007, Aamir's extended family issued a media statement, saying: 'It is deeply distressing and saddening to see the depths to which Aamir's father and brother have sunk, with the express intention of causing Aamir hurt. Their offensive allegations, malicious lies and pathetic behaviour are truly shameful. Their behaviour is all the more appalling given that Aamir has supported both his father and brother in every way possible for the last fifteen years, and has on numerous occasions bailed them out of their various crises. Unfortunately, Aamir's goodness has only earned him their envy and hatred.' Aamir, they said, was 'the pillar of strength of our family, supporting and protecting us, and always doing the best by us. He is a person of extraordinary gifts, of the highest moral integrity and honesty, and someone who has always put his family before himself. He has our deepest respect and all our love, and we support him and stand by him in whatever he does. We are proud of him for his courage and his dignity, which he continues to maintain despite all of this.'

The statement went on to say: 'We strongly condemn the comments and allegations made by Tahir Husain and Faisal

Khan against Aamir and our family. Faisal is unwell and is in need of urgent medical attention. Aamir's attempt to take custody of Faisal was so that he could help him and take care of him. However, seeing that all Aamir's efforts have been met with such hostility, we think it's all for the best that Tahir Husain has been given custody of Faisal Khan. He should now take complete responsibility for Faisal's care and actions.'

It was signed, among others, by his wives, former and current, his mother, his sisters Nikhat and Farhat, as well as his cousins Mansoor and Nuzhat.[24] Faisal reportedly moved back with Aamir after the death of their father in 2010, reconciling with the actor during the shoot of *3 Idiots*. But not for long.

Aamir also had a troubled relationship with his father, on account of the latter's infidelities. In a December 2000 article, *Stardust* referred to a public notice Aamir had issued against his father's company, TV Productions, stating that he had nothing to do with his father's business interests. The article blamed a young actress, Divya Palat, for the differences between father and son, saying Aamir had questioned his father's decision to sign her for five films. It said Aamir was already miffed with his father for his second marriage. It also quoted Tahir Hussain saying he had launched eighteen newcomers in the course of his career and this was no different. 'Just because we (Divya and I) are fond of each other doesn't mean we are having an affair.' He also explained Aamir's public notice as a consequence of him asking Aamir to resign as director of his company because he had got busy with work on *Lagaan*. 'Since Aamir is very systematic about everything, he issued a public notice to make everyone aware. I'm sure he didn't realise *ki log rai ka pahad bana denge* (people will make a mountain of a molehill).'

Aamir's second marriage has, however, remained strong even in the face of rumours of him seeing a co-star. Kiran and Aamir had a child through surrogacy in 2011. They named him Azad.

Kiran had had a painful miscarriage in 2010 and the couple decided to opt for surrogacy after medical advice. In a 2013 interview, Kiran said that it 'was the last resort for us as it wasn't possible for me to have a child the natural way'. She also said it was suggested as an option to them by Dr Firuza Parikh, their doctor and dear friend. Both she and her husband, Dr Rajesh Parikh, had helped them understand the process and counselled them through their doubts. Their openness about the decision came in for praise from doctors, who felt they had done much to remove the stigma from the procedure. For Kiran, though, transparency was the obvious choice. As she said in the same interview: 'We knew that being in the public eye we would be asked about it anyway, and we have never felt defensive about our decision, so we opted to be open about it. Of course if our experience is useful for people to know, then all the better.'[25]

Kiran's presence in Aamir's life has given him a partner who understands him fully as an artiste. She provides him the space needed to be creative and also allows him to remain integrated with his family and friends. I remember her coming to the India Today Conclave in 2018, to listen to Israeli author Yuval Noah Harari, with Junaid, Aamir's oldest son, and apologising for her husband's absence—he was sad to have missed the event as he is a huge fan of the author. The next year, she made up for his absence again by accepting a Safaigiri award from *India Today* for the work done by Paani Foundation, which they had set up in 2016 to help make Maharashtra drought free. Aamir's old friend, Satyajit Bhatkal, who directed *Satyamev Jayate*, is the CEO of the foundation. Kiran was also chairperson of the MAMI Mumbai Film Festival of India till she stepped down in 2019 to focus on her own work. She had taken over the position in 2014 from veteran director Shyam Benegal, and did much over the years to put it on the cultural map of the city.

Aamir is a supportive father but has allowed his children to make their own mistakes and find their own paths. Junaid, his eldest, is making his debut in a Yash Raj Film, *Maharaja*, directed by Siddharth P. Malhotra, after several years spent in theatre. Aamir's daughter, Ira, has also been acting, on stage, even directing her version of Euripedes' *Medea*, produced by veteran actress Sarika and starring actress Hazel Keech and her brother, Junaid. In 2021, she became her father's manager, the only way to reach him when he gave up his cellphone, calling it the 'black hole of time'.

Salman remains a bachelor, and though it is widely believed that he is dating and living with the Romanian actress-singer, Julia Vantur, he is yet to confirm it. He also clearly shares a close friendship with actress Jacqueline Fernandez, who spent much of the 2020 lockdown with him on his Panvel farm. He continues to work with former girlfriend Katrina Kaif, who had come to his rescue by taking on the part of Kumud (Madam Sir) Raina in old friend Ali Abbas Zafar's *Bharat* (2019) after Priyanka Chopra chose to walk out. Apart from running the Being Human Foundation, Salman now runs Salman Khan Films, which produces and distributes movies, produces TV shows like the popular *Kapil Sharma Show*, and runs a talent agency, Uniworld Being Talented.

The relationship between the three Khans remains complex. The famed frostiness between Salman and Shah Rukh seems to have melted under a mutual need. Shah Rukh did a cameo as a magician in Salman's 2017 film *Tubelight*, while Salman returned the favour by starring in a song in *Zero*, '*Isaaqnazi*'. He was given a dramatic entry, with Shah Rukh looking up at him. Since then, the two have decided to strengthen their support for each other. In 2021, it was announced that Salman would make an appearance as Tiger in Shah Rukh's *Pathan*. Both are Yash Raj Films productions. Salman has also used Shah Rukh's VFX studio for the special effects for his film, *Radhe: The Most Wanted Bhai*.

Aamir Khan remains friends with Salman, and though there is no enmity between him and Shah Rukh, they are not exactly best mates. But each of them has shown resilience in the face of challenges, both on account of changes in society and in the face of growing competition from their contemporaries, Akshay Kumar and Ajay Devgan, as well as younger stars. Kumar and Devgan have also had successful careers, and they have the added advantage of being on the right side of the current regime. Hrithik Roshan, who debuted in 2000, continues to stay relevant despite the setback of a much-publicised divorce from interior designer Suzanne Khan Roshan and an ugly spat with his *Krrish 3* (2013) co-star, Kangana Ranaut. She claims they had an affair; he vehemently denies it. The battle between the two began when Hrithik sent Kangana a legal notice after she referred to him as her 'silly ex' during an interview.[26]

There appears to be a new star system in place, especially post the COVID-19 lockdown. Younger actors such as Ranveer Singh and Ranbir Singh are facing tough competition from actors like Nawazuddin Siddiqui and Pankaj Tripathi, who appear regularly in streaming series and independent movies. Amitabh Bachchan and Anil Kapoor are making movies written especially for them, such as *Gulabo Sitabo* (2020) and *AK vs AK* (2020). The death of Irrfan in 2020, after a prolonged battle with cancer, has stripped the film industry of a major talent. The actor had built a healthy career for himself in the West too, with big, showy turns in blockbusters such as *Jurassic World* (2015) and *Inferno* (2016), as well as quieter acts in independent movies such as *The Namesake* (2007) and *The Lunchbox* (2013).

By the time 2020 opened, it was clear that the Khans were slowing down. The film industry, fuelled by their innovation and imagination over three decades, would have to look for new stars and new stories. This was not to say that the era of the Khans was over. Each of them had their constituency.

Shah Rukh could be absent from the big screen for two years and still be the cynosure of all eyes when he appeared, either accepting a philanthropy award in Davos for advancing women's rights in 2018 or on David Letterman's *My Next Guest Needs No Introduction* in October 2019. Aamir could make a terrible film like *Thugs of Hindostan* but win hearts by apologising to his fans for it and plunging into work on his next magnum opus. Salman seemed determined to extract every ounce of life left in a career rebuilt on the return of the mofussil hero. His movies would still routinely be blockbusters but not every film was hitting the mark now. Like Shah Rukh, he had broadened his business interests with 'Being Human' becoming a merchandiser as well as a not-for-profit foundation raising money for those in need.

The three Khans had shown tremendous strength and flexibility, changing with the times and with the audience. Could they last another decade, their fourth in the public eye?

6

A New Order for a New India

It was around October 2016, I was working with *India Today*, and we had organised a series of conversations between two film legends from different generations. There was Ranveer Singh, who came in early and locked himself up in a conference room in a suburban hotel to work on pages of notes, which he would then edit and put on index cards. Back then, Ranveer was totally involved in the character, Alauddin Khilji, that he was to play in *Padmavati* (the film's title had to be later changed)—he had grown his hair, sported a moustache and worked on his diction. 'Alauddin Khilji was from so many different places that the accent was difficult to nail down,' he explained, as he sat at a table strewn with his notes, waiting for Aamir Khan to arrive. Aamir came straight from recording an episode of *Koffee with Karan*, accompanied by his two young co-stars in *Dangal*, Fatima Sana Shaikh and Sanya Malhotra. They were working as his assistants in the post-production phase of the soon-to-be-released film.

Ranveer was excitable, asking questions, admiring the depth of Aamir's eyes and talking about some of Aamir's best performances. Stroking his moustache and beard, Aamir looked embarrassed, but asked suitably interested questions, especially about those of Ranveer's films that he had watched: *Band Baaja Baarat*, *Dil Dhadakne Do* and parts of *Bajirao Mastani*. It was like watching a master and his pupil, guru and devotee.

Two years later, the two generations represented by Aamir and Ranveer went head-to-head at the box office. Data from media analyst Karan Taurani shows that in 2018, stars like Ranveer Singh, Ayushmann Khurrana, Vicky Kaushal, Shahid Kapoor and Ranbir Kapoor out-performed the over-forty stars in the number of film releases (forty-six against thirty-eight) and did better at the box office (₹136 crore vs ₹108 crore), suggesting that there was now, in terms of casting, an alternative for producers, who were accustomed to taking home only 10 per cent of the total revenue because of the high cost attached to having A-list stars. Now there was clear evidence that entertainment did not necessarily mean the Khans.

When 2020 dawned, for the first time since 1988, when the three Khans made their debut, none of the three was the subject of popular conversation in India.

Shah Rukh Khan was nursing self-inflicted wounds from the dismal failure of *Zero* (with its unfortunate title) and taking his time to decide on his next project. Aamir Khan had started shooting *Laal Singh Chadha*, a remake of *Forrest Gump*, in an effort to make it in time for his customary December release. Salman Khan was manfully trying to keep it together, taking his muscles and the bags under his eyes to the sets of *Radhe: Your Most Wanted Bhai*, which was meant to be out on Eid 2020.

After three decades of entertaining India, and increasingly the diasporic world, the era of the Khans, all born in 1965, seemed to be petering out. The 'Actor Forever in Search of a Character' had not had a single release after the disastrous attempt at playing the is-he-good-or-is-he-bad thug in *Thugs of Hindostan* in 2018. 'Rahul/Raj the Romantic' looked increasingly tired and worn out. And yet, his innate intelligence shone through whenever he was himself, as evident in the *TED Talks India: Nayi Soch* or *My Next Guest Needs No Introduction* with David Letterman. Suddenly, as he showed off his cooking skills to Letterman and spoke of growing up in Delhi, India realised why it had fallen in love with this man, with his odd hair and unnerving intensity. It was the same with Salman Khan, whether he scolded *Bigg Boss* contestants for misbehaving, flirted with Katrina Kaif on-screen in *Bharat* or adjusted the dress of co-actor Saiee Manjrekar who, at twenty-one, was young enough to be his daughter, at a promotional event for *Dabanng 3*.

In the dying light of the Khan Kingdom, a new India was establishing itself. It is an India that seems to have little patience with the old platitudes of pluralism and multiculturalism. It is an India where the Mandal, mandir and market mobilisations of the 1990s have merged with the rights-based legislation of the 2000s to create a new narrative of populist aggression. What was once considered a privilege is now seen as a necessity, whether it is a telephone connection, a gas cylinder or a toilet. In this India, Prime Minister Narendra Modi, having been re-elected in 2019 with an even bigger majority in the Lok Sabha than in 2014, embodies the newly assertive way of dealing with the domestic margins and the global mainstream.

This is an India where identities are being transformed and internal borders are being redrawn. As promised by the BJP in its election agenda, in August 2019, Union Home Minister Amit Shah announced the abrogation of Article 370 and 35A in Parliament, which resulted in the bifurcation of the state of Jammu and Kashmir into two union territories: Jammu and Kashmir and Ladakh. The Kashmir Valley was placed under a virtual lockdown with all communication snapped and political leaders placed under house arrest. In November 2019, the Supreme Court's final judgment in the Ayodhya dispute ordered the disputed land to be handed over to a trust (to be created by the Centre), which would have the authority to oversee the building of the Ram Janmabhoomi temple. The court also ordered the government to give five acres of land, elsewhere in the state, to the Uttar Pradesh Sunni Central Waqf Board, for building a mosque as a replacement for the demolished Babri Masjid. Completing this sweeping transformation of the political and social landscape was the Citizenship (Amendment) Act, 2019, which provided a pathway to Indian citizenship for refugees from Afghanistan, Bangladesh and Pakistan who were Hindus, Sikhs, Buddhists, Jains, Parsis or Christians, and had arrived in India before the end of December 2014. Not only did this ignite a furious debate and spark nationwide protests, but it also meant a loss of citizenship for many.

By articulating ideas from political meritocracy to menstrual hygiene, by implementing decisions long pledged by the BJP, Prime Minister Modi has colonised the Indian imagination, leaving very little space for other icons. His relentless publicity machine has ensured that he, more than any other public figure, now helps India understand itself. This was what the Three Khans had once done, in their own ways, helping Indians navigate from tradition to modernity, as they themselves moved from the callowness of youthful romances to bigger themes. India had seen itself in the three of them.

But by associating their stardom with Prime Minister Modi's various projects, whether it was Swachh Bharat, demonetisation, or even the celebration of Mahatma Gandhi's 150th birth anniversary where both Aamir and Shah Rukh made flattering speeches and took obedient selfies, the Khans have effaced their own primacy in the cultural space.

Add to this the fact that the old certainties that created the conditions for the three-decade domination of the three stars has vanished. As sociologist Shiv Visvanathan says, 'The triangle of contemporary Khans has to be understood within a rough genealogy of heroes. The Fifties saw the dominance of Dev Anand, Dilip Kumar and Raj Kapoor. There was something urban and urbane about them. The first two embodied the middle class hero while Raj Kapoor brought a hint of Charlie Chaplin's tramp to add a touch of socialism. The late Sixties provided the space to two heroes who dominated the screens as individuals. The first was Rajesh Khanna who exuded a poetics of romance. This gave way to the myth of urban violence, epitomised by Amitabh Bachchan as the Angry Young Man. The next triangle was a set of composite, equivocal figures whose heroism needed time to develop. These were the Khans. Each began with a touch of adolescence which they then tried to shrug off in their own way.'

Salman became the eternal adolescent, says Visvanathan, the boy-next-door who never grew up. Aamir, the autodidact, matured the most, attempting a more serious sense of himself in experimenting with a historical movie like *Lagaan* (2001) and *Dangal* (2016), the biography of a wrestling family. Shah Rukh was more ambivalent. Growing old seems to be the toughest for him, caught between the changeless Khan and the perpetually changing Khan. And time has been hard on him. 'People watching his movies often ask, "How did I like this guy?" Yet the lives of millions, from youth to middle age, have been marked by him in some way. He marks all of us growing up. He is the common denominator of the Khan in all of us, a middle-class hero, an outsider, a man who has made it on his own,' says Visvanathan in an email to me.

2020 was expected to be the year in which there would be a resurgence. There were rumours that Shah Rukh would start, and perhaps complete, a film with Raju Hirani that would restore his street credibility, and Salman and Aamir would be back with entertaining blockbusters. But it was not to be. COVID-19 struck the world and by 14 June, when thirty-four-year-old Sushant Singh Rajput died, apparently by suicide, the industry had changed beyond recognition. Suddenly, from a huge sympathy wave for a young death, conspiracy theories began doing the rounds, creating a media storm. It was said that yet another promising outsider had fallen at the barricades erected by the powerful in Bollywood. Clips of Rajput being mocked on Karan Johar's *Koffee with Karan* by other guests went viral. Stories that made the rounds suggested that Aditya Chopra had short-circuited Sushant's career by dropping the idea of making *Paani*, directed by Shekhar Kapur, in which the young actor was cast in the lead.

At a time when the Khans could have spoken up for the hurt and rage within and outside Bollywood, they chose to be silent, and that included Shah Rukh, the man whom Sushant had most publicly admired and emulated. Starting by questioning the suicide theory, the Sushant case soon became about money laundering by his girlfriend, actress Rhea Chakraborty, and when that couldn't be proved, it became a drugs investigation in which a series of top stars, male and female, were named and shamed.

The discourse went from the survival of the Khans to damning the whole of Bollywood itself. Apoplectic anchors, whose channel ratings rose with their continued coverage of the Sushant Singh Rajput case, exposed the underbelly of the industry, from its deep-seated sexism and its celebration of mediocrity, to its rampant drug use. They provided a platform to voices like that of Kangana Ranaut, who threw in the narrative of anti-nationalism, a clever ploy to bring religion into the conversation. The deification of the mafia in movies, the outpouring of support from the industry when Sanjay Dutt was accused of terrorist activities under TADA in 1993, and the rule of male actors who allowed women only item songs and a couple of romantic scenes while also expecting them to behave like their wives on the sets—Ranaut's list of harsh accusations against the industry were many, and if some were self-serving, she admitted as much. 'If I won't destroy my enemies, who will?' she asked on Twitter.

The anger against Old Bollywood got powerful extra-territorial support from Rajya Sabha MP Subramanian Swamy, whose supporters saw in it yet another opportunity to boost his image as the hero of the Virat Hindu Samaj. At the same time, BJP leader Muralidhar Rao, BJP general secretary and great proponent of family values, and Prasoon Joshi, the chairman of the Central Board of Film Certification and the BJP's unofficial poet laureate, saw in all this upturning of reputations an opportunity for Bollywood to craft a new form of storytelling inspired by ancient texts and contemporary history, rather than the narratives it had always fed off on.

Most of the Bollywood biggies, among them Aamir and Shah Rukh, were participants in one such conversation with Prime Minister Narendra Modi in October 2019 in Mumbai, where the latter spoke of cinema's potential for 'nation-building'. Pro-establishment actors such as Akshay Kumar jumped in, even if somewhat late, asking for Bollywood to look within, at its own faults and flaws. As Visvanathan notes, 'It is clear that Bollywood needs to fix itself, having come apart as myth and grammar. The old oppositions do not work. Violence is no longer heroic, the epic act that Amitabh Bachchan dreamt of to resolve a social crisis. It is all-pervasive, inventive, endemic and institutional. The imagination of the city as holding together rural and urban is over. The city dominates as a demography but not as an ideology. The small town is offered as an intermediate solution, but it inspires as sociology, as market, but not as myth. The family and the mother are sacred but given domestic violence, this plot does not hold. Friendship and peer groups seem more logical and more important today. The personal and the public have got separated, so there is no Bollywood balance between the two.'

Bollywood tried taking to historical movies to solve the problem of a disconnect between the audience and itself. But that genre tried to look at the past more as a costume ball, dressed by Sabyasachi and designed by Sanjay Leela Bhansali, rather than as an examination of history. There is a highlighting of forgotten stories but a failure to work the epic as metaphor. Also, figures in history have become fragmented among caste groups. Bollywood has no answer to technology, no sense of science fiction. Music, Hindi cinema's great strength, has taken a backseat in recent films, which means that songs cannot carry a film as they once used to. The solo scriptwriter and even the solo lyricist is fast disappearing, and in their place, a team of writers and more than one songwriter are given the task of writing the songs—but, ultimately, if the script fails to surprise or entertain, even the stars can't save it.

Bollywood has failed to create a convincing kind of entertainment which can subsume the changes one sees in the body, sexuality, gender, desire and even the erotic. The myth of youth does not work. They do not challenge the establishment, they want to be co-opted.

Sadly, the Khans—who, as their co-star Twinkle Khanna notes, have nothing in common except their surnames—had little to offer during the COVID-19 crisis, except a few tepid songs from Salman, who was clearly bored in his Panvel farmhouse. They have aged happily in their personal life as larger-than-life epic characters. They have degenerated into weaker versions of themselves, points out Visvanathan, mimicking themselves into oblivion, somewhat like Dev Anand.

Bollywood has to compete with the growth of streaming services, which are fast emerging as an alternative to the theatrical experience. The COVID-19 lockdown has changed audience tastes to a considerable extent.[1] Not only have people got used to watching long-form storytelling with diverse characters and intriguing storylines, but they have also been exposed to a new world of global TV series and movies. Even the more popular entertainment meant for the masses, the equivalent of the proverbial front benchers, has acquired some degree of authenticity and sophistication. As the protagonist of ALT Balaji's *Bichoo Ka Khel* puts it: '*Aap apni kahaani likho, nahin to koi aur likhega.*' (Write your own story, otherwise someone else will write it for you).'

Consumers are creatures of habit, and even at the so-called bottom of the pyramid, entertainment is being absorbed mindfully. *Coolie No. 1*, Varun Dhawan's duet with dad David, may have premiered on Amazon Prime, but how many watched it till the end? According to OrmaxMedia word-of-mouth rankings, the film was nowhere in the all-time top ten—it is topped by Sushant Singh Rajput's last film, *Dil Bechara*, followed by *Ludo, Lust Stories, Kaagaz, Chhalang, Shakuntala Devi, Khuda Haafiz, Love Per Square Foot, Serious Men* and *Lootcase.* There are at least twenty serious OTT players in India, homegrown and foreign, and audience numbers are rising for streaming services: Disney+Hotstar (launched as Hotstar in 2015) has 26 million subscribers, Amazon Prime Video, which started in 2016, has between 10 and 15 million subscribers and Netflix, which began the same year, has 5 million.

This has led to a democratisation of talent, making stars of actors traditionally referred to as 'character actors'. So Nawazuddin Siddiqui, Pankaj Tripathi, Neeraj Kabi and Jaideep Ahlawat have seen stellar successes in streaming series, especially during the months of lockdown. With no theatres, no exorbitant ticket prices and no restricted windows for smaller films, the playing field for actors has levelled. Movie premieres on streaming services, long-form series that require characters to have greater depth and the need to reflect the diversity among audiences has led to the emergence of a new hero.

Nawazuddin Siddiqui shone as Inspector Jatil Yadav in Honey Trehan's directorial debut, *Raat Akeli Hai* and in Sudhir Mishra's *Serious Men* based on Manu Joseph's novel of the same name. Pankaj Tripathi, *Gangs of Wasseypur* alumnus, was tender and tough as Janhvi Kapoor's father in Netflix's *Gunjan Saxena: The Kargil Girl*; hilarious as the singing ganglord in Anurag Basu's *Ludo*, and at his inscrutable best as Kaleen Bhai in *Mirzapur*. Yet another *Gangs of Wasseypur* alumnus, Jaideep Ahlawat, was the star of Amazon Prime Video's irresistibly dark series, *Paatal Lok*, where he matched wits with Neeraj Kabi in his role as a suave and narcissistic TV anchor.

The new hero can disappear into the role he plays with such felicity that it is sometimes difficult to recognise him. Kabi is one such self-taught actor, who came to Mumbai in 1998 and waited for twenty-one years, doing a series of odd jobs which he refuses to elaborate on, saying he has nurtured his secrets for many years. A student of management at Symbiosis University who dreamt of a corporate career, Kabi fell in love with the movies in Pune, home to the Film and Television Institute of India (FTII). When he couldn't get into the National School of Drama (NSD), he took the FTII syllabus and taught himself, finding his own gurus in various arts such as Kathak and Kalaripayattu. While doing theatre and acting workshops, he attracted the attention of visionary director Anand Gandhi, who cast him as a mournful monk in *Ship of Theseus* (2013). Kabi's performance immediately won him fans. From being on the periphery, he was suddenly being courted by two well-known directors. Vishal Bhardwaj wanted to cast him as Tabu's second husband in *Haider* while Dibakar Banerjee was keen to cast him as the villain in *Detective Byomkesh Bakshy!* Kabi recalls Banerjee saying to him: 'People are going to grab you now, but don't give yourself to just anybody.' He waited for *Detective Byomkesh Bakshy!*, following up that role with several others. He played the father in Meghna Gulzar's *Talvar* (2015), DCP Parulkar in Netflix's *Sacred Games* (2018) and National Security Advisor Shailesh Malviya in SonyLIV's *Avrodh* (2020).

Actors such as Kabi and Ahlawat are characterised not only by their patience and perseverance, but also by the refreshing 'otherness' they bring to an industry with a small gene pool and self-referential storytelling. Ahlawat, whose Hathi Ram Chaudhry became an instant hit when *Paatal Lok* was aired, brings with him the lived experience of Rohtak, Haryana, which he left in 2008 to make his way in Mumbai. It is a place that he still goes back to, to hang out and have tea and samosas at the canteen of the Maharshi Dayanand University.

Ahlawat studied acting at the FTII, an experience that opened his heart and mind to the best in world cinema. After twelve years and pivotal roles in movies such as *Raees* (2017) and *Raazi* (2018), he accepted *Paatal Lok* with grateful hands. With his walk modelled on his father's gait, paunch in place, and speaking the kind of language he had heard many police officers use, Ahlawat's Hathi Ram was the kind of loser everyone loves.

They've all had their struggles. At some point in 2004, after a year of cooking for a senior actor so he could stay in his home for free, Nawazuddin Siddiqui said to himself: 'Have I come to Mumbai to be an actor or a cook?' He took his few belongings and decided to redouble his efforts looking for work. Nothing much had changed from the time when he had first come to Mumbai in search of work, armed with a diploma from the NSD, but slowly and surely he made his way through the innards of Mumbai cinema to emerge into the light. He'd been limited to a bit role in *Black Friday* (2004), a cult song, 'Emotional Atyachaar', in the cult movie *Dev D* (2009), a 9/11 detainee in *New York* (2009) and a small-town journalist in Anusha Rizvi's *Peepli Live* (2010), produced by Aamir Khan. But his world changed in 2011 when *Patang,* a Prashant Bhargava movie, won him rave reviews at international film festivals. *Gangs of Wasseypur* happened the same year and Faisal Khan, the character he played in the film, became the first of many fully-realised iconic characters.

Siddiqui says he was prepared to wait for as long as it was necessary. 'I am an artist, I have come here to work. There is no timeline for success here,' he says. And this, despite the understanding that 'with my kind of face' the roles that would come to him were limited. The advent of streaming has altered the game for those with unusual faces and unique backgrounds, but 'formulaic cinema in India hasn't changed. It still needs a good-looking boy, a good-looking girl, five songs and a happy ending,' says Siddiqui.[2]

With his love for Hindi literature, Pankaj Tripathi brings another kind of authenticity to his roles. Born in Belsand, Bihar, he too studied at the NSD—having got in on his third attempt—before moving to Mumbai in 2004, he trained in hospitality at the Institute of Hotel Management, Patna, and became an assistant chef in a hotel in the city. 'I told my wife to get a BEd so that she could teach,' he says. They knew the struggle was going to be long and the earnings erratic. 'I had trained to be an actor so I came to Mumbai to survive,' he adds. It took eight long years before he was noticed in *Gangs of Wasseypur*, but he seemed to possess the same equanimity then as he does now.

Some of the new streaming devices and several production houses are headed by women, which means that women's voices are becoming a lot more audible. Women's stories are also being told with a vengeance, partly because there are only a few male stars who can open a movie wide. Crafting smaller movies around interesting stories can be worn as a badge of honour, and on top of that, they now make commercial sense. The story has increasingly become the star, especially in the so-called indie film, and the characters are often true-to-life. You can find many examples, including Alankrita Shrivastava's *Dolly, Kitty Aur Woh Chamakte Sitare* with Konkona Sen Sharma and Bhumi Pednekar (who is emerging as a champion of sisterhood movies). Or Ashwiny Iyer Tiwari's *Panga* where Kangana Ranaut plays a young mother who takes another shot at life. Or Taapsee Pannu's roles in movies from *Thappad* to *Haseen Dillruba*.

Filmmaker Rahul Dholakia loves the fearlessness of the current generation of young women in the industry, their can-do attitude and their sistas-over-mistas style. Plus, there is a strong audience of young women with dreams and aspirations that match those of their on-screen heroines, who are often seen playing real-life women: take Janhvi Kapoor, who played a Kargil war pilot in *Gunjan Saxena: The Kargil Girl*, a character based on a young, small-town woman. Or Deepika Padukone, who played Laxmi Agarwal, an acid-attack survivor, in *Chhapaak*. It is the same with long-form series, whether it is the racy *Four More Shots Please* on Amazon Prime Video, the stark *Bombay Begums* on Netflix, or the intriguing *Aarya* on Disney+Hotstar. All three have ensemble casts led by strong women.

Data supports the hypothesis that progressive tales about women are the rising stars on the story telling firmament. Zee5 found that their content was dominated by women-centric shows in 2019, at 34 per cent of the total content produced, followed by thrillers at 25 per cent, 'edgy, young adult' series at 24 per cent, crime at 11 per cent and experimental movies at 6 per cent. Viewers seem to be willing to experience greater range, and like the traffic on Indian streets, are indicating their ability to cohabit several platforms, whether it is cinema screens, TV or digital screens.

Therein lies the problem.

At the core of the current power struggle in cinema between the old establishment, still largely run by families, and the new India is the question of who gets to be the storyteller, the influencer of the future. As actors become brands, standing for varieties of social values, they are expected to have a worldview. This worldview is disseminated not only through their movies and social media, but also through the issues they choose to add their names and support to. As long as such opinions coincide with those of the establishment—as in the case of most cricketers, Bollywood's only rivals in terms of popularity—there is no outrage.

If they don't, the voices—and the actors—are seen as anti-establishment, or worse, anti-national, and they become problematic. Therefore the unusual spectacle of Uttar Pradesh Chief Minister Yogi Adityanath inviting senior members of the film industry to participate in creating a new 1,000-acre hub on the Delhi-Yamuna expressway, an alternative film industry redistributing value to the tune of ₹3,000 crore. The move was welcomed by those on the right of the political spectrum, like Anupam Kher and Ashoke Pandit.

So far, Mumbai cinema's hold on the collective imagination of the nation has been unparalleled, as has the ability of its heroes to define contemporary India, beginning with the Nehruvian triumvirate who embraced the romance of post-Independent India. There was Raj Kapoor's wide-eyed socialism, Dev Anand's smooth urbanity and Dilip Kumar's deep-seated sense of tragedy. Cut to the '60s, when Shammi Kapoor, with his raw sexuality and even bolder mannerisms reduced the polite ’50s to cinders. Here was a hero who was not afraid of winning, warring and wooing with energy, one pelvic thrust at a time.

As India changed, so did the hero who articulated its angst. Suddenly, nothing was good enough—there was unchecked crime on the streets, the politician was morally corrupt, families were becoming dysfunctional, and there was poison in the air. All of this had to be channelled through the evidently posh persona of Amitabh Bachchan, but then, Hindi movie audiences have never been hung up on realism. Even in his darkest moments, we (and the camera) looked up to him to know how to negotiate our modernity in the ’70s and ’80s, from the width of our flares to the length of our sideburns.

Cut to three decades later, a time dominated by three men with a common surname, each appealing to a different constituency with consistency and charm. The evolution of the three Khans, their personal lives, public spats and professional accomplishments have held India spellbound. But the nation has changed, unleashing forces both positive and pessimistic. Where there were easy definitions, there are divisions; where there was a definitive national identity, there are multiple diversities; and where there was one kind of audience, there are as many as there are platforms.

As we enter the third decade of the century, will Ranveer Singh and Ayushmann Khurrana become the superheroes and everymen of our paradoxical times? India is not the country it was when the Khans burst on to the screen, or even when they were at their peak. Noted academic Ashis Nandy told me recently that he doubts whether such a moment in India’s history will return where three Muslims could be unparalleled cultural heroes. He believes a large majority of Indians have travelled too far down the road of regarding the Muslim as the ‘other’.

Also, the business of Bollywood heroes is one of diminishing returns. The Khans at their finest could never repeat what Amitabh Bachchan had achieved at the height of his fame. Any new star will find it impossible to imitate the universality of the Khans. The audience is far less tolerant of ordinary scripts bolstered by star power. It demands more compelling narratives. It has an increasingly schizophrenic attitude to the consumption of glamour—those whose controversies it follows are not necessarily the ones whose movies it watches. And it has a wide array of platforms to choose its entertainment from. So an unheralded Vicky Kaushal could seemingly come out of nowhere with a well-made war movie, *Uri: The Surgical Strike* (2019), which would go on to make ₹240 crore and counting. And equally, a consistently good but low-key Khurrana could become an audience favourite with a ₹140 crore box-office hit, *Badhaai Ho!* (2018), about his on-screen mother's late pregnancy, a subject that, twenty years ago, would have been unthinkable as a crowd-pleaser.

In today's Bollywood, nothing is certain. You can bare your bottom, dance frenetically in Paris, and mouth ridiculous dialogue that passes for cool, but you cannot get a *Befikre* (2016) to succeed, even though it is directed by Mumbai's most powerful producer, Aditya Chopra. Ranveer Singh realised this when the film that was studio-designed to get him to slip into Shah Rukh Khan's shoes flopped. Ranbir Kapoor, the other star touted to replace the Khans, had become aware of this even earlier, when his movies with the two Kashyap brothers—Abhinav Kashyap's *Besharam* (2013) and Anurag Kashyap's *Bombay Velvet* (2015)—brought his early, hard-won stardom crashing down to earth. Ranbir had perfected the boy-man trope which he initiated in 2009 with the coming-of-age movie, *Wake Up Sid!*. Directed by Ayan Mukerji, who soon became Ranbir's best friend, the film established the idea of the boy waiting to be rescued by the woman so that he could become a man. The idea was explored again in Mukerji's *Yeh Jawaani Yeh Diwani* (2013) as well as in Karan Johar's *Ae Dil Hai Mushkil* (2016). Raju Hirani's *Sanju* (2018) was the ultimate in this line of munna-babies. Ranbir Kapoor's star waned somewhat because of the prolonged shoot of Ayan Mukerji's *Brahmastra*. But a fresh set of movies, starting with the dacoit epic *Shamshera*, may well restore his lost sheen.

Ranveer Singh, once Ranbir's direct rival, is aware of the fickleness of stardom, but he is both hungry for more and careful about its orchestration. A natural actor, he is a constructed, method star. Indeed, Ranveer is forever in performance mode, boom box for company, energy on high, and an effusive embrace for everyone. Even journalists who have interviewed him at length have rarely been invited into his private space, his 'apna time', be it his home or inside his vanity van.

Ranveer's preparation for his roles has become almost as iconic as that of Aamir Khan. For the role of Kapil Dev in Kabir Khan's *83*, he underwent four months of intensive training, says Khan, learning how to bowl like the World Cup winning captain. Balwinder Singh Sandhu from the 1983 squad was his coach, with Kapil adding his inputs. Kabir Khan calls him a chameleon, saying, 'He's that rare actor today who is able to totally and completely transform himself into the character he is portraying. His face seems to change with every character. From Khilji *(Padmavat)* to *Simmba* to *Gully Boy*, we just don't see the same person—they are three different and unique people on-screen.' He looks for the key in every character and struggles until he is satisfied with it—while he was preparing to play Khilji, he locked himself up in his new flat in Goregaon for twenty-one days to isolate himself and find the darkness within.

Ranveer takes his celebrity status almost as seriously as he does his acting. His flamboyant suits, witticisms, and networking are all carefully plotted. From the time he attended parties with his boom box to get noticed among a sea of newbies, he has aimed to be the life and soul of every celebration—witness his wild dancing at Sonam Kapoor's wedding reception with Anil Kapoor, the father of the bride. Equally well-orchestrated is the image he presents as one half of Bollywood's premier power couple, since his Lake Como wedding to Deepika Padukone. She is higher paid, has worked longer in the industry, and is clearly the bigger star. But he is comfortable enough in his skin to accept this and revel in it—the perfect man in the Age of #MeToo. He even moved into her house post-marriage, to blend seamlessly into her life. From picking her up from restaurants with paparazzi in full attendance to colour coordinating their airport looks, Ranveer never misses a beat while playing the part he has assigned to himself—a knight in shining armour to the 'most beautiful girl in the world', even when it involves travelling from Goa to Mumbai when she was summoned for interrogation by the Narcotics Control Bureau. And where images go, words and emojis follow, with the couple routinely exchanging messages with each other and the world on Instagram. You are unstoppable, she gushes to Ranveer. You are my superpower, he responds. Talk about a match made in social media heaven.

Backed by hard work—who can top a prep of ten months, training with rappers Divine and Naezy for 2019's *Gully Boy*?—Ranveer's star seems set to ascend higher, even in an increasingly crowded sky where a new star boy is born every year. Yet there is the lurking anxiety of more discerning audiences learning to distinguish between a star and an influencer.[3]

Then there is Everyman Khurrana, who has become a past master at negotiating the complexities of what it means to be an ordinary man in the extraordinarily complex India of today, with its deep social divisions, increasingly independent women, harsh economic realities and traditional systems of managing conflict. With an ease born of five years of travelling to different college festivals with his two theatre groups, meeting a variety of people, and working in radio and TV as a presenter, Khurrana finds himself uniquely placed to embody the fluid masculinity demanded of the once invincible Hindi film hero. Alpha Male, move over: meet the Alphabet Male, reconstructing himself bit by bit, letter by letter.

Nowhere did he portray this flawed, vulnerable, not-a-hero better than in his fourth film, *Dum Laga Ke Haisha* (2015), which saved his career from spiralling into a freefall after a successful debut in 2012, in *Vicky Donor*. *'Krantikari banenge. Makkhi toh maari na sake hai inse,'* (They want to be revolutionaries, but they can't even kill a fly), says the father of the character played by Khurrana in *Dum Laga Ke Haisha*. The father is talking of an organisation suspiciously like the Rashtriya Swayamsevak Sangh (RSS) which instructs boys on how to be men and whom to follow as role models—Bhagat Singh, Subhas Chandra Bose, Shivaji and Atal Bihari Vajpayee. It's a confusing list. It has a communist, a lapsed Congressman, a Maratha warlord and a poet-prime minister under whom India triggered its second series of nuclear tests.

It's the kind of masculinity Indian men grow up with, in the shadow of their fathers' expectations, usually coddled by overprotective mothers and taught by society to feel entitled. Listen again to Khurrana's father, Chandrabhan Tiwari, played by Sanjai Mishra: *'Dasvin toh nikaal nahin paaya, Juhi Chawla ke sapne dekh raha hai.'* (He couldn't clear Class X and he's dreaming of Juhi Chawla.) The film is set in the '90s, the heroine (played by Bhumi Pednekar) is better educated than he is, and yet he believes he can do better than her in life and is superior to her.

Between the toxic man best exemplified by Salman Khan in his portrayals of men who are tone-deaf to women and most recently reprised by Shahid Kapoor in *Kabir Singh*, and the nationalistic man whose heart beats only for India, epitomised by Akshay Kumar and Ajay Devgan, Khurrana has opened the gates for male actors such as Rajkummar Rao and Vikrant Massey, who are also willing to try out new personas. Whether Khurrana is a young man embarrassed by his inability to perform in bed in *Shubh Mangal Saavdhan* (2017), a writer unsure of winning the woman of his dreams in *Bareilly Ki Barfi* (2017), an adman facing the prospect of his middle-aged parents having a baby in *Badhaai Ho!* (2018), or a store-keeper who is obsessed with staying on in a crumbling haveli in Lucknow and is routinely insulted by his better educated sister and lover in *Gulabo Sitabo* (2020), this actor symbolises the man in the middle, torn between a patriarchal upbringing and a rapidly transforming society.[4]

For Juhi Chaturvedi, who wrote *Vicky Donor* and *Gulabo Sitabo* (where Khurrana was cast opposite Amitabh Bachchan), Khurrana is the messiah of all small-town stories, a real face who convincingly transforms into the part. 'We all may know him as an actor first,' she says, 'but for me it seems that's just the last and an obvious culmination of all the talents he is born with. His expression, be it in his voice, in what he sings or what he chooses to say in his poetry, all that must have been inside him even during his days in Chandigarh where he grew up. When your pitcher is full of observations from life, experiences that have pushed you to introspect, it is bound to happen and your craft will be honest.' This is evident in *Article 15*, the most political of Khurrana's films.

Khurrana has often said that success follows 'when preparation meets opportunity'. The child of a homemaker mother and an astrologer father, he says he always wanted to be an actor, even though he had to jump over many hurdles along the way: winning Roadies in 2002, being a radio host for two years, becoming an MTV VJ, fronting reality shows such as

India's Got Talent, Just Dance, Music ka Maha Muqabla and, finally, IPL Season 3. He wasn't desperate so much as determined to be an actor and when *Vicky Donor* was offered to him, director Shoojit Sircar didn't even screen-test him first.

His directors, past and present, adore him. Rohan Sippy, who cast him as a theatre director in *Nautanki Saala!* (2013), says that from the beginning of his career, Khurrana found an opportunity to redefine masculinity in Hindi cinema. As Sippy said to me, Khurrana is armed with perhaps the best script sense and instinct since Aamir Khan. 'He has managed to flourish and engage with his audience and expand it with each film too,' Sippy told me. Khurrana says he reads scripts as though he were a member of the audience. He was, after all, an outsider to films. He was someone who queued up to buy cinema tickets, sometimes even acquiring them in black. His desire to be a hero was sparked after watching *Tezaab* (1988) at the age of four, and the hunger continues to manifest as he avidly seeks out directors who would not normally have cast him, given his Mr Nice Guy image.

Prabhat Chaudhary, founder of two of Mumbai's biggest communications agencies in entertainment, Spice and Entropy, believes nothing has gone out of fashion and everything can be attempted. Anything well told has the potential to make money at the box office. Digital, he says, brings audacity and imagination to the subjects. 'Southern cinema is bringing its own grammar of mass appeal. High social awareness will mean more real life stories. The content palette is getting more diverse.' So, women's stories such *as Shakuntala Devi*, starring the wondrous Vidya Balan, can co-exist with misogynistic movies from the Luv Ranjan School of Filmmaking, such as *Jai Mummy Di*. And sporty biopics such as *Sania* can be released along with five-hankie remakes of Hollywood's *The Fault Is in Our Stars*, called *Dil Bechara*.

The challenge to match the best in the West is unrelenting. Also, as Dholakia pointed out to me in an interview, our culture is casual and happy-go-lucky, so the entertainment quotient has to be high. Biopics will work provided the character or the story is interesting. Nationalistic stories will win, provided they are well made. There will be fewer big films, and film shoots will be wrapped up in forty-five to sixty days, which means more drama and less action. Unless it's a film that stars Tiger Shroff or Hrithik Roshan—or both, like 2019's biggest hit, *War*. Limited locations, social commentary, an interesting cast and experimentation that is palatable to the Central Board for Film Certification could well be the elements of a new formula.

The big boys will continue to play by their own rules, within certain parameters suggested by the establishment. If Akshay Kumar plays a police officer in Rohit Shetty's *Sooryavanshi*, he will make sure he is the head of an anti-terror squad with enough opportunities for flag waving. When he plays a historical figure, he will be the beloved Prithiviraj Chauhan, who may have lost against Mohammed Ghori but is revered for having put up a fight. In his annual nod to the disenfranchised and disempowered in 2020, he played a transgender in *Laxxmi Bomb*. He goes retro as well in the forthcoming *Bell Bottom*, which casts him as a spy in a story inspired by real events, complete with '80s swag.

'Mera Bharat mahaan' will work, but with diminishing returns and entirely dependent on the quality of the film. Not all of it is voluntary. Some of it will be very much within Prime Minister Narendra Modi's request to the industry to create 'nation-building' content. It could be Ajay Devgn's *Tanhaji* or his *Bhuj: The Pride of India* about 300 Gujarati women who helped an IAF wing commander reconstruct an airstrip during the 1971 war. Or even Ranveer Singh's *83*, to remind everyone of a time when India was a cricketing underdog and Kapil Dev an unalloyed hero. Or Kangana Ranaut's *Thalaivi*, on the life of Jayalalithaa.

Anubhav Sinha, one of the few directors who has chosen to make films his conscience can be proud of, said to me, 'Instructions have been given to actors and filmmakers to make more films that feed into the current political narrative.' But for how long? That is the big question, as entertainment becomes democratic, and every kind of content gains an audience. If it's a great time to be an actor, it's the best time to be a storyteller. Directors are experimenting with style and structure, even though the government has created a '3-stair' regulatory mechanism for streaming services which will enable it to classify content. Creators will have to work within the acceptable parameters and as *Bombay Begums'* creator Alankrita Shrivastava told me, 'be as subversive as possible'. The opportunities are tremendous. Take Zoya Akhtar, who moves seamlessly from co-creating the delicious *Made in Heaven* for Amazon Prime to making the gritty but sublime *Gully Boy* for cinemas, and then filming a gorgeously shot episode in Netflix's anthology, *Ghost Stories*, which focuses on her very own fears of abandonment and ageing.

Or Anurag Kashyap, who can make movies, streaming series and short films at one go, and still feel renewed. The world is changing, he says. India is on the move, migrating to nuclear families in crowded cities. 'We don't look up from our phones, we need drivers and Google Maps to get around,' he told me. 'The Google generation has changed cinema and television. They're kinder now. In one or two years, they won't be. They'll demand higher standards from Indian filmmakers.'

It's a good time to be a consumer in India's Age of Diversity.

But Bollywood's inability to speak up for itself has eroded its reputation, with divisions sown deep in 2014, says Anupam Kher, when a group of artistes signed a letter protesting the election of Modi. Those who supported the government have been rewarded in various ways. The most obvious are sinecures. The willingness to be co-opted did not arise with the Modi government or indeed, the BJP. The faces of the current cultural establishment may be new—Prasoon Joshi as Chairperson of the Central Board of Film Certification, Paresh Rawal as Chairperson of the National School of Drama, Shekhar Kapur as President of the Film and Television Institute of India and Vivek Ranjan Agnihotri as cultural representative of the Indian Council for Cultural Relations—but the practice of Bollywood artists playing ideologues is an old one.

Bollywood also has to get rid of its safety net. One that makes it tread familiar territory or cast star kids who come prepared with their own social media following and grooming entourages. After a soft launch in her mother's reality show, *Fabulous Lives of Bollywood Wives,* Shanaya Kapoor (daughter of Sanjay Kapoor) will soon be launched by the same production house, Karan Johar's Dharma Productions. Bollywood reprises don't even stretch too far back. *Bhool Bhulaiyaa* (2007), *Bunty Aur Babli* (2005), *Dostana* (2008), *Love Aaj Kal* (2009) and even *Coolie No. 1 (*1995) belong to the '90s and the noughties, when the directors were young and the actors in their infancy.

Old Bollywood with its Uncle Brigade and Auntie Squad guiding the next generation of stars born into film families is still a safe space, a bubble far removed from the changes sweeping through the country. The film world is entrapped by its own repeat-worthy item songs and well-visited pairs. Consider this: not only is Saif Ali Khan teaming up with his *Hum Tum* co-star Rani Mukerji in a reprise of *Bunty Aur Babli*, but he also sang a new version of his *Yeh Dillagi* (1994) chartbuster 'Ole Ole' in *Jawaani Jaaneman*. As if that was not enough, his daughter Sara Ali Khan acted in an update of Saif Ali Khan's romance, *Love Aaj Kal*, with the same title and the same director, Imtiaz Ali.

With the safety net fraying rapidly, this is as close as it gets to a guarantee of success. It explains the casting of youngsters with those who have famous last names, the buying of remake rights from Hollywood and south Indian studios, and sequels. It makes sense in a world where millennials and centennials are increasingly exposed to the best of world entertainment on their phones, laptops and television-screens making it easy to find ready material, which is tried and tested, and high on recall value.

After *Radhe: Your Most Wanted Bhai* released on pay-per-view in India and in theatres in the rest of the world, Salman has a slate of movies waiting, some of them part of the Salman Khan Family Employment Scheme such as *Antim* which co-stars his brother-in-law Ayush Sharma. Shah Rukh's year-long sabbatical has turned into two, but he is now in the thick of shooting *Pathan* which will have an extended cameo by Salman as Tiger, the RAW spy of the popular franchise. Both movies are produced by Yash Raj Films and if all goes well, both franchises will extend the cinematic lives of the two Khans. Aamir is likely to start a biopic of T-Series founder Gulshan Kumar after completing *Laal Singh Chadha*. His constant reinventing of himself places him beyond the problems associated with ageing.

Or they might reinvent themselves, perhaps even collaboratively, to stay relevant for another decade. Salman Khan's role as action star, especially in the Tiger franchise, suggests a fairy-tale future where India and Pakistan can co-exist as he and Zoya do in the film. He's all heart encased in India's most beloved body. To repeat his dialogue in *Kick*, the 2014 film where Devi Lal (Salman) defeats Devil (also Salman): '*Mere baare mein itna mat socho. Mein dil mein aata hoon, samajh mein nahin.*' (Don't think so hard about me. I appeal to hearts, not minds.) . Aamir Khan, all head, tells the stories he believes in, no matter the cost to himself psychologically or financially. It could be replacing southern superstar Vijay Sethupati from *Laal Singh Chadha* for putting on weight or refusing to commit on director Subhash Kapoor when the latter was accused of a sexual assault until he had studied the charges in detail. Shah Rukh, a complex man governed by both his head and heart, remains the great global gambler, hoping *Pathan* will cater to his international audience—every taxi driver I met in Dubai on a recent visit was a Pathan from Peshawar and was a fan of the actor, partly because he was a Pathan too. *Pathan* may well restore Shah Rukh's box office stature, especially overseas.

Filmmaker Mahesh Bhatt is optimistic. 'The people of India and the world are not the same as the government of India,' he said to me recently.

But for that distinction to remain, the three Khans will have to tell stories that matter to India and the world. The world is ready for it, with its emphasis on greater diversity in storytelling. The Khans have to step out of their comfort zones. Salman Khan is an action star who can create a *Fast and Furious* franchise that rises from the East. Aamir can play homegrown epic characters instead of borrowing heroes from foreign studios. Shah Rukh can start playing romantic hero to women his own age in mature love stories.

The Three Khans have built their legacies. Now they have to build a brighter future for themselves and for Indian entertainment. India and the world aren't done with them yet.

Notes

INTRODUCTION

1. Indian National Congress passes through a crisis of self-confidence', Ajay Kumar and Prabhu Chawla, 15 January 1986, *India Today*, https://www.indiatoday.in/magazine/special-report/story/19860115-indian-national-congress-passes-through-a-crisis-of-self-confidence-800477-1986-01-15
2. *Encyclopaedia of Indian Cinema*: Ashish Rajadhyaksha and Paul Willemen, Routledge India, 2014
3. *The Film That Revived Hindi Cinema: Qayamat Se Qayamat Tak*, Gautam Chintamani, Harper Collins, 2016
4. *India After Gandhi: The History of the World's Largest Democracy,* Ramachandra Guha, Picador, 2007
5. Brothers-in-law because Kumar Gaurav married Sanjay Dutt's sister, Namrata
6. 'From Subjectification to Schizophrenia', Ranjani Mazumdar, *Making Meaning in Indian Cinema,* Ravi S. Vasudevan (editor), Oxford University Press India, 2001
7. Rajadhyaksha and Willemen (2014)

8. *Freedom and Destiny: Gender, Family and Popular Culture in India*, Patricia Uberoi, Oxford University Press India, 2009
9. *Passionate Modernity: Sexuality, Class and Consumption in India,* Sanjay Srivastava, Routledge India, 2020
10. *Music, Masti, Modernity: The Cinema of Nasir Husain*, Akshay Manwani, Harper Collins, 2016
11. 'Conversations Over Chai', https://anuradhawarrier.blogspot.com/
12. *Ideology of the Hindi Film: A Historical Construction*, M. Madhava Prasad, Oxford University Press India, 1998
13. *Yash Chopra: Fifty Years in Indian Cinema*, Rachel Dwyer, Roli Books, 2002
14. Urdu, Awadh and the Tawaif: The Islamicate Roots of Indian Cinema', Mukul Kesavan, Zoya Hasan (editor), *Forging Identities: Gender, Communities and the State in India,* Routledge India, 2020
15. *Global Bollywood*, Anandam P. Kavoori and Aswin Punathambekar (editors), New York University Press, 2008
16. *Talking Films and Songs*, Javed Akhtar in conversation with Nasreen Munni Kabir, Oxford University Press India, 2017
17. 'Aamir Khan in Mahabharata? Javed Akhtar rips apart communal rant on Twitter', *The Week***,** 24 March 2018**,** https://www.theweek.in/leisure/society/2018/03/24/aamir-kha-mahabharata-twitter-war-over-muslim-man-remake-epic-javed-akhtar.html
18. 'Of *Earth* and a star', Alpana Choudhary, 3 June 1998, https://www.rediff.com/movies/1998/jun/03am.htm

1. THEN THERE WERE THREE

1. 15 December 1988, *India Today*, Simran Bhargava
2. Ibid.
3. Aysha Iqbal Viswamohan, 'Mansoor Khan: Narrative and Aesthetic Impulses of a Director now in "Self-exile"', *Behind the Scenes: Contemporary Bollywood Directors and Their Cinema*, Aysha Iqbal Viswamohan and Vimal Mohan John (Editors), Sage Publications India, 2017
4. Jyotika Virdi, *The Cinematic ImagiNation: Indian Popular Films in Social History,* Rutgers University Press, 2003
5. *The Film That Revived Hindi Cinema: Qayamat Se Qayamat Tak*, Gautam Chintamani, Harper Collins, 2016

6. 'If *Maine Pyar Kiya* was my first film, perhaps I would have failed', Sonil Dedhia, 9 July 2015 https://www.rediff.com/movies/interview/if-maine-pyar-kiya-was-my-first-film-perhaps-i-would-have-failed/20150709.htm
7. Ibid.
8. Ibid.
9. 'The DD Files: When Shah Rukh Khan stole hearts and the show in "Fauji"', Chandrima Pal, 7 Dec 2015, https://scroll.in/reel/800500/the-dd-files-when-shah-rukh-khan-stole-hearts-and-the-show-in-fauji
10. 'Blast from the Past', *Filmfare*, May 1990
11. *I'll Do it My Way: The Incredible Journey of Aamir Khan*, Christina Daniels, Om Books International, 2012
12. May 1990, *The Times of India*
13. *The Illustrated Weekly of India*
14. In an interview to *Filmfare*
15. 'Gandhi Visit to Pakistan Signals Thaw', Steve Coll, *The Washington Post*, 17 July 1989, https://www.washingtonpost.com/archive/politics/1989/07/17/gandhi-visit-to-pakistan-signals-thaw/1a6148e3-83d4-48f4-a377-e27ec6c9c1c7/
16. 'Being Salman', Anna M.M. Vetticad, *Caravan*, November 2017, https://caravanmagazine.in/reportage/salman-khan-dangerous-innocence-bollywood-controversial-star
17. 'My SRK Story', Bharathi Pradhan, *Telegraph*, 8 November 2015, https://www.telegraphindia.com/7-days/my-srk-story/cid/1313738
18. 'Was Sanjay Dutt a terrorist?: It's grey, says Rajdeep Sardesai as he recalls Mumbai's '92-'93 trauma', Rajdeep Sardesai, 9 July 2018, https://scroll.in/article/885790/was-sanjay-dutt-a-terrorist-rajdeep-sardesai-recalls-10-facts-about-mumbais-trauma-in-1992-93
19. Once, Bollywood Fought For What Was Right. Wonder What Stops Them Now, Rohit Khilnani, 28 May 2018, https://www.ndtv.com/entertainment/blog-once-bollywood-fought-for-what-was-right-wonder-what-stops-them-now-1858825
20. 'Was Sanjay Dutt a terrorist?: It's grey, says Rajdeep Sardesai as he recalls Mumbai's '92-'93 trauma', Rajdeep Sardesai, 9 July 2018, https://scroll.in/article/885790/was-sanjay-dutt-a-terrorist-rajdeep-sardesai-recalls-10-facts-about-mumbais-trauma-in-1992-93

21. 'Indian actors join real world: Communal strife is intruding on the world's largest film industry', Tim McGirk, Independent, 2 February 1993, https://www.independent.co.uk/news/world/indian-actors-join-real-world-communal-strife-is-intruding-on-the-worlds-largest-film-industry-tim-1470395.html
22. Amitabh Bachchan on Bal Thackeray: If not for him, I would not have been alive', 21 January 2019, https://www.indiatoday.in/movies/bollywood/story/amitabh-bachchan-on-bal-thackeray-if-not-for-him-i-would-not-have-been-alive-1435916-2019-01-21
23. 'While in jail, Sanjay Dutt used to get THIS message every day from Bal Thackeray', 21 January 2019, https://www.timesnownews.com/entertainment/news/bollywood-news/article/while-in-jail-sanjay-dutt-used-to-get-this-message-everyday-from-bal-thackeray-watch-video/349950
24. 'Indian actors join real world: Communal strife is intruding on the world's largest film industry', Tim McGirk, *The Independent*, 2 February 1993, https://www.independent.co.uk/news/world/indian-actors-join-real-world-communal-strife-is-intruding-on-the-worlds-largest-film-industry-tim-1470395.html

2. A SPLIT NATION, DIVIDED STARS

1. 'Culture of Suspicion: Riots and Rumour in Bombay 1992-93', Radhika Subramaniam, *Transforming Anthropogy*, Volume 8, Numbers 1&2, 1999
2. *King of Bollywood: Shah Rukh Khan and the Seductive World of Indian Cinema*, Anupama Chopra, Hachette, 2007
3. Ibid.
4. 'I will never ever do a film with Aamir Khan—Ram Gopal Varma, https://www.indiaglitz.com/-i-will-never-ever-do-a-film-with-aamir-khan—ram-gopal-varma-hindi-news-40578.html
5. 'Salman Khan has a go at the media' (1998), https://www.bing.com/videos/search?q=salman+khan+1998+interview&docid=608012135850313013&mid=828A90F5C5C4E974DBF7828A90F5C5C4E974DBF7&view=detail&FORM=VIRE (https://www.youtube.com/watch?v=6KEmUyug0Eg)
6. 'Salman Khan's funny dance With Karishma on Tan Tana Tan Tan Taara Song', https://www.youtube.com/watch?v=I11tMYrA5eE

3. THE YEAR OF RESET

1. 'Well-planned attack on the Khans of Bollywood', 15 July 2000, https://www.milligazette.com/Archives/15-7-2000/Art6.htm
2. 'Dharma Cola: The RSS conjures up a Muslim conspiracy in Bollywood', Priya Sahgal, *Outlook*, 3 July 2000, https://magazine.outlookindia.com/story/dharma-cola/209625
3. *Unsettling India: Affect, Temporality and Transnationality*, Purnima Mankekar, Duke University Press, 2015

4. MARCHING TOWARDS STARDOM, GOING GLOBAL

1. 'Lagaan: As race for Oscars draws to a close, Aamir Khan proves his marketing acumen', Anna M.M. Vetticad, *India Today*, 18 March 2002, https://www.indiatoday.in/magazine/society-the-arts/films/story/20020318-lagaan-as-race-for-oscars-draws-to-a-close-aamir-khan-proves-his-marketing-acumen-795737-2002-03-25
2. 'Lagaan wins Audience Award at Locarno', Uma Da Cunha, *The Times of India*, 13 August 2001, http://timesofindia.indiatimes.com/articleshow/1283912159.cms?utm_source=contentofinterest&utm_medium=text&utm_campaign=cppst
3. 'Aamir Khan: questions from the floor', *The Guardian*, 27 October 2002, https://www.theguardian.com/film/2002/oct/27/bollywood.features
4. 'External Affairs', Laila Chandok, 27 January 2003, https://www.outlookindia.com/magazine/story/external-affairs/218676
5. 'Statement of Stardust editor regarding Aamir Khan and Jessica Hines controversy', https://bollywoodjournalist.com/articles-i-like/supporting-pages/statement-of-stardust-editor-regarding-aamir-khan-and-jessica-hines-controversy/
6. Stardust has always told facts, not gossip!' An interview with Nari Hira, founding editor of Stardust Magazine', Piyush Roy, Vol 2 No 3 (2013), *The South Asianist*, http://www.southasianist.ed.ac.uk/article/view/696/1010
7. 'Aamir Khan: Mr Blockbuster', Kaveree Bamzai, *India Today,* 18 January 2010, https://www.indiatoday.in/magazine/cover-story/story/20100118-aamir-khan-mr-blockbuster-741731-2010-01-07

8. Ibid.
9. 'Aamir and I became 2 a.m. friends when we started dating: Kiran Rao', https://www.news18.com/news/india/aamir-and-i-became-2-am-friends-when-we-started-dating-kiran-rao-607971.html
10. 'Blood, death and dancing girls', Geoffrey Macnab, 5 August 2005, *The Guardian*, https://www.theguardian.com/film/2005/aug/05/1
11. 'Talent manager sent "fat f****** pig" Harvey Weinstein a trough filled with Diet Coke after he asked her what he had to do to get her client Aishwarya Rai alone with him', Jeniffer Smith, 14 October 2017, *The Daily Mail* https://www.dailymail.co.uk/news/article-4980806/Agent-sent-fat-pig-Weinstein-trough-Diet-Coke.html
12. Ibid
13. 'Sanjay Leela Bhansali takes a huge risk by making most expensive Hindi film ever, "Devdas"', Sheela Raval and Anupama Chopra, *India Today*, 20 May 2002, https://www.indiatoday.in/magazine/cover-story/story/20020520-sanjay-leela-bhansali-bollywood-take-a-huge-risk-by-with-devdas-795250-2002-05-20
14. 'Salman harassing me, says Aishwarya', Afsana Ahmed, Smrity Sharma, 27 September 2002, *The Times of India*, https://timesofindia.indiatimes.com/entertainment/hindi/bollywood/news/Salman-harassing-me-says-Aishwarya/articleshow/23402266.cms
15. 'Automatic Bodies', Paromita Vohra, *Indian Quarterly*, https://indianquarterly.com/?p=3401
16. 'Movie review: 'No Entry' starring Anil Kapoor, Salman Khan, Bipasha Basu', *India Today*, Anupama Chopra, 12 September 2005 https://www.indiatoday.in/magazine/your-week/story/20050912-movie-review-no-entry-starring-anil-kapoor-salman-khan-bipasha-basu-787120-2005-09-12
17. *The Caravan*, November 2017
18. 'Patriotic films: Bollywood redefines flag-waving, xenophobic patriotism of the past', Kaveree Bamzai, *India Today*, 11 October 2004 https://www.indiatoday.in/magazine/cover-story/story/20041011-patriotic-films-bollywood-redefines-flag-waving-xenophobic-patriotism-of-the-past-789213-2004-10-11
19. 'Shooting with SRK, Rani', Aseem Chhabra, 3 August 2006, https://in.rediff.com/movies/2006/aug/03aseem.htm

20. SRK to Amar Singh: Don't you scare my kids', 16 March 2007, https://www.rediff.com/movies/2007/mar/16srk.htm
21. 'Shah Rukh Khan talks about Salman Khan', 1 February 2010, https://www.bing.com/videos/search?q=shah+rukh+khan+2008+inteview+on+salman+khan&docid=608047011090337749&mid=6E45355793D395F1B92A6E45355793D395F1B92A&view=detail&FORM=VIRE
22. 'Salman Khan talking about Shah Rukh Khan', 31 May 2014, https://www.bing.com/videos/search?q=salman+khan+interview+on+fight+with+shah+rukh+khan&docid=608032975192918586&mid=6D7C6DD0E333038DD32F6D7C6DD0E333038DD32F&view= detail&FORM=VIRE
23. 'Happy Birthday Salman Khan: A look at Bhai's 'dumdaar' stint on the small screen', Sana Farzeen, *The Indian Express*, 27 December 2019, https://indianexpress.com/article/entertainment/television/happy-birthday-salman-khan-a-look-at-bhais-dumdaar-stint-on-the-small-scree-6186965/
24. Aamir Khan on Narendra Modi—'Walk The Talk', 9 April 2015, https://www.bing.com/videos/search?q=aamir+khan+walk+the+talk+with+shekhar+gupta&docid=608022538419505201&mid=8C166DD48D38F1F8C6A28C166DD48D38F1F8C6A2&view=detail&FORM=VIRE
25. 'Rang De Basanti: Consumption, Citizenship and the Public Sphere', Meghana Dilip, University of Massachusetts Amherst, February 2014, https://scholarworks.umass.edu/cgi/viewcontent.cgi?referer=https://www.bing.com/&httpsredir=1&article=1116&context=theses
26. Aamir on Narmada: I won't apologise, 25 May 2006, https://www.rediff.com/movies/2006/may/25aamir1.htm
27. Aamir Khan's tryst with Narmada (Aired: May 2007), 26 February 2014 https://www.bing.com/videos/search?q=aamir+marriage+over+2007&docid=608016001552616506&mid=6186D05BEB1C28EB5C 616186D05BEB1C28EB5C61&view=detail&FORM=VIRE
28. Fareed Kazmi and H,M. Sanjeev Kumar, 'The Politics of Muslim Identity and the Nature of Public Imagination in India: Media and Films as Major Determinants', *European Journal of Economic and Political Studies*, Vol. 4 (1): 171–87), 2011

29. 'Yes, I have directed *Taare Zameen Par*—Aamir Khan', Harneet Singh (*Screen Weekly*), 21 May 2007, https://web.archive.org/web/20101113130244/http://www.bollywoodhungama.com/features/2007/05/21/2665/index.html
30. '*Taare Zameen Par* inspires people, institutions into action', 12 April 2008, Ambika Naithani, https://www.webcitation.org/5tf3QkTbC?url=http://economictimes.indiatimes.com/Business_of_Bollywood/Taare_Zameen_Par_inspires_people_institutions_into_action/articleshow/2946132.cms
31. 'Shah Rukh Is Licking My Feet', When Aamir Khan Referred To SRK As His Dog #Throwback, Basyukta Basuprava, 24 October 2020, https://odishatv.in/ entertainment/ shah-rukh-is-licking-my-feet-when-aamir-khan-referred-to-srk-as-his-dog-487534

5. REVENGE, RETRIBUTION AND SELF-REFERENCE

1. 'The Good Bad Boy', Kaveree Bamzai, *India Today*, 22 October 2010, https://www.indiatoday.in/magazine/latest-headlines/story/20101101-the-good-bad-boy-744529-2010-10-22
2. *Salaam Bollywood: Representations and Interpretations*, Routledge India, 2019, Edited By Vikrant Kishore, Amit Sarwal and Parichay Patra
3. 'Bandra cartel exists: Director Abhinav Kashyap attacks Salman Khan, family for "sabotaging" his career', 16 June 2020, *The New Indian Express* https://www.newindianexpress.com/entertainment/hindi/2020/jun/16/bandra-cartel-exists-director-abhinav-kashyap-attacks-salman-khan-family-for- sabotaging-his-career-2157245.html
4. 'I am giving up my security: Uddhav Thackeray', 10 February 2010, *Hindustan Times*, https://www.hindustantimes.com mumbai/i-am-giving-up-my-security-uddhav-thackeray/story-eyBhLhJ4tgbcDksiuXZx7M.html
5. 'His name is Khan', 18 February 2010, Kaveree Bamzai, *India Today*, https://www.indiatoday.in/magazine/controversy/story/20100301-his-name-is-khan-742122-2010-02-18
6. 'Religious and National Identity, in *My Name is Khan*', Kathleen Erndl, *Journal of Religion and Film*, 2015
7. 'Precarious Inclusions; Re-Imagining Disability, Race, Masculinity and Nation in *My Name is Khan*', Nadia Kanani, https://scholarspace.manoa.hawaii.edu/handle/10125/58592

8. 'Mondo Pop: the Challenge of Popular World Cinema', *Phoenix Fry*, http://framescinemajournal.com/article/mondo-pop-the-challenge-of-popular-world-cinema/
9. 'Increasing Hindu Protest against Anti Hindu Film "PK". Hundreds FIR lodged. Demand to ban and boycott the film.' https://hinduexistence.org/2014/12/29/increasing- hindu-protest- against-anti-hindu- film-pk-hundreds-fir-lodged-demand-to-ban-the-film/
10. 'An Insider's View: Why is Bollywood Going Bust?' A. Krishna, 14 March 2018, https://www.thequint.com/entertainment/bollywood-studios-economy-disney-india-utv-motion-pictures-balaji-motion-pictures-dharma-shut-down
11. 'An Insider's View: Why is Bollywood Going Bust?', A. Krishna, 14 March 2018, https://www.thequint.com/entertainment-bollywood-studios-economy-disney-india-utv-motion-pictures-balaji-motion-pictures-dharma-shut-down
12. 'Not Sushant Singh Rajput, Paani shelved due to creative differences with Shekhar Kapur: Aditya Chopra tells police', *Hindustan Times*, 20 July 2020.
13. 'Salman Khan not bothered about the religious protests over *Bajrangi Bhaijaan*!', Sreeju Sudhakaran, 4 July 2015
14. In a personal email to the author
15. Ibid.
16. 'Vedanta brain and Islam body—only hope for our motherland', Swami Vivekananda, https://www.swamivivekananda.guru/2017/02/19/vedanta-brain-and-islam-body-only-hope-for-our-motherland/
17. 'Aamir apologises for *Thugs of Hindostan* failure: I take full responsibility', 26 November 2018, https://www.indiatoday.in/movies/bollywood/story/aamir-apologises-for-thugs-of-hindostan-failure-i-take-full-responsibility-1396663-2018-11-26
18. SRK Responding To Priyanka Chopra & His Alleged Affair', 19 November 2018, https://www.bing.com/videos/search?q=shah+rukh+khan+interview+on+priyanka+chopra+on+IBN&docid=608028719640478308&mid=4FCC34B22E07FFE514804FCC34B22E07FFE51480&view=detail&FORM=VIRE
19. 'SRK wants kids to first finish studies then enter Bollywood', 22 April 2016, https://news.rediff.com/commentary/2016/apr/

22/srk-wants-kids-to-first-finish-studies-then-enter-bollywood/b77a13411cf512734fc9f9b6f4486195

20. 'Suhana Khan's *Vogue India* cover triggers jokes, memes on Twitter', 6 August 2018, https://indianexpress.com/article/trending/trending-in-india/suhana-khans-vogue-india-cover-5289003/
21. 'Gauri Khan Designs: This sought-after design brand will be exhibiting at the AD Design Show 2019', Pallavi Mehra, 7 October 2019, https://www.architecturaldigest.in/content/gauri-khan-designs/
22. 'Arjun Rampal And Mehr Jesia Separated Because Of Sussanne Khan? "It's News To Me," Says Actor', Divya Goyal, 6 June 2018 https://www.ndtv.com/entertainment/arjun-rampal-and-mehr-jesia-separated-because-of-sussanne-khan-its-news-to-me-says-actor-1862996
23. 'When Aamir Khan made headlines after losing his brother's custody battle against father Tahir Hussain', https://www.pinkvilla.com/entertainment/nostalgia/when-aamir-khan-made-headlines-after-losing-his-brothers-custody-battle-against-father-tahir-hussain
24. 'Aamir's family condemns father, Faisal', 2 November 2007 https://www.rediff.com/movies/report/aamir/20071102.htm
25. 'Surrogacy was our last resort: Kiran Rao', 22 July 2013 https://www.indiatoday.in/magazine/special-report/story/20130722-aamir-khan-azad-kiran-rao-surrogacy-764710-1999-11-30)
26. 'Explained: A look at the Kangana Ranaut versus Hrithik Roshan legal battle', Ektaa Malik, 21 December 2020, https://indianexpress.com/article/explained/kangana-ranaut-hrithik-roshan-court-case-7105959/

6. A NEW ORDER FOR A NEW INDIA

1. 'Changing Habits', Kaveree Bamzai, 5 March 2021, *Open,* https://openthemagazine.com/cinema/changing-habits
2. 'The New Hero', Kaveree Bamzai, 18 September 2020, *Open,* https://openthemagazine.com/cinema/the-new-hero/
3. 'Ranveer Singh: The Hybrid Star', Kaveree Bamzai, 14 March 2019, *Open,* https://openthemagazine.com/cover-stories/ranveer-singh-the-hybrid-star/

4. 'Ayushmann Khurrana: Mr Everyman', Kaveree Bamzai, *Open,* 5 July 2019, https://openthemagazine.com/cinema/ayushmann-khurrana-mr-everyman/
5. 'Fatima Bhutto on her new book, Asia's cultural influence and why Shah Rukh Khan tops the charts', Surbhi Gupta, *The Indian Express,* 26 November 2019, https://indianexpress.com/article/lifestyle/books/fatima-bhutto-new-kings-of-the-world-book-srk-6136621/

Acknowledgements

One of my earliest memories of going to a theatre involved not seeing the movie. We were in Mumbai and there was a kung-fu movie my brother was keen on. My father took both of us and my two cousins came along too, but the usher refused to let my younger cousin and me into the theatre, saying the film was too violent. My father obeyed instantly, left my brother and older cousin at the theatre, promising to pick them up when the show ended. My cousin and I were compensated, and how! My dad took us to the Mumbai Taj Mahal Hotel's iconic restaurant Shamiana, where in between bites of our pastries, we watched the crowd around us, including Dimple Kapadia.

Needless to say, by the time we picked up my brother and my older cousin, we sounded quite supercilious. My father, who was once a film critic for the *Patriot* newspaper, was a great movie buff and even when we didn't have much, he always made sure we got to watch the latest movie in whichever city we lived in. He would also buy film magazines for my mother every month even though she protested that she didn't have time to read them. She did eventually, and so would I, wondering at how Devyani Chaubal and Shobhaa De (aka 'Neeta's Natter') wrote about stars with so much insouciance and irreverence.

This book is the result of my parents' love for movies and books as well as magazines. It is a love I have tried to pass on to my two lovely boys, Samvit and Kartikeya, with varying degrees of success. It is also a tribute to the various bosses I have had, pre-eminently Aroon Purie, who never treated cinema as irrelevant to *India Today* and always advocated his journalists meeting the subject of any profile, even if it meant flying down to Mauritius for my first almost-cover story on Amitabh Bachchan in 2002. It was pipped to the cover by Omar Abdullah's defeat in the assembly elections in the then state of Jammu and Kashmir. At *India Today*, where I worked for a total of 21 years over two stints, starting as a rookie sub-editor, there was a fine tradition of film writing with Madhu Jain, Simran Bhargava, Maseeh Rahman and Anupama Chopra. You will understand now why I have so often used the magazine as my source in writing this book.

This book would not have been possible without people who have helped shape my love for cinema writing over the years, from my husband and sometime colleague, Sourish Bhattacharyya; my former colleague S. Prasannarajan, who lets me write for the *Open* magazine, of which he is the editor; my boss at *The New Indian Express* and an inspiration to all journalists, Prabhu Chawla; my former colleagues and friends—Shekhar Gupta, Unni Rajen Shanker, S. Ranjit Sahaya, Sandeep Unnithan, Prachi Bhuchar, Kaushik Deka, Kunal Pradhan, Gayatri Jayaraman, Jairaj Singh (who let me write copious amounts for *DailyO.in*), and Jessica Hines. This is a shoutout also to my agent, Anuj Bahri Malhotra, my publisher V.K. Karthika and my editor Karthik Venkatesh for their immense patience and ever-accessible guidance.